QUALITY OF WORKING LIFE IN SUGAR INDUSTRY

QUALITY OF WORKING LIFE IN SUGAR INDUSTRY

Prof. (Dr.) Sudhir Chandra Das
Anil Kumar Gope

GenNext Publication

Published by

GenNext Publication
5, Ansari Road
Daryaganj, New Delhi-110002
Phone: 011-47034999, 9811692060
E-mail: gennextpublication@hotmail.com

Distribution Network
gyanbooks.com
India, USA, Canada, UK, Australia, France

ISBN: 978-93-5663-884-6 (PB)

First Published, 2024

Printed at: Gyan Press, Delhi.

Quality of Working Life in Sugar Industry

Author: Prof. Dr. Sudhir Chandra Das, Anil Kumar Gope

Contents

List of Tables

List of Figures

List of Abbreviations

ANOVA	Analysis of Variance
BIFR	Board for Industrial and Financial Reconstruction
BPL	Below Poverty Line
DGFT	Directorate General of Foreign Trade
ETOP	Environmental Threat and Opportunity Profile
FF	Financial Factor
HRM	Human Resource Management
ISEC	Indian Sugar Exim Corporation Ltd.
ISMA	Indian Sugar Mills Association
ISGIEC	Indian Sugar and General Industry Export-Import Corporation Ltd.
JF	Job Factor
MT	Million Tonnes
OCP	Organisational Capability Profile
OGL	Open General License
PDS	Public Distribution System
QWL	Quality of Work Life
QOL	Quality of Life
RF	Relational Factor
SAP	State Advised Prices
SMP	Statutory Minimum Prices
SWOT	Strength Weakness Opportunity and Threats
SY	Sugar Year
TCD	Ton Crushed per Day
TIEL	Triveni Engineering and Industries Ltd.
UNESCO	United Nation Educational, Scientific and Cultural Organisation

UP	Uttar Pradesh
UPSSCL	Uttar Pradesh State Sugar Corporation Ltd.
UPCSFFL	Uttar Pradesh Co-operative Sugar Factories Federation Ltd
WEF	Working Environment Factor

Preface

Quality of Work Life (QWL) is becoming an increasingly popular concept in recent times. It basically talks about the methods in which an organisation can ensure the holistic well-being of an employee instead of just focussing on work related aspects. In the broadest sense, the term Quality of Work Life (QWL) aims at enhancing the entire organisational climate by humanising work, individualising organisations and changing the structural and managerial system. It takes into consideration the total values, both material and non-material, attained by a worker throughout his career life. QWL includes aspects of work-related life such as wages and hours, work environment, benefits and services, career prospects and human relations which is possibly relevant to workers satisfaction and motivation. Its main aim is to create a work environment where employees work in co-operation with each other and contribute to organisational objectives.

The book is an application of structured dimension of QWL in sugar mills. The Indian sugar industry is the second largest agro-processing industry in India, accounting for 15 per cent of the total world consumption. India's average recovery rate at 10.27 per cent is quite low in comparison with the international average. Uttar Pradesh, Maharashtra, Tamil Nadu, Karnataka, Punjab and Gujarat contribute more than 90 per cent of the total domestic sugarcane production, while Uttar Pradesh and Maharashtra have contributed 30 per cent to total production. The Indian sugar industry is divided into organised and unorganised sectors with the former accounting for 20 per cent of the total production.

The present book is an endeavour of understanding the Quality of Working Life (QWL) of Employees in Sugar Industry. In the case of QWL of Indian sugar industry is of recent origin and individual as well as organised efforts are required to improve the quality of work life for millions of workers in the industry. The book originally address crucial issues as rampant sickness in the industry, the workers quality of life as well as performance of mills will be benefitted through redefining the structure of QWL.

The main objective of this manuscript is to assess the effectiveness of the various dimensions (namely, working environment, relational, job and financial) of Quality of Working Life of Employees in Sugar Industry. The book has made a broader comparison QWL practices in multi-angle namely, private vs co-operative, permanent vs seasonal workforce and among zones, i.e., eastern, western, and central.

The entire communication of the book has been segregated into nine chapters. The first chapter **(QWL- An Introduction)** deals evolutionary stages of QWL in abroad and India, different dimensions of QWL and techniques of improving and measuring QWL, etc. The second chapter **(Review of Literature and Research Strategy)** shows the comprehensive literature at national and international levels with exploration of research gap. The detailed problem and research design including art of sampling have been categorically projected in this chapter. The evolution, growth and development of Sugar Industry in India vis-a-vis Uttar Pradesh have been captured in the third chapter **(Indian Sugar Industry – An Overview)**. The fourth **(Working Environment Factor –An Analysis)**, fifth **(Relational Factor – An Evaluation)**, sixth **(Job Factor: An Appraisal)** and seventh chapter **(Financial Factor –An Assessment)** depicts analytical preview of individual variables of QWL with geographical location-wise and nature of organisation/employment-wise. The eighth chapter **(Factors of QWL – An Effectiveness and Impact Analysis)** predicts relationship of independent QWL variables with nature of employment/organisation and also different locations. The impact of thirty-six independent variables on five different outcome variables namely employees productivity, workers participation in management, job satisfaction, motivation and organisational loyalty are analysed using binary logistic regression, and the ordinal regression model. Finally, the last chapter **(IX- Summary of Findings, Conclusions and Suggestions)** summarises the entire study with mentioning conclusive remarks and suggestions. This chapter also mentions categorically the further scope of the study.

At the last but not the least, the book projects good number of variables (issues) which really effects positively on productivity, and also traced differences in QWL practices among private and co-operative sugar employees' causes industrial sickness and unrest. The zone-wise asymmetrical QWL initiatives also major concern needs immediate action by mills owners and policy-makers. The overall empirical study depicts real picture of QWL initiatives in broad perspectives with advanced statistical methods.

Prof. S.C. Das
Faculty of Commerce
Banaras Hindu University

Acknowledgements

The writing of Research-based book is a long-drawn and multi-stage process before getting culminated into a final shape. Inevitably, right from its take-off to its final stage, the author has to incur debts of several kinds at different junctures. Though, it is very difficult to convey in words, I wish to express my sincere and deep sense of gratitude to former Deans **Prof. Shyam Chandra,** and **Prof. V.S. Singh,** Faculty of Commerce, BHU, Varanasi, who supported the fully through-out my pursuit. I owe an equal debt to **Prof. A.R. Tripathi (Head and Dean)**, Faculty of Commerce, Banaras Hindu University for their generosity, wisdom, vision and diligence towards the final completion of the book.

I express my deep sense of indebtedness to my teacher and mentor **Prof. M.N. Mishra** and colleagues of the faculty for offering their valuable idea, suggestions and constructive criticism for improving the quality of this book.

I am deeply indebted to all of sugar mill owners and officers of eastern, western and central zones for their constant support and encouragement by providing necessary feedback and guidelines in the path of completion of the writing of the manuscript.

My special thanks to all of my research scholars namely, Mr Wasif Ali, Mr Pradip Ram, Dr Sanjay Kumar Sah, and Ms Shivani Kushwaha for their extensive co-operation to shape the work in the final phase.

My cordial thanks are due to all of employees of seasonal and permanent category (respondents), who have rendered all possible assistance and kind co-operation in the collection of primary/secondary data and relative information.

I express my deep sense of gratitude to all of previous researchers in the area of Quality of Work Life (QWL), since their valuable contribution has helped me a lot to enhance the area of study.

Lastly, my heartfelt gratitude to my wife, **Dr Seema Das** (Assistant Professor, Political Science, Banaras Hindu University), who have inspired, encouraged and motivated me constantly in completing this book.

Prof. S.C. Das
Faculty of Commerce
Banaras Hindu University

1

Quality of Work Life — An Introduction

1.1 Introduction

Human Resources (HR) have always been central to organisation. Recently, they have acquired an even more key role in building sustainable competitive advantage for the corporation. Economic, social and cultural development of any country mostly depends upon the human resources it has. Herbert contends, "The product of work is people". According to him, it is the people who constitute the core of an organisation; and it is again the people for whom we work. The modern management has been increasingly aware of the fact that "Human Factor" is the most important factor of all factors of production. Therefore, Rensis Likert (1967), who rightly observes, "All the activities of any enterprise are initiated and determined by the person who make-up that institution, plants, offices, computers, automated equipment and all else that make a modern firm uses are unproductive except for human effort and direction of all the tasks of management, managing the human component is the central and the most important task, because all else depends on how well it is done."

The future success of any organisations relies on the ability to manage a diverse body of talent that can bring innovative ideas, perspectives and views to their work. Today, the most important aspect of a successful business is to understand and manage its human resources strategically and competently. Rapid social and technological changes have been accompanied by changes in the relationship between the worker and the job. This created a negative impact on the working environment among the employees and has started developing the feeling of powerlessness, meaninglessness, formlessness, social isolation and self-estrangement. Such a feeling has resulted into lesser increase in productivity as compared to what was envisaged at the time of adopting a new technology. These symptoms are often associated with decreasing motivation and increasing counter-productive behaviour and worker demands on the workplace. Although these symptoms can certainly be found in the most workplaces, whether they are factories or offices, public or private organisations, the extent to which they are reported to exist in the workplace varies greatly (Mills, 1975). This led to the emergence of concept of quality of work life which aims at integrating the socio-psychological needs of people in the organisation, the unique requirements of a particular technology, the structure and processes of the organisation and socio-cultural milieu.

QWL is a recent concept for the behavioural scientists. The thought has then travelled through to be considered as a 'movement', 'reform' and 'policy' for increased productivity in an organisation (Promonis and Baumgratel, 1980). Therefore, QWL programmes have been receiving widespread attention in more and more organisations, both in developed and developing countries, for their contribution to job satisfaction, productivity and organisation success (Biswas, 1993). QWL is concerned with how the relationship between individuals, their physical, social economic work environment affect their attitude and behaviour that society considers to be important both on and off the job (Gupta, 1993). Moreover, QWL has been increasingly used to describe certain environmental and humanistic values neglected by the industrial societies in favour of technological advancement, industrial productivity and economic growth.

In the aforesaid context, the present study planned to assess the various facet of quality of working life such as demographic variables, working environment factor, relational factor, job factor and financial factor of employees in Uttar Pradesh sugar industry which can be broadly classified into two sub-sectors, the organised sector, i.e., sugar factories and the unorganised sector, i.e., manufactures of traditional sweeteners like *gur* and *khandsari*.

1.2 Quality of Work Life — Concept and Indicators

The notion of Quality of Working Life (QWL), as an English idiom is closely related to the quality of life concept. Both emerged relatively recently in the industrialised nations where English was the primary language. Parallel concepts and innovative moves towards life goals developed, however, almost simultaneously in several other industrial countries.

Humanisation of work, for instance, is often used in a number of languages as a synonym for quality of working life. In Europe, the most usual expression is "improvement of working condition", "working environment", "democratisation of work place" while the socialist countries, the term is "worker's protection" and in case of Japan, similar concept of *hatarakigai* and *ikigai* are used. However, the English concept of "quality of work life" is broadly understood in all industrial countries, even if it is sometimes barely used (Thorsrud, 1976).

Historically, it can be traced back to the quality of working life momentum that largely consisted a number of industrial psychologists in response to a perceived disenchantment with the organisation work in the late 1960s and early 1970s (Walton, 1973; Littler and Salaman,1984). A number of reports published in both US and UK sought to develop models of job redesign that aimed to improve utilisation of worker initiative and reduce job dissatisfaction thereby offering an alternative to the technocratic rigidity and inflexibility of Taylorism. QWL has also been associated with organisational changes aimed at increasing the levels of job enlargement (greater horizontal task flexibility) and job enrichment (greater vertical task flexibility including the taking of new responsibilities). Crucially, the idea is that of attaining the higher-level of participation and thereby motivation by improving the attractiveness of work itself rather than through improving the term and condition of work (Hertzberg *et al.,* 1959). QWL consists of opportunities for active involvement in group working arrangements or problem solving that are of mutual benefit to employees or employers, based on labour management cooperation. People also conceive of QWL as a set of methods, such as autonomous work groups, job enrichment and high-involvement aimed at boosting the satisfaction and productivity of workers (Feuer, D. 1989). Thus, QWL is a comprehensive construct that includes an individual's job- related well-being and the extent to which work experiences are rewarding, fulfilling and devoid of stress and other negative personal consequences (Shamir and Salomon, 1985).

Early work on QWL was strongly rooted in psychology with a focus on the individual. The historical context for this has been identified as the breakdown of the illusion of industrial consensus identified as occurring from the 1960s onwards (Thompson, 1983). The term Quality of Working Life (QWL) was probably coined originally at the first international conference on QWL at Arden House, New York, in 1972; that sought to share knowledge and initiate a coherent theory and practice on how to create the condition for a "Human Working Life" (Ryan, 1995). This conference set-up a task force to develop a model-based on four dimensions of integrity: (1) integrity of body, (2) integrity of social growth and development, (3) integrity of self, and (4) integrity of life roles.

It really got momentum in the beginning of 80's. From 1972 to 1980, the concern for QWL has gained momentum and has assumed the proportion of a movement. Some of the members of ICQWL wanted during 80s to hold another international conference. In Canada, QWL researches were gaining attention. The first open international conference was organised in Toronto in August, 1981 with the theme of 'QWL and the 80's. A large number of people – managers, union representatives, and academician, attended the conference. Jenkins (1981) observed that the Toronto Conference demonstrated that QWL is no longer the exclusive concern of academics but is becoming more and more an issue of ongoing organisational reality. During the twentieth century, our social science conceptualisations regarding work have been labelled scientific management, human relation, socio-technical systems theory and now possibly holistic learning organisation. QWL owes its origins to the marriage of the structural, system perspective of organisational behaviour with the interpersonal, human relation, supervisory-style perspective. In North America, Europe and Japan, QWL has been quite well received as an approach leading to greater democratisation and humanisation of work place as well as to greater productivity on the part of the work force.

The work on QWL had begun in India four decades ago with differences in the social, cultural, political and economic spheres. A major thrust in this area was a though proposition but social scientists have gradually weaned their way and the efforts of Ganguly (1976), Joseph (1978), De (1977, 1980), Mehta (1976), Sinha (1977), and Sayeed and Sinha (1981). It is further interesting to note that most of the work in Indian setting dealt with the QWL in theoretical and descriptive framework, or mostly in an action research context to bring about some desirable change in the design of work system (De, 1980).

For instance, QWL is a philosophy, a set of principles, which holds that people are the most important resource in the organisation as they are trustworthy, responsible and capable of making valuable contribution and they should be treated with dignity and respect (Straw and Heckscher, 1984).

Keith Davis says, "QWL refers to the favourableness or unfavourableness of a job environment for people." The basic purpose in this regard is to develop jobs aiming at human resource development as well as production enhancement. The QWL approach is a large step forward from the traditional job design of scientific management, which focussed mostly on specialisation and efficiency for the performance of narrow task. Basically, two reasons have been pointed out for redesigning jobs and organisation for better QWL: (i) classical designs originally give inadequate attention to human needs, and (ii) the needs and aspirations of workers themselves are changing.

Rosow (1974) explains the importance of work more in detail and relates it to success and failure of a man in society. According to him, "work is the core of life considering the deeper meaning of work to be individual and to life's values; work means being a good provider, it means autonomy, it plays off in success and it establishes self-respect or self-worth. Within this frame-work, the person who openly confesses active job satisfaction is virtually admitting failure as a man, a failure in fulfilling his moral role in society".

Richard Walton (1979), who had taken up extensive research on Quality of Work Life made significant contribution for the conceptualisation of the theme QWL. In fact, measuring QWL has become easy and practicable with the factors that he proposed. According to him, "Quality of work life is the work culture that serves as the corner stone". Hence, work culture of an organisation should be recognised and improved to improve Quality of Work Life of that organisation.

Robert H. Guest (1979) a noted behavioural scientist talks about feelings of an employee about his work while defining Quality of Work Life. The learned author points out the effect of Quality of Work Life on person's life. According to him "Quality of Work Life is a generic phrase that covers a person's feelings about every dimension of work including economic rewards and benefits, security, working condition, organisational and interpersonal relation and its intrinsic meaning in person's life". It is a process by which an organisation attempts to unlock the creative potential of its people by involving them in decision affecting their work lives.

Robert F. Craver (1983), a senior executive of American Telephone and Telegraphic Company (AT & T) says "Quality of Work Life is more than an attempt to pacify the growing demands of impatient employees. For the corporation involved productivity is at a stake, for the management, quality of work life offers new challenges, opportunity, growth and satisfaction". According to Fred Luthans, (1981) QWL is the socio-technological approach in job design. It is concerned with overall climate of work. It has been defined as a process of joint-decision making, collaboration and building mutual respect between management and employees. The purpose is to change the climate at work, so that the human technological organisational interface leads to better QWL Luthans, (1981). Another author Sangeeta Jain (1991) defines that any conscious effort that is aimed at improving working conditions, work content and its attendant conditions like safety, security wages and benefits can legitimately qualify as QWL activity. Ultimately, QWL is a concern not only to improve life at work, but also life outside work. Sharma and Ghosh (1993) give their general perception about improvement in QWL. Improved QWL leads to improved performance. Performance means not only physical output but also the behaviour of the worker in helping his colleagues in solving job related problems accepting orders with enthusiasm, promoting team spirit and accepting unfavourable work condition without complaints. M.G. Rao (1993) stated the essence of QWL in the following words: "The QWL is co-operative rather than authoritarian, evolutionary and open rather than static and rigid, informal rather than role-bound; impersonal rather than mechanistic; mutual respect and trust rather than hatred against each other'. The major factors that affect the QWL may be stated thus: salary, benefit, job security, alternative work schedules, and occupational stress, etc. De (1976) pointed out, "QWL is an indicator of how free the society is from exploitation, injustice, inequality, oppression and restrictions on the continuity of growth of man, leading to his development to the fullest".

The psychological factors have been seen from the angle of labour problems by Delamotte and Takezawa (1974) in their report for International Labour Organisation on QWL. They defined QWL as a set of new problems and their counter-measures which has gained recognition as important determinants of worker satisfaction and productivity in many societies during the period of their sustained economic growth. It was noted that traditionally QWL and job redesign have been used synonymously by professionals in India. It was noted that improvements in QWL in India can be brought about not only in work re-organisation and job re-design but also in several other areas which affect the QWL of an individual working in an organisation. In this connection, the ILO list of areas concern in improving QWL was noted. It was also suggested that QWL activities could be initiated in any of the areas listed below:

- Hours of work and arrangement of working time;
- Work organisation and job content;

- Impact of new technologies on working condition;
- Working condition of women, young as well as old workers including those employed in special categories;
- Work-related welfare services and facilities;
- Shop floor participation in the improvement of work performance and working condition; and
- Occupational safety and health.

QWL is much broader and more diverse than organisational development, in ensuring adequate and fair compensation, safe and healthy working conditions, opportunities for personal growth and development, satisfaction of social needs at work, protection of employee rights, compatibility between work and non-work responsibilities and the social relevance of work-life (Davis *et.al.,* 1975). There are three distinctive elements of QWL related interventions: (1) a concern about the effect of work on people as well as organisational effectiveness, (2) the idea of worker participation in organisational problem solving and decision-making and (3) the creation of reward structures in the workplace which consider innovative ways of rewarding employee input into the work process such as gain sharing, etc. (Lawler, 1982). Some of the elements that are relevant in determining an individual's quality of work life would include the task, the physical work environment, social environment within the organisation, administrative system and relationship between life on and off the job (Che Rose, Beh, Uli and Idris, 2006). A study conducted in Malaysia by Che Rose *et. al.* (2006) further concluded that the most important predictor of QWL is organisational climate, followed by career achievement, career satisfaction and career balance. Carr *et. al.* in their (2003) study used Ostroff's (1993) taxonomy to organise dimensions labelled as workplace climate and then used meta-analytic techniques to test a path analytic model. The results suggest that there are three higher order facets of climate (affective, cognitive, and instrumental) that affected individual level outcomes of job performance, psychological well-being, and withdrawal through their impact on organisational commitment and job satisfaction. A number of indicators are used to measure quality of work life of people. Following were the indicators used in Swedish (1974) survey of employment and work place relationship (UNESCO):

(a) Hours of Work: hours per day and week, overtime, rest-period, travel time, arrangement of work time (work-shift, days of week, desire for change in work time).
(b) Periods of unemployment (last five years).

(c) Desire for employment (obstacle to employment), early retirement.
(d) Domestic work.
(e) Physical work environment: physical strain, climatic and lighting provisions, dirt, dangerous substance, noise, accident risk.
(f) Psycho-social environment: mental strain, freedom in one's work, knowledge and skills originating in one's work, attitude to work.
(g) Preventing safety and health examination, type of remuneration.

Attempts at defining the concepts of QWL have been made by many. Taylor's (1973) and Sprin's (1975) viewpoint can be considered for an operational definition which describe QWL as "the degree of excellence in work and working conditions which contribute to the overall satisfaction of the individual and enhance individual as well as organisational effectiveness". Prominent among those who have contributed to the area are Harrik and Maccoby (1972), Heizel, Geodale, Jayner and Burke (1973), Cherns (1973, 1975), Davis and Cherns (1975), Emery and Thorsrud (1976), Macy and Marvic (1976), Green, Cashman, Ginsburg and Schiemann (1973) and Miller (1977).

Thus, precisely, in the broadest sense the term Quality of Work Life (QWL) aims at enhancing the entire organisational climate by humanising work, individualising organisations and changing the structural and managerial system. It takes into consideration the total values, both material and non-material, attained by a worker throughout his career life. QWL includes aspects of work-related life such as wages and hours, work environment, benefits and services, career prospects and human relations which is possibly relevant to workers satisfaction and motivation. Its main aim is to create a work environment where employees work in cooperation with each other and contribute to organisational objectives.

1.3 The Evolutionary Stages of Quality of Work Life

The evolution of the concept QWL was mainly in three phases:

(i) Scientific Management Movement
(ii) Human Relation Movement, and
(iii) Socio-technical Movement.

1.3.1 Scientific Management Movement: Federick W. Taylor (1947) was the advocate of scientific management movement. He viewed that the burden of planning and designing the work should be removed from the shoulders of workers. They should be given specific task and clear instruction as to how a particular job should be done before hand. He also advocated "Division of Work" which means that instead of assigning a worker entire job, divide it into parts and assign each part to a different worker. With the help of time, work and motion studies, Taylor viewed that workers can be briefed exactly what is to be done, when, where and how, leaving practically nothing to their discretion. Taylor had put his thoughts in point in his work "The principles of scientific management" in 1911 which was the most popular work of that period and influence not only the American industry, but industry all over the world for at least quarter of the century. Taylor, through his time and work study, division of labour and incentive schemes, tried to improve work life of employees. Thus, through incentive schemes and division of labour Taylor contributed towards Quality of Work life.

1.3.2 Human Relation Movement: The 'Human Relation' movement became popular in the 1940s, where much attention began to be paid to the workers' need and in realising the importance of human beings in total productivity. This approach was a significant departure from the "Taylorian Scientific Management" approach. Human relation movement was mainly concerned with inter-personal and group-relationship among workers and advocate participatory and democratic style of supervision to achieve work effectiveness. Maslow (1954), Hertzberg (1959), Mc-Gregor (1960) etc., were all important members of human relation school who contributed towards this view. Quality of Work Life has its roots in the theories of Maslow, Hertzberg and McGregor. The needs for fulfillment as that of Abraham Maslow's motivational theory of need hierarchy are comparable with those of the factors of Quality of Work Life. Basic needs like monetary benefits came first followed by good working condition. Later, it comes in career planning growth and development of human capabilities to satisfy. Maslow's esteem needs are comparable with opportunity to use and develop human capabilities. Lastly, challenging work is advocated by Walton to satisfy self-actualisation need in need hierarchy. Quality of Work Life concern itself with satisfying both hygiene factors and motivators as identified by Hertzberg to improve the work life of employees. The assumption of Mc-Gregor can be divided into two sets, i.e., Theory 'X' and theory 'Y'. Theory X is based on the traditional approach of human behaviour. Theory Y represents the democratic approach and gives to the employee's scope for creativity and responsibility. This assumes that the average human being does not inherently dislike work. Quality of Work Life assumes that all employees are basically active and reliable because of theory Y. Thus, it is evident that the quality of work life has had its origin in these theories of motivation.

1.3.3 Socio-technical Movement: In order to understand QWL, it is also essential to understand socio-technical approach to organisation and action research as methodology of change. Socio-technical approach is an improved school of thought from human relation movement which forms actual basis for present Quality of Work Life.

The Tavistock Institute of Human Relation (1947), conducted a series of studies in coal-mines. There was a subsequent research in Calico Textile Mills in Ahmedabad which was conducted by Prof. A.K. Rice. These two studies form basis for socio-technical movement. The basic features of socio-technical approach to organisation have been enunciated as ten principals by Chern (1979). They may not be considered a blue print. These are followings:

- Compatibility,
- Minimal Critical Specification,
- Variance Control,
- Multi-functional Principle,
- Boundary Location,
- Information Flow,
- Support Congruence,
- Design and Human Value,
- Transitional Organisation, and
- Incompletion: The Fourth Bridge Principle.

1.4 Development of QWL Programmes in India

In the developmental process, the term, Quality of Work Life, has acquired different definitions that the term has led to confusion. Nadler and Lawler (1983) brought out the confusion thus:

First Definition	1969-1972	QWL = Variables,
Second Definition	1969-1975	QWL = Approach,
Third Definition	1972-1975	QWL = Methods,
Fourth Definition	1975-1980	QWL = Movement,
Fifth Definition	1969-1982	QWL = Everything.

In Indian context, the QWL as a movement may be considered rising in comparison to Western, where there are a wide variation in Indian and Western culture. The set of industrial norms are quite different in both the civilisation and on top of this as compared to West, India's industrial growth is in developing stage. In India, despite efforts were being initiated by the Government and the private sector, the unorganised sector still existing this is as vast as the organised sector. India is a country with different culture, values, systems and varied interest. As such it is difficult to assess the impact of a particular concept in the country as a whole. For example, Lahiri and Srivastawa (1976) had found out from their study in one of the industry that extrinsic rewards are more important to the workers, whereas Dayal and Sharma (1975), in another similar study carried out in still another study conducted that intrinsic reward are more important to the workers. In another study, Dayal says that Indian labours prefer paternalistic approach of management while Srivastawa contradictory says that workers would like to participate in decision-making given an opportunity, based on one of his studies. Thorsrud, in this context says, "Even within the same country, there may be importance cultural differences with regard to the relative importance of motivating factors and therefore, there is a need to find local solutions to QWL problems rather than applying uniform principal which cannot be adopted to local requirement".

A recognition of the widening implication of 'Quality of Working Life' is reflected in the recommendations of The National Seminar on improving QWL in India was held in 1982 which made specific recommendations delineating the responsibilities of managers and employers, trade unions, professional organisations and Government in the development of QWL efforts. It was noted that the concept, although relevant in the Indian context, needs to be enlarge in its scope and coverage in view of somewhat divergent conditions prevailing in the country; this enlargement of the concept should manifest in several directions:

- Additional areas of concern for improving QWL in an organisation.
- Modification of the concept of organisational boundaries to indicate its permeability and interaction with the surrounding environment.
- Inclusion of the concern for creation of work for the unemployed and semi-employed.
- Recognition of the fact that the concern for QWL cannot be separated from improvement in the quality of life of the people.

Another National Symposium on Quality of Working Life (1983) was held in Hyderabad. Some case studies of QWL project in Indian enterprises and public system were represented and discussed. The delegates felt that presently there was a lull in the QWL movement in the country, and concerned efforts were needed to revive and revitalise it, and secure greater involvement of social and behavioural scientists, social thinkers, managements, trade unions, and the government. The delegates participating in the symposium raised a number of issues related to QWL concepts, goals and strategies of interventions. Some of these issues are listed below:

(a) Conceiving, installing and sustaining QWL in an organisation as a whole involving all its members across the various hierarchical levels.
(b) Developing QWL programmers for non-industrial setting (e.g., academic and research institution, the service sector, Government departments and agencies, etc.).
(c) Developing QWL programmers for specific categories of members in an organisation (e.g., women, ex-servicemen, schedule cast/tribe employees, the physically handicapped, first generation migrants from rural areas, etc.) without upsetting the cohesiveness and effectiveness of the organisation.
(d) Introducing "Flexi-time" as an integral part of a QWL project: what is the Indian experience.
(e) Linkages between QWL and productivity: how to bring about a consensus on this issue between management and the trade unions, at the national level, unit level, and shop floor level. Is QWL a means, or an end, or both.
(f) Evaluating the impact and continuity of the QWL processes and systems in an organisation.
(g) Roles and motivations of the external consultant in a QWL project; how to develop mechanism for continuity of QWL effort in an organisation, when the external consultant leave.
(h) Tactical and strategic issues in developing a QWL project; how to define the goals and indicators of QWL (and who decides?); the point of entry in an organisation; issue and diffusion from the experimental sub-system of the organisation; mechanism of self-review and mid-course correction.
(i) Relationship between the Quality Circle approach and the QWL strategies: how to integrate the two in an organisation.

The Commulative Digest prepared by International Labour Organisation (1982) records only nine studies on Quality of Working Life being conducted at different organisations in India. However, since last four decades the prominent among those who have contributed to the area are De (1975), Majumdar (1976), Ganguli (1976), Sinha (1977), Bharadwaj (1983), Singh (1983), Singhal (1983), Pestonjee (1983), D'Souza (1984), Rehman (1984), De (1984), Rao (1986), Mehta (1987), Khalique and Rahman (1987), Gupta and Khandelwal (1988), Sengupta and Sidique (2001), Varadaraj and Sellappan (2008), etc.

1.5 Dimensions of QWL

QWL is the relationship between the worker and his environment. Varying conditions of employment such as healthy work environment, importance of decision made, recognition at work, job security, job satisfaction, etc., form important dimensions of QWL. QWL dimensions which are described by some of the authors in brief are as follow:

Boisvert(1977)

- Control over work,
- Extent of use of own judgement,
- Importance of decisions made,
- Learning opportunity,
- Use of skills and abilities,
- Control over criteria of work adequacy,
- Feedback on performance,
- Challenges in the job,
- Work variety,
- Interaction with co-workers,
- Recognition at work,
- Possibilities for taking pride in one's work,
- Possibilities for relating work to final products of the organisation,
- Extent of preparation of the job for a desirable work future, and
- Participation in organisational decision-making.

Sinha (1982) stated four main dimensions:

- Job satisfaction,
- Job attractiveness,
- Intrinsic motivation, and
- Control and influence.

Sinha and Sayeed (1980)

- Economic benefits,
- Physical working condition,
- Mental state,
- Career orientation,
- Advancement on merit,
- Job stress,
- Effect on personal life,
- Union-management relation,

- Self-respect,
- Supervisory relationship,
- Intergroup relations,
- Apathy,
- Confidence in management,
- Meaningful development,
- Control, influence and participation,
- Employee commitment,
- General life satisfaction, and
- Organisational climate.

The American authors **Klatt, Mudrick and Schuster (1985)** identified eleven specific issues in general which we can also adopt. They are:

- Pay and Stability of Employment,
- Occupational Stress,
- Organisational Health Programmers
- Alternative Work Schedule,
- Participative Management and Control of Work,
- Recognition,
- Superior- Subordinate Relations,
- Grievance Procedure,
- Adequacy of Resources,
- Seniority and Merit in Promotion and Employment,
- Employment on Permanent Basis.

Rao (1993) stated the following factors that affect the QWL:

- Pay benefits,
- Job-security,
- Occupational stress,
- Worker participation,
- Social integration,
- Work and total life space and,
- Alternative work schedule.
  - Flexi-time,
  - Staggered hours,
  - Compressed work week,
  - Job enrichment, and
  - Autonomous work group.

Chander (1993)

- Decision-making authority,
- Growth and development,

- Job security,
- Organisational prestige,
- Feeling of worthwhile accomplishment,
- Pay and allowances, and
- Recognition and appreciation.

1.6 Measurement of Quality of Working Life

In view of dearth of systematic work in the area of Quality of Work Life, the measurement of the same seemed to be a practical difficulty. Various criteria are evolved in the past four decades. Majority of the studies in this area are theoretically oriented. Though, the list of QWL dimension to be considered for its measurement is quite exhaustive, with the exception of general motor survey (Carlson, 1978). Boisvert (1977) identified fifteen dimensions for measuring QWL. On the other hand, Walker's (1975) quality of working life involved the task, the physical work environment and social environment within the organisation, the administrative system of the enterprises and the relationship between life and the job.

Similarly, Ghosh and Kalra (1982), Ganguly (1979), Joseph (1978), Carlson (1977) etc., took different dimensions for their study of quality of working life. The important of all these studies are by Carlson and Walton in American set-up and Sinha and Sayeed in Indian set-up. Very little, however, has been done at the empirical level to relate QWL dimension with various processes of the organisation. Employees' source of stress and level of satisfaction regarding several aspect of work are also measured to get a better understanding of the overall QWL in the institution and although these aspects are not work life on their own, perception of quality of work life is often assessed using job satisfaction and organisational climate surveys (Krueger, Brazil, Lohfeld, Edward, Lewis, Tjam, 2002).

Sashkin and Lengermann (1984) have taken a combination of two factors, i.e., conditions of the work and the feelings aroused and the impression of the worker to each of the condition with emphasis on the productivity in an organisation. The conditions of work were measured by autonomy, work speed and routine, task-related interaction, personal growth opportunity and work complexity. The feelings have been measured by asking certain questions about various activities of the work. Verwayen (1978) has reported that the organisation for Economic Cooperation and Development, Paris had initiated Social Indicators Development Programme in some of the countries to measure quality of life on the assumption that similarities of well-being and methodological principals of these surveys will be consent for all the countries under study. The areas that have been selected for his intensive work were:

(i) Healthfulness of life,
(ii) Measurement of learning,
(iii) Employment,
(iv) Quality of working life,
(v) Time and leisure,
(vi) Income, wealth and material deprivation,
(vii) Housing condition,
(viii) Quality of natural environment,
(ix) Measurement of victimisation,
(x) Inequality,
(xi) Economic accessibility,
(xii) Comprehensive survey,
(xiii) Methodological issue in data collection,
(xiv) Presentation of social indicators and statistics, and
(xv) Applicability of selected social concern and indicators to particular national contexts.

The dimension taken by Sayeed and Sinha for the measurement of QWL were, economic benefits, physical working condition, mental state, career orientation, advancement on merit, job stress, effect on personal life, union-management relations, self-respect, supervisory relations, apathy, confidence in management, meaningful development, control, influence and participation, employee commitment, general life satisfaction and organisational climate. However, various researchers who carried on studies in this area came up with various criteria which are not entirely different from each other. Walton (1973) gives us a model of analysis of important experiments on QWL and considers eight conceptual categories that include factors of motivation summarised as following table:

Table 1.1: Walton Model of Quality of Work Life

Dimensions	*Indicators*
I. Adequate and Fair Compensation	- Internal and external fairness - Justice in the compensation - Allotment of productivity profits - Proportionality between wages
II. Safe and Healthy Working conditions	- Reasonable hours of working - Safe and healthful physical environment

(Contd.)

(Contd. Table 1.1)

Dimensions	*Indicators*
III. Opportunity to Develop Human Capacities	- Autonomy - Relative self-control - Multiple qualities - Information on the total process
IV. Opportunity for Career Growth	- Possibility of career - Personal growth - Perspective of wage advance - Job Security
V. Social Integration in the Work force	- Absence of prejudice - Equality - Mobility - Relationship - Communitarian sense
VI. Constitutionalism	- Rights of protection to the worker - Personal privacy - Labour laws - Freedom of expression - Impartial treatment
VII. Work and Quality of Life	- Balanced paper in the work - Stability of schedules - Few geographic changes - Time for leisure of the family
VIII. Social Relevance	- Image of the company - Social responsibility of the company - Responsibility for the products - Job practices

Source: Walton (1973).

(I) Adequate and Fair Compensation: In spite of the importance gained by the other factors during the last four decades, the compensation plays a greater role in employee's satisfaction. Especially, in a country like India, where the employee welfare programmers and well-being programmers take back seat, the compensation is the main sources of satisfaction to the employee. Organisation at rural and semi-urban regions can satisfy their employees with comparatively lower levels of compensation than their urban-based counterpart. The urban-based organisation usually compensates the extra cost of living through higher dearness allowance, keeping basic the same. The level of fair wages also changes depending upon cost of living. As the cost of living increases, employee demand for more pay.

(II) Safe and Healthy Working Condition: Physical working condition is the second most important aspect in measuring Quality of Work Life as Walton has rightly categorised. Employees who spend a lot of time at their work-place consider the physical working condition as an important factor, especially chemical industries, engineering industries, fertiliser industries, etc., where potential possibility of danger exist. Proper seating arrangement, water facility, fresh air and good sanitary conditions are important to the employees, who engage themselves in desk-work. Absence of such good conditions may result in ailments, back pain and rheumatic pain which in turn frustrate the employee who may develop stress. Physical conditions at work places which are second home for employees are thus an important factor in measuring Quality of Work Life.

(III) Opportunity to Develop Human Capacities: An employee must satisfy, given an opportunity to use and develop his capabilities. According to Maslow, people want to satisfy their high-order needs once they are satisfied with their basic needs like fair pay and good physical conditions. These high-orders needs include recognition and social status. More regulations and control mechanism by the management may dissatisfy the employee. This was the very reason why Taylor was criticised. An employee provided optimum degree of freedom in work can improve himself on the job which gives him immense satisfaction. Periodic discussion with the employee, calling for suggestion and forming work group like 'Quality Circles' help the employee in improving his capabilities on job.

(IV) Opportunity for Career Growth: The employees seek career growth more and more recently. Job security ceased to satisfy employees. Employee tends to drift from jobs which do not promise career growth more and more organisations are helping employees in this direction by helping them draw their career paths. The organisations have a counsellor for this purpose who helps the employees. Not only drawing career paths, but the organisations also help employee achieve next position through training. Organisational chart is so prepared to accommodate employees in next higher position. Internal promotion system is gaining importance. The employee is prepared to take-up a higher position where there is possibility. Prolonged employment in the same position may cause employee develop stress. Care is to be taken to chart proper career charts for employees at some level so as a balance of human resource in the organisation is maintained.

(V) Social Integration in the Work Force: According to Walton, a satisfying ideality and self-esteem are influenced by a five characteristics of the workplace. Freedom from prejudice, egalitarianism, and upward mobility are the steps to be necessarily taken by the management for ensuring higher QWL. Though, the initiative is to be from management. The employees also should give their complete support and co-operation to make the efforts of management a success.

An organisation can possess supportive work groups and interpersonal openness in other words 'Industrial Democracy' through establishing 'Work Committees' which intend to "promote measures for securing and preserving amity between employer and workmen and to that end to comment upon matter of their common interest or concern and endeavour to settle any material difference of opinion in respect of such matters" (Sharma, B.R., 1987). Another step in this direction could be setting up of 'Joint-Management Councils'. These were first set-up by Industrial Dispute Act, 1947 in 1958. 'Joint-Management Councils' meant to (a) improve working condition, productivity and communication, (b) assist in the administration of law and collective agreements, (c) encourage suggestions from workers, and (d) create a sense of participation.

(VI) Constitutionalism: Bias on part of management, lack of privacy, improper process of discipline, etc., tamper the constitutionalism of an organisation. The constitutionalism can be considered as hygiene factor, i.e., though it may not satisfy or motivate the employees considerably. The absence of it is definitely felt by the employees and may have adverse effects. Though employees consider work place their second home they may not want to disclose their private lives at work place. As such management should take steps to maintain its employee privacy unless he himself comes out with his problems, where the management can offer some counselling or any other helps. So as in case of bias, it is the most dissatisfying to an employee to find out that his colleague is being treated differently from him, which will have an adverse effect on his QWL.

(VII) Work and Quality of Life: The very purpose of worker being at work place is his work. As such work itself is of great importance. Satisfactory work can influence the employee's Quality of Work Life immensely. A challenging tasks which utilises the capabilities of employees' plays important role in QWL. Right person for right job is the motto gaining importance. Emery and Thorsurd (1969), identified six psychological requirements of working peoplc.

(a) The need for variety in the content of a job.
(b) The need for being able to learn on the job and go on learning.
(c) The need for some minimal area of decision-making that the individual can call his own.

(d) The need for some minimal degree of social support and recognition in the work place.
(e) The need for individual to be able to relate what he does and what he produces to his social life.
(f) The need to feel that the job leads to some sort of desirable future.

(VIII) Social Relevance of Work: The employees feel a need to relate their work socially. For example, those in service-oriented organisation who directly relate their jobs socially and can gain immediate recognition in a group are more satisfied. If his organisation is attracted/criticised by the Government or public on any aspect, the employee develops stress and is frustrated. As such, social relevance of the work of each employee is very important in measuring his Quality of Work Life. Organisation is an interdependent social and technical system. Socio-technical system requires social and technical system to be jointly optimised. It is from this notion of socio-technical system that the Quality of Work Life emerged.

1.7 Benefits from Improved QWL

There are various elements which influence the individual's work experience. Therefore, it is certain that an improved QWL will affect these variables. As the perception of QWL differs from individual to individual so is the gain perceived in various terms. QWL programmers incorporate a number of critical elements including a commitment from top management-acknowledgement from both management and employees that a voluntary desire from both sides to cooperate is essential. From the organisations point of view the gain of QWL improvement is significant because there is:

(i) Improved quality,
(ii) Increased output,
(iii) Reduced absenteeism,
(iv) Decrease higher turnover, and
(v) Better labour management relation, etc.

From the employee's point of view the gains of improved quality of work life are:

(i) Job satisfaction,
(ii) Greater control over one's own job,
(iii) Recognition,
(iv) Increased self-esteem,
(v) A sense of accomplishment, and
(vi) Fewer mental health problems, improved physical and psychological health.

In short, we can say that a higher quality of working life can often lead to decrease absenteeism and higher turnover, few accidents and higher quality and quantity of output of goods and services. The most direct and immediate gain from an improved QWL is job satisfaction. These two phenomenons are so closely related that they are often assumed to be one of the same, and people sometimes use it interchangeably. But the term job satisfaction refers to an individual's affective reaction or feelings towards his or her job and the term QWL refers to the individual work experiences. Job satisfaction is determined largely by how well an individual's actual rewards and experience on his job are compared to his desired or expected rewards and experience. Quality of work life is a broader concept than job satisfaction in the sense that it includes both the job content and job context.

Generally, the workers having high QWL experience high job satisfaction. Individuals, whose important needs are being satisfied by their job- related activity, invariably express positive feelings about these jobs and hence, there are increased in individual productivity. Individual productivity and quality of work life are closely related, especially when productivity is defined in terms of individual's internal work standards. Improved quality of working life improves the organisational effectiveness on the whole. If the interest of workers and goals of the organisation are mutually supportive, improvement in quality of work life will result in gains for both parties.

1.8 Changing Technology and its Impact on QWL

QWL has been taken as a new approach to provide careful balance of human imperative and technological imperative. The emergence of post-industrial era is stimulated by ever-increasing rate of change in technology. The traditional organisations follow the technological imperative, which regard man simply as an extension of the machine and therefore as an expendable spare part, thus rendering the meaning of QWL-vain. By contrast, the emergent new work paradigm is founded on the principal of joint optimisation, which regards man as complementary to the machine and values his unique capabilities for appreciative and evaluating judgment. The difference between the two can be visualised as follow:

The high rate of change of technology has consequences for organisation and job structure. On the product side, frequent new developments are leading to the growth of shorter production runs with the resulting need for adaptability of organisation and workers to more

Table 1.2: Old Paradigm vs. New Paradigm of HRM

Sr. No.	*Old Paradigm*	*New Paradigm*
1.	The Technological imperative.	Joint optimisation.
2.	Man as the extension of the machine.	Man as complementary to the machine.
3.	Man as an expendable spare part.	Man as a resource to be developed.
4.	Maximum task breakdown, simple narrow skills.	Optimum task grouping, multiple broad skills.
5.	External controls (supervisors, specialist staff, and procedures).	Internal controls (self-regulating sub-system-systems).
6.	Tall organisation chart, autocratic style.	Flat organisation chart, participative style.
7.	Competition, gamemanship.	Collaboration, congeniality.
8.	Organisation purpose only.	Members and society purpose also.
9.	Alienation.	Commitment.
10.	Low risk- taking	Innovation.

Source: Trehan, R. (2008), 'Work Environment and Quality of Life', Regal Publication, New Delhi, pp.15-16.

changes. On the production side, there is the phenomenon of more sophisticated machines and simpler manual activities embedded within automated complex production processes. The advanced technology presents us with a number of opportunities to develop new and more human organisational forms and jobs leading to a high QWL.

Restructure the workplace and redesigning job is one of the two major thrusts of 'Quality of Working Life' (QWL) movement. Many social observers argue that dissatisfaction has emerged from the routinisation of work and a scientific management mentality in the design of jobs. To confront what appears to be a steady decline in work-related satisfaction (Cooper, *et.al.,* 1979), many jobs have been restructured, so that employees will take more of an interest in their work and subsequently perform better (Jonson, 1981).

Ford (1973) states that 17 out of 18 experiments with clerical and other telephone company employees showed positive improvement after jobs were enriched. A study of technicians, engineers and sales representatives indicated that job enrichment pays off in better performance and greater satisfaction (Paul *et. al.,* 1969). Through a series of studies (Hackman and Lawler, 1971; Hackman and Oldham, 1975), a model of job characteristics was developed which states that work motivation is fraction of at least three sets of variables: Job core characteristics, psychological states of employees and employees' growth need strengths. Davis (1957) had delineated 23 criteria for job design. Out of this nine were adopted by the socio-technical group. The item such as desirable future was translated into job design terms as promotion prospects. The work of Davis in America on job design provides information about developments within the socio-technical school in the early 1960s. He has sought to praise highly the concept of socio-technical system, joint optimisation, and responsible autonomy to show that many studies lend them empirical support (Davis, 1972 a, b, c, d; 1976). Davis has argued very clearly that job specifications are connected with the satisfaction of general human needs such as the need for variety, for learning and for control over one's environment. He also put forward his views in the context of alleged growing demands for meaningful work (Davis, 1972).

It was often asserted that effective socio-technical changes cannot be introduced without the commitment of top management. A number of cases demonstrated that this is not always the case. A remarkable case of this kind has been reported from Corning and Glass Workers (Beer and Huse, 1972). The R and D department of the plant introduced a change programme with the assistance of behavioural scientists. Other departments were impressed with the success of the programme and tried out the changes for themselves. Since then, widespread corporate support has been obtained for work redesign based on socio-technical research. Thus, QWL emphasises on participative mechanism in view of giving freedom to employees in their tasks performance. Traditional jobs have various negative effects on social system and make an individual psychologically sick. This resulted into high absenteeism, low output, indiscipline, low productivity, high rework and rejection, demand for more money, finding fault in the organisational system (Gupta, 1993).

1.9 Quality of Work Life and Organisational Variable

Quality of work life programmers when assessed reveals their effect on the different HRM variables of an organisation. Because of poor design of socio-technical system, employees also experience alienation. Alienation is a feeling of powerlessness, meaninglessness, loneliness, and boredom, lack of involvement and lack of attachment to job (Keith Davis). This job discontent and job pressure may in turn affect employees' health giving way to general unhappiness. Hence, it is viewed that QWL should be designed along with all activities of HRM. Quality of Work Life and employee's performance often go hand in hand. For one thing, most conditions that contribute to performance (like equitable salaries, financial incentives and effective employee selections) will also contribute to the QWL. In fact, every personnel-related action affects the QWL in some way.

Table 1.3: Effect of HRM Activities on QWL

Sr. No.	*Management Activities*	*Effect on the QWL*
1.	**Job Analysis**	Finding out what human requirement are necessary so that people with the necessary skill and aptitudes can be placed into the jobs where they can perform best and be satisfied.
2.	**Selection**	Placing the right person on the right job should provide that person with a more satisfying, rewarding and motivating experience.
3.	**Job Evaluation**	Having adequate, equitable wages is a major consideration of most people in defining the Quality of their work life.
4.	**Job Enrichment**	By tapping 'Higher order' needs to encourage the employees to grow and use all his or her abilities.
5.	**Safety and Health**	A safe, healthy work environment is an obvious element contributing to the QWL.
6.	**Grievance Procedure**	Helps protect employee's rights and dignity and therefore contributes to the QWL.
7.	**Equal Employment Opportunity**	Protects rights of minority workers and thereby contributes to their QWL.
8.	**The Reward System**	Adequate rewards and wages that are equitable externally and internally and individuality of incentive systems and benefits.

Source: Gary Dessler, "Personnel Management Modern Concept and Techniques", p. 83.

1.10 Relationship between Quality of Working Life and Quality of Life

For working individual 'Quality of Life' cannot be separated from the 'Quality of Work' that he does. The quality of work is a basic and decisive indicator of life quality (De N.R. 1984). Quality of works depends on the share of creative activity in the working process. When we show our preference for quality of work, we include quality. The higher this share, the higher the quality of work and consequently, the quality of life. While reading literature on Quality of Life (QOL), one comes across terms like needs, social indicators, and social well-being, good or bad working condition, etc. The concept of "Quality of Life" is said to encompass all the maternal aspect of human life and may even extend beyond it to cover the physical and psychological dimensions. Operationally, Quality of Life was defined in a UNESCO Report (1977), as an inclusive concept which covered all aspects of living including material satisfaction of vital needs as well as more transcendental aspect of life such as personal development, self-realisation and a healthy eco-system (Parthasarthy, 1988).

The quality of work life has an important bearing on the overall health or well-being of an individual. Chavdar Kiuranov Szalai, ed. (1980), emphasised the relation between the quality of work life and quality of life:

(a) quality of life depends on the socio-economic character of work. It depends on the relations of production of the people enter in the societal reproduction of their life.

(b) Some features of quality of work are reflected in the quality of life such as whether the work in question is interesting and challenging for the person doing it. An individual may lack interest in work that is merely the accomplishment of a routine, repetitive dull task evolving nothing but boredom. Another characteristic of quality of work is the satisfaction with the kind of work done.

It is by no means surprising that social scientists, who are not directly immediate concerned with work redesign, socio-technical system or the quality of work life devoted to an organisational setting only, describe their concern for the future of work on a more comprehensive framework that do the applied behavioural scientists:

- Within the organisation itself there is scope for extending critical consciousness of the members from work place to their immediate environmental context. There are examples in support of this proposition. Workers at the grassroots, participating in work system redesign, picking up the key lesson from their experience, showed interest in the company-run school system for children, so that the quality of education can improve. Large number of welfare services, healthcare, food supply, immediate environment and the workers residential colonies could be looked upon with a new perspective.
- Employees of productive organisation can become leading parts in influencing the quality of decision-making, planning process and

implementation machinery by their productive intervention. It is postulated that an apathetic work culture would not have succeeded in raising and mobilising some collective consciousness.

- Quality of work life in micro-organisations can derive its substance and broaden its horizon by drawing upon the insights of the quality of life movements.
- Need to perceive the life-sized burning problems which cast deepening shadow of threats upon quality of life and work (Trehan, R. 2008).

Quality of life acquired sociological importance and become a topic of social research which coverage largely on people's welfare and well- being, their living conditions, their style of life, their standard of living. It is a new branch of socio-economic investigation took a formal shape called "study of social indicator system".

1.11 Techniques for Improving QWL

The Quality of Work Life movement is of recent origin and has a long way to go. Individual as well as organised efforts are required to improve the quality of work life for millions of workers in the country. According to Subba Rao, the strategies for improving quality of work life are self- managed work teams, job redesign and enrichment, effective leadership and supervisory behaviour, career development, alternative work schedule, job security, etc. All the above steps depict the importance of management's efforts in this regard. By implementing such changes, the management can create a sense of involvement, commitment and togetherness among the employees which paves way for better Quality of Work Life. In advocating a restricted, rather than a global view of QWL in Indian organisations, Singh (1982) suggested that organisations can be classified into three categories.

(A) Organisations in which physical working conditions are poor or hazardous.

(B) Organisations in which physical working conditions are good, but work is psychologically frustrating.

(C) Organisations in which both physical and psychological conditions are good but work is organised in a traditional manner.

Research evidence indicates that a large number of organisations fall in the second category, in which the concerns of employees relate to psychological need satisfaction (Dayal and Sharma, 1975; Mehta, 1982). In such organisations, QWL efforts need to be directed towards satisfying the higher order social and psychological needs of the employees through methods such as job enlargement, job enrichment,participation in work- related matters and the like. As for the third category of organisations the major concerns would be those pertaining to new forms of work organisations that would allow a richer QWL. However, some of the techniques used to improve the QWL are as given below:

(i) Flexible Work Schedule: There should be flexibility in the work schedule of the employees. Alternative work schedule for the employees can be flexi-time, staggered hours, compressed work week, etc. Flexi-time is a system of flexible working hours, staggered hours schedule means that different group of employees begin and end work at different intervals. Compressed work week involves longer hours of work per day for fewer days per week.

(ii) Job Enlargement: This entails the extension of job duties and rotation that might, for example, a company a switch to some form of team working or more functional flexibility. Clearly, such moves will require training (Littler and Salaman, 1984).

(iii) Job Enrichment: Job enrichment or job redesigning improves the quality of jobs. It attempts to provide a person with existing, interesting stimulating and challenging work. It helps to satisfy the higher-level needs of the employees. This entails a vertical extension of duties, normally consisting of a greater proportion of one's duties being those traditionally associated with supervisory or managerial roles in the traditional Tayloristic model of workplace design. Such duties might include daily and weekly planning of work, quality control, problem identification and solving, maintenances, budgeting and supplier and customer contact. Again, training in new competencies is required (Kuhlmann, 2002).

(iv) Opportunity for Development: This concept entails the notion of worker input into and discretion over developmental processes at the workplace in the spirit of socio-technical system theory. Career development is very important for ambitious and achievement-oriented employees. If the companies are provided with opportunity for their advancement and growth, they will be highly motivated and their commitment to the organistion will increase.

(v) Autonomous Work Group: Autonomous work group is also called self-managed work teams. In such group, the employees are given freedom of decision-making. Here employees are granted powers of self-regulation in areas such as the pace of work, job methods and sequencing without reference back (*Ibid*). They are themselves responsible for planning, organising and controlling the activities of their groups. The groups are also responsible for their success or failure. In much of the literature such notions are termed 'empowerment' (Senge, 1990; Willmott, 1993).

(vi) Employees Participation in Management: People in the organisation should be allowed to participate in the management decision affecting their lives and the labour process and design of the work place. The notion of consultative participation is intended here whereby channels are established for employees to give a voice on matters that affect them and thus some degree of influence (EPOC, 1997). Quality circle, management by objective, suggestion system and other forms of employee's participation in management help to improve the QWL.

(vii) Job Security: Employees want stability of employment. Adequate job security provided to the employees will improve the QWL to a large extent.

(viii) Equitable Justice: The principle of equitable administrative justice should be applied in disciplinary action, grievance procedure, promotion, transfer and work assignment, etc. Partiality and biasness at any stage can discourage the workers and affect the QWL.

To sum up, the more psychological-based dimensions of QWL outlined by Davis and Cherns, Walton and others are seen here as the stakeholder outcomes afforded to employees from a process of change in an organisation. The impact of such change on QWL is mediated by certain organisational outcomes in terms of job redesign. Thus, employees who are provided with good 'Quality of Work Life, can more and more concentrate on their development. Good quality of work life creates such cordial atmosphere where human resource development programmes becomes easy and encouraging. A good understanding between employees and management can be brought out with the help of quality of work life. More and more attention is to be paid towards improving quality of work life to form a firm basis for human resource development.

References

Beer, M. and Huse, E.F. (1972). System approach to organisation development, *Applied Behavioural Science, 8*, 79-109.

Biswas, S.K. (1993), Quality of Work Life, What Is It? *The Indian Journal of Labour Economics,* Vol. 36 (4), 759-64.

Boisvert, M.P. (1977). The quality of working life: An analysis. *Human Relation, 30 (II),* 155-160.

Carr, J.Z., Schmidt, A.M., Ford, J., and Deshon, R.P. (2003). Climate perceptions matter: A meta-analytic path analysis relating molar climate, cognitive and affective states, and individual level work outcome, *Journal of Applied Psychology, 88*, 605–619.

Chander, Subash and Singh, Parampal (1993), Quality of Work Life in a University: An Empirical Investigation, Management and Labour Studies, 18 (2), 97-107.

Che Rose, R.; Beh L.S., Uli, J., Idris K. (2006), An Analysis of Quality of Work Life (QWL) and Career-related Variables, *American Journal of Applied Sciences 3*, (12): 2151-2159.

Cherns,. A.B. (1973). 'Belter Wasking Lives; A Social Scientists View', *Journal of Occupational Psychology, 47*, 23-28.

_____(1975). 'Perspective on the Quality of Working Life, *Journal of Occupational Psychology, 48*, 153-167.

_____(1979). "Using the Social Sciences," London: Routledge and Kegan Paul.

Cooper, M.S., B.S. Morgan, P.M. Foley, and L.B. Kaplan, (1979). "Changing Employee Values: Deepening Discontent?" *Harvard Business Review*, 57:1 pp. 117-25.

Davis, L.E. (1957). Job Design Research, *Journal of Industrial Engineering*. Nov - Dec.

______(1972a). The coming crisis for production management. In L.E. Davis and J.C. Taylor (eds.), Design of Jobs Harmondsworth: Penguin.

______ (1972b). Readying the Unready: Post-industrial jobs. In L.E. Davisand J.C. Taylor (eds.), Design of Jobs Harmondsworth: Penguin.

______ (1972c). The design of jobs. In L.E. Davis and J.C. Taylor (eds.), Design of Jobs Harmondsworth: Penguin.

______(1972d). Job satisfaction research: The post-industrial view. In L.E. Davis and J.C. Taylor (eds.), Design of Jobs Harmondsworth: Penguin.

______(1975). Work revamping can help workers and efficiency. LMRS, *Newsletter*. National League of Cities, Washington, D.C., 6 (12), 3.

______(1976). Developments in job design. In P.B. Warr (ed.), Personal goals and work design. London: Wiley.

______(1977). Evolving alternative organisation design: Their socio-technical bases. *Human Relations,* 39 (3), 261-273.

Davis, L.E. and A.B. Cherns *et. al.*, (1975). The Quality of Working Life. Volume One: Problems, Prospects and the State of the Art. New York: The Free Press.

Dayal and Sharma (1975), The Meaning of Work to Bank Employees, Jamshedpur, XLRI (*Mimeographed)*.

Delamotte, Y. and Takezawa, S. (1974). 'QWL in International Perspective', International Labour Organisation, Geneva.

De, N.R. (1976). 'Some Dimensions of Quality of Working Life', paper presented at the National Seminar on Quality of Working Life, Bombay, pp.-22-27.

_______ (1977). 'Diflusion of Work System Redesign on Participative Design in a Large Complex Engineering Factory, (mimeo), National Labour Institute, New Delhi.

_______ (1980). 'Redesign of work system and Quality of Work Life', Joshi, N.C. and Kesary, V.G. (eds), Reading in Managements. Allahabad: A.H. Wheeler.

_______ (1984). "Towards an Appreciation of Quality of Life and Quality of Work Life." *Economic and Political Weekly,* 19 (20-21): M46- M57.

E.F. Huse, Organisation Development and Change (Minneapolis: West, 1980), p. 508.

Emery, E.F., and Thorsurd, E (1969). "Form and the Content in Industrial Democracy" Tavistock, London.

EPOC (1997), New Forms of Work Organisation: Can Europe Realise its Full Potential? Dublin: European Foundation.

Feuer, D., 1989. Quality of work life: a cure for all ills? Training: *The Magazine of Human Resources Development, 26*: 65-66.

Ford, R. (1973), "Job Enrichment Lessons for At and T", *Harvard Business Review,* Vol. Jan- Feb., 15-20.

Guest R.H. (1979), 'Quality of Work Life -- Learning from Terry-town', Harward Business Review, July-August, 28-39.

Gupta, T. K. (1993). Quality of Work Life, *The Indian Journal of Labour Economics, Vol. 36* (4), 770-77.'

Hackman, J.R. and G.R. Oldham *et. al.,* (1975), A New Strategy for Job Enrichment, California Management Review.

Hackman, J.R. and Lawler, E.E. (1971), Employee Reactions to Job Characteristics, *Journal of Applied Psychology,* Vol. 53(3), 259-86.

Heizel, M.F., Geodale, J.G. Joyner, R.C. and Burke, R.J. (1973). 'Development of a Quality of Working Life Questionnaire: Item Discrimination Study', Department of Labour, Ottawa, Canada.

Hertzberg, F. Maunser, B., Snyderman, B.B. (1959), The Motivation to Work, New York: John Wiley and Sons.

Herrick, N. and Maccoby, M. (1972). Humanising Work: A priority Goal of the 1970's, Paper presented at the International Conference on the Quality of Working Life, Adren House, Harrison, New York.

International Labour Organisation (1982). Condition of Work: *A Cumulative Digest*, ILO, Geneva.

Jain, Sangeeta (1991), Quality of Work Life, Deep and Deep Publication.

Janson, R. "Work Redesign: A Result-oriented Strategy That Works," in J.H. Donnelly, J.L. Gibson, and J. M. Ivanceich (eds.) Fundamentals of Management (Plano, Tex: Business Publication, Inc., 1981), pp. 199-204.

Jenkins, D. (1981). QWL: Current Trends and Directions. A series of occasional papers No. 3. Ontario: Quality of Working Life Centre.

Keith Davis, (1981). 'Human Behaviour at Work', Tata McGraw Hill Publishing Co. Ltd., New Delhi, p. 273.

Klatt, Murdick and Schuster, (1985). Human Resource Management, Chartex E. Merrill Publishing Company, Ohio, 585-592.

Kuhlmann, M. (2002), Group Work and Democracy, in Docherty, P., Forslin, J., Shani, R. (eds). Creating Sustainable Work System: Emerging Perspectives and Practice, London: Routledge.

Lawler, E.E. III., (1982). Strategies for improving the quality of work life. *Am. Psychologist,* 37: 486- 493.

Littler, C., Salaman, G. (1984). Class at Work: The Design, Allocation and Control of Jobs, London: Bastford.

Likert, Rensis, (1967). The Human Organisation, Its Management and Value, McGraw-Hill Book Company, New York, p.1.

Luthans, Fred (1981), Organisational Behaviour, McGraw-Hill International Book Company.

Macy, B.A. and Mervis, P.H. (1976) 'A Methodology for Assessment of Equality of Working Life and Organisational Effectiveness in Behavioural Economic Terms' *Administrative Science Quarterly,* 21, 215-226.

McGregor, D. (1960). 'The Human Side of the Enterprise,' McGraw-Hill, New York.

Mathur, R.N. (1989) QWL of women construction workers, pp. 22-24.

Mehta, P. (1976) 'From Economism to Democratic Commitment, The Role of Working Participation', *Vikalpa, 1 (4)*, 39-46.

Nadler, D.A. and Lawler E.E. (1983). 'Quality of Work Life, Perspective and Direction', Organisational Dynamics, W*inter, 11 (3),*20-30.

National Seminar on Improving the Quality of work life (1982), Proceeding and Recommendation. New Delhi: Participation and Development Centre, *Mimeographed.*

National Symposium on Quality of Working Life (1983). Summary of Deliberation and Recommendation, July 25-26, Hyderabad. *Mimeographed.*

Parthasarthy, J. (1988). "Resources and Quality of life: A case study of the Irulas of Nilgiris." *The Eastern Anthropologist.* Vol. 41, July-Sep. 3; 240-249.

Paul, W.L. *et. al.* (1969), "Job Enrichment Pays Off", *Harvard Business Review,* Vol. March- April, 1-15.

P. Subba Rao and Anitha (1991). 'Stress Management' in V.S.P. Rao and Srilatha, 'Organisation Stress', Discovery Publishing House, New Delhi, p. 263.

Rao, M.G. (1993), Quality of Working Life and Quality Circles, Vol. 1. Human Behaviour at Work,43-54.

Rice, A.K. (1953). Productivity and Social Organisation in an Indian weaving shed. *Human Relation,* 6, 297-329.

________. (1958). Productivity and Social Organisation: The Ahmedabad Experiment. London and: Tavistock.

Richard Walton, E. (1977). Criteria for Quality of Working Life, in Davis L., *et. al.* The Free Press London, 91-112.

Robert F. Craver, AT and T, (1983). QWL Experiment. A Practical case study, *Management Review,* Summer, 91-112.

Rosow, J.M. (1977) 'Quality of Working Life and productivity', The double pay off, A paper presented at Conference held at America Institute Inc., Chicago.

Ryan, G.M. (1995). Theoretical Basis for the QWL Concept. University of Siena: Quality, (Esprit Project 8162), Working Paper.www.yahu.com.

Sashkin, M. and Lengermann, J.J. (1984). 'Quality of Work Life Conditions/ Feelings, (ed.) Pfeiffer, J.M. and Goldstein, L.D. (1984), *Annual Developing Human Resources*, 13th Annual, University Associates Inc., California,131-144.

Senge, P. (1990), The Fifth Discipline: The Art and Practice of Learning Organisation, New York: Double-day.

Shamir, B. and I. Salomon, 1985. Work-at-home and the quality of working life. *Acad. Manag.*, 10: 455-64.

Sharma, Ajay and Ghosh, Siladitya (1993), Quality of Work Life and Productivity, *The Indian Journal of Labour Economics*, Vol. 36 (4) 785-88.

Singh, J.P. (1982), Improving Quality of Working Life in the Indian Context, *Productivity*, Vol. 22 (4), 13-20.

Singhal, Sushila (1983), Quality of Work Life: A re-examination of Assumptions, Hyderabad: National Symposium on Quality of Working Life, *Mimeographed*, 25-26.

Sinha, J.B.P., (1977). 'Quality of Working Life in the Indian setting' *Journal of Social and Economic Studies, 2*, 235-247.

Sinha, Prakash (1982). Quality of Working Life and Quality of Life, *Indian Journal of Industrial Relation, 17(3),* 373-394.

Sinha, Prakash and Sayeed, Omer Bin (1980). Measuring Quality of Work Life: Development of An Inventory, *Indian Journal of Social Work, 41(3)* 221-26.

Sprin, P. (1975). 'Some Comment on the Quality of Working Life', *Journal of Occupational Psychology, 48*, 179-184.

Straw, R.J., and C.C. Heckscher, 1984. QWL: New working relationships in the communication Industry. *Labour Studies Journal,* 9: 261-74.

Taylor, J.C. (1973) 'Concept and Problems in Studies of the Quality of Working Life': Graduate School of management, UCLA.

Thompson, P. (1983), The Nature of Work, London: Macmillan.

Thorsrud, E. (1976). 'Democracy at the Work and Prospective on the QWL in Scandinavi, Research Studies, No. 8, IIIL S, Geneva.

Turner, A.N. and P.L. Lawrence (1965). Industrial Jobs and the Worker, Boston, Harvard Graduate School Business Administration.

UNESCO 38. "Indicators of Environmental Quality and Quality of Life" Reports and Papers in the Social Sciences.

Verwayen, H. (1978). 'The Specification and Measurement of the Quality of Life in OECD Countries, The Quality of Life, Comparative Studies, (Ed.) Szalai, A. and Andrews, F.F., Sage Publication, California, 235-24.

Walker, K.F. (1975), 'Worker's Attitude, A Key to the Quality of Life', L.E. Davis and Cherns, A. The Quality of Working Life. Vol. 1. The Free Press, 1-2.

Walton, R.E. (1973). 'Quality of Working Life: What Is It?' *Sloan Management Review, 15(1)*:11-21.

Walton R.E., (1977). 'Criteria for quality of working life' in Davis L., *et. al.*, The Free Press London, 91-112.

Willmott, H. (1993). "Strength is Ignorance, Slavery is Freedom: Managing Culture in Modern Organisations", *Journal of Management Studies, 30 (4)*, 515-52.

Yusuf, Anwar (1996), Evaluating the Quality of Working Life, *Management and Labour Studies*, 21(1), 8-15.

2

Review of Literature and Research Strategy

2.1 Review of Literature

The evolution of quality of work life began in late 1960s stresses the human dimension of work by focussing on the quality of relationship between the worker and the working environment. QWL as discipline began in the US in September 1972, when the phrase was coined at a "democratisation of work" conference held at Columbia University's Arden House to discuss two movements. The first was a political movement in Western Europe called 'Industrial Democracy'. Militant, socialist labour unions were lobbying the Parliaments and Assemblies of England, France, West Germany, Sweden and Italy to legislate worker participation in corporate decision-making. The second movement was the emergence in the US of number social science theories about "humanising the workplace". The Quality of work-life is important to organisational performance. Sirota (1973) found that under-utilisation of workers skills and abilities cause low Quality of work life and suggested job enrichment programme to correct the problems of worker's skill and abilities. Very few studies could be cited in the context human relation to review how good relationship superior and subordinate enhances quality of their working life. Walton (1973) suggested eight major conceptual areas for understanding quality of work life. These were adequate and fair compensation, safe and healthy working conditions, development of human competencies, growth and security, social integration, constitutionalisation and total life space and social reliance. Delamotte and Walker (1974), indicated that the number of emphasis have been made in the humanisation of work including the need to protect the worker from hazards to health and safety, the wage work bargain, the protection of workers from hazards of illness and unemployment and the protection of the worker from arbitrary the authority of management.

Johnston (1975) viewed that workers often value factors such as job interest and good working condition above pay. Katzell *et. al.* (1975), mentioned that the worker enjoys the quality of working life when he has positive feelings towards his job and its future prospects is motivated to stay on the job and performs well and feels his working life fits well with his private life. Walton (1975) suggests that Quality of Work Life requires employee commitment and an environment in which this commitment can flourish. Katzell *et. al.* (1975), viewed quality of work life more broadly as an individual's evaluation of the outcome of the work relationship. They observed that a employee may be said to enjoy a high quality of working life when he has positive feelings towards his job and its future prospects, is motivated to stay on the job and performs well and feels his working life fits well with his private life to afford him a balance between the two in terms of his personal values. Ganguly *et. al.* (1976), in his study identified those economic factors like income, promotional opportunities, social security as important factors in employee's sense of life satisfaction. Factors like working hours and nature of job did not find same importance as salary, security and advancement. Glassier (1976) thinks that quality of work life implies job security, good working conditions, adequate and fair compensation, more even than equal employment opportunity all together.

Mirvils and Mehta (1977) in his studies pointed out that, employees perception regarding availability influence and autonomy, economic compensation, inter-personal support, respectful supervisory behaviour are important factor of general life satisfaction. Majumdar (1978), in his study found that the quality of working life directly affect the output from an individual. He remarked that the worker spends about eight hours of his day time at the work place and 16 hours outside the factory. The scholar argues, the environment outside his work place is also very important in his life. Joseph (1978) indicates that attitudes towards that nature of work is clearly associated with QWL and future co-workers have the potential to make QWL high or low but attitudes towards supervision and pay appears to be least associated with QWL. Livneh (1978) study on quality of work experience found that patterns of change in work values, job reward are contingent on specific facet of work involved, rather than age being uniformly a significant determining factor.

Robert (1979) points out the effect of Quality of Work Life on person's life. According to him, Quality of Work Life is a generic phrase that covers a person's feelings about every dimension of work including economic rewards and benefit, security, working condition, organisational and interpersonal relation and its intrinsic meaning in person's life. Runcie (1980), remarked that an employee have positive perception of the quality of work life in the company, will probably strive to further improve the working condition, increase production and quality of products. Singh and Maggu (1980), revealed that QWL was considerably low across all the categories of respondents and across all the parameters of work system, perceived QWL being the poorest in the case of democratisation of work process. It was further observed that the variation in managerial hierarchy, income and experience do not significantly influence the perception of the QWL. Hackman and Oldhams (1980), highlight the constructs of QWL in relation to the interaction between work environment and personal needs. The work environment that is able to fulfill employees' personal needs is considered to provide a positive interaction effect, which will lead to an excellent QWL. They emphasised the personal needs are satisfied when rewards from the organisation, such as compensation, promotion, recognition and development meet their expectations. Runcie (1980) remarked that should an employee have positive perception of the quality of work-life in the company, he would further probably strive to further improve the working conditions, increase production and quality products.

In a more comprehensive study of Sayeed and Sinha (1981) examined the relationship between QWL and job satisfaction and performance. The result indicates that higher QWL leads to greater job satisfaction and better performance. Sanyal and Singh (1982) attempted to study QWL as a well thought out corporate strategy for optimising the productivity of the Rashtriya Chemicals and Fertilisers Limited. The company has realised that with its high technology production system with high task specialisation, commitment, moral, initiative and creative urge of its employees are must for higher productivity. QWL directly helps in building-up these variables. Singh (1982) reviewed that current status of quality of working life activities and suggest a need to enlarge the concept of QWL to include search for work. Sinha (1982), studied that the quality of working life and quality of life had to direct relationship but this relationship varied with socio-culture effect. Tandon (1982) presents four key areas of concern for India:

(a) Improving QWL implies improvement in wages, poor working conditions, worker's amenities and safety and occupational health;

(b) There is need for systematic analysis prior to change;

(c) Dynamics of implementation: willingness for participation; and

(d) Diffusion and strategic consideration.

De (1982) started from the premise that quality of life and quality of work life are systemically inseparable, particularly in face of problems like poverty, malnutrition, unemployment and inequitable distribution of wealth. Ghosh and Karla (1982) in their studies found that significant perceptual differences only in relation to four factors, i.e., employee welfare, advancement based on merit, absence of under job stress, and union-management relation.

Singhal (1983) commented that quality of working life will be meaningful only if the people working in organisation live happy and healthy life in society. The economic, familiar and health strains, etc., to which employees remain exposed as member of the larger society will continue to threaten the peace at work. He further remarked that quality of working life is a time and situation related concept and will require constant revision and modification as socio-organisational contexts change over time. Singh (1983) concludes that the overall perceived quality of work life in the Indian industries is considerably poor. He found that QWL was perceived to be poorer by private sector employees in compression to the public sector employees. De (1984) indicates that quality of work depends on the share of creative activity in the working process. The higher this share, the higher the quality of work and consequently, the quality of life. Rahman (1984) in his study found that subject having low education background and lower income has better perception of QWL then those having higher education and higher income. D'souza *et. al.* (1984) attempted to view the state of art pertaining to QWL as the result of development that have taken place over time in models of man and organisation. The classical, neo-classical and system school of thought in organisation theory provided different conception of man and organisation which resulted in the broadening of the scope of QWL theory and application. Mirvis and Lawler (1984) suggested that Quality of Working Life was associated with satisfaction with wages hour and working condition, 'describing the basic element of good quality of work life' as safe work environment, equitable wages, equal employment opportunities' and opportunity for advancement. De (1984) worked on productivity criteria in different industrial, commercial and service organisations and found that the grassroots employees have responded positively to work related issue. But there were limited sign of progress towards quality of working life. Many factors contribute to QWL which includes adequate and fair remuneration, safe and healthy working conditions and social integration in the work organisation that enables an individual to develop and use all his or her capacities; it holds that people are the most important resource in the organisation as they are trustworthy, responsible and capable of making valuable contribution and they should be treated with dignity and respect (Straw, R.J. and C.C. Heckscher, 1984).

Sekaran (1985), empirically established through this survey that QWL in banks was not high and the reason for this were fairly well-recognised but considered by managers to be beyond the control of institution. Rao (1986) study shows a significantly higher composite quality of working life score for men than women employees. Man employees had significantly higher score for opportunity to learn new skill, challenges in job and discretionary elements in work. Khalique and Rahman (1987) in their study of job satisfaction of workers of Jute industries found that older, married and more educated workers were more satisfied than younger, unmarried and more educated workers. Mehta (1987) found that the composite perceived quality of work life showed a gradual decline with increasing activities. The finding also revealed that greater the proximity to development, the lower was the perceived quality of work life.

Gupta and Khandelwal (1988) found a significant positive relationship between quality of work life and role efficiency. They also found that supervisory behaviour is the most important dimension of the quality of work life contributing 21 per cent of the variance in the employees' role efficiency. Cunningham and Eberle (1990) suggests that the elements that are relevant to an individual's quality of work life include the task, the physical working environment, social environment within the organisation, administrative system and relationship between life on and off the job. Baba and Jamal (1991) listed some typical indicators of quality of working life, including job satisfaction, job involvement, work role ambiguity, work role conflict, work role overload, job stress, organisational commitment and turn over intension. Loscocco and Roschelle (1991), suggested that the most common assessment of QWL is the individual attitudes. This is because individual work attitudes are important indicators of QWL. Individual selectively perceive and make attribution about their job in accordance with the expectation they bring to the work place.

Singh (1992) concludes that it is high time for managements of UP sugar mills to realise the situation and strive to find possible solution for job satisfaction, job evaluation, group assignment, participative management, work design and work procedure and such improvement of work environment and other measures for job enrichment of the workers. Quality of work life is an important factor that affects motivation at work (Ghosh *et. al.,* 1992). Igbaria and Greenhaus (1992) in their study indicated that two measures of QWL, job satisfaction and organisational commitment, had the strongest and most direct influence on turnover intentions, and the impact of other variables on turnover intentions was primarily mediated by these two variables. Haque (1992) observed that QWL was positively correlated with job satisfaction. He also found that there was a significant positive correlation between QWL and performance.

Rao, M.G. (1993) stated the essence of QWL in the following words, "The QWL is co-operative rather than authoritarian, evolutionary and open rather than static and rigid, informal rather than role bound, impersonal rather than mechanistic, mutual respect and trust rather than hatred against each other. The major factor that affect the QWL may be stated thus - salary, benefits, job security, alternative work schedule and occupational stress.

Gani (1993) argues that employee perception of their quality of work life is heavily affected by the treatment they receive from their supervisors and managers. Much of the research available on the subject has supported the contention that the subordinates are directly related to employee orientation by their supervisors and managers.

Tomar (1993) pointed out that absenteeism is the biggest problem of workers in UP sugar mills especially during off season. Non-availability of residence near factory premises and sufficient welfare measures to the labourers, inadequate medical, educational facilities are responsible for labour absenteeism and turnover. Chander *et. al.* (1993) opined that the selected university was functioning in an environment where four major determinants of QWL, i.e., decision-making authority, growth and development, recognition and appreciation and promotional avenues were largely missing and the teachers would like an environment that included these determinants. Wadud (1996) in a study found that QWL was significantly higher among the private sector women employees than their counterparts in the public sector. Hossain (1997) found a significant influence of age, experience and income on overall QWL. A positive correlation was also found between QWL and performance. Studies have proven that organisations offering better QWL are more likely to gain leverage in hiring and retaining its valuable work force (May, Lau, and Johnson, 1999). Hossain and Islam (1999) revealed that there was a significant positive correlation between QWL and job satisfaction. A significant positive correlation was also found between QWL and performance and job satisfaction and performance.

Winter *et. al.* (2000), viewed QWL for academician as an attitudinal response to the prevailing work environment and posited five work environment domains that include role stress, job characteristics, and supervisory, structural and sectoral characteristics to directly and indirectly shape academician's experience, attitude and behaviour. Sen Gupta and Sidique (2001) of their study with a view to investigate the effect of quality of work life (QWL) on group cohesiveness (GC), in sugar industry in Bangladesh. The results reveal that there was significant positive correlation between QWL and GC and most of the QWL factors are positively contributing towards group cohesiveness. Singh (2001) revealed that discharge/dismissal of employees, non-payment of wages according to wage board and compensation, poor medical facilities are the major disturbing elements of effective working environment in sugar mills. Sirgy *et. al.* (2001) suggested that the key factors in quality of working life are need satisfaction based on job requirement, need satisfaction based on work environment, need satisfaction based on supervisory behaviour, need satisfaction based on ancillary programmes and organisational commitments. Lau, Wong, Chan and Law (2001) operationlised QWL as the favourable working environment that supports and promotes satisfaction by providing employees with rewards, job security and career growth opportunities. Wyatt and Wah, (2001) has emphasised QWL to a far lesser degree than North America and Europe. Thus, not only there is probably fewer organisation operating QWL programmes, but there are also fewer published QWL research papers in the Southeast Asia region. Rhoades and Eisenberger (2002), found that QWL have a positive impact on organisational commitment, employee performance as well as job satisfaction. Ellis and Pompli (2002), identified a number of factors contributing to job dissatisfaction and quality of working life in nurses including poor working environment, resident aggression, workload, unable to do delivery of quality of care preferred, balance of work and family, shift work, lack of involvement in decision-making, professional isolation, lack of recognition, poor relationship with supervisor/peers, role conflict, lack of opportunity to learn new skills. Johnsrud (2002) revealed that job satisfaction has been viewed as an attitudinal disposition that is studied as an outcome of the quality of work life. A high quality of work life is essential for organisations to continue, to attract and retain employees (Sandrick, 2003). Saklani (2004) has pointed that QWL is a measures of quality of human experience which is a matter of individual organisation interface. Rainye (2005), concluded on the basis of 18 independent variables in quality of work life in banking industry that employee perception of their quality of work life, its heavily affected by the treatment they receive from there supervisor and managers. Non-fulfillment of these expectations could mean employee frustration, discouragement, anxiety and even bitterness, all negatively related to quality of work life, the study pointed out. A study conducted in Malaysia by Che Rose *et. al.* (2006), concluded that the most important predictor of QWL is organisational climate, followed by career achievement, career satisfaction and career balance. Worrall and Cooper (2006), reported that a low-level of well-being at work is estimated to cost about 5-10 per cent of gross national product per annum, yet quality of working life as a theoretical construct remains relatively unexplored and unexplained within the organisational psychology research literature. Attaining a reasonable level of QWL poses a significant impact on individual's organisational commitment (Huang, Lawler and Lei, 2007; Kalbers, Kalbers and Cenker, 2007; Razali, 2004; Saklani, 2004). Varadaraj and Sellappan (2008), concludes that qualities of work life of employees are related to an individual's expectation of different characteristics of the job and perception of how much is attained. This accounts for the conflicting result with regard to effect of these variables on quality of work life. Kaushik and Tonk (2008) have argued that QWL is also determined by the intersection of personal and situational factors, that is individual organisational fit, where it involves both personal (subjective) and external (objective) aspect of work- related rewards, work experience and work environment.

Exploration of Research Gap

The literature cited above in national and international context makes it clear that the most important indicator of quality of work life in India is the context of fulfillment of the basic needs of employees in manufacturing and service sector. There is a strong evidence of conclusive research especially scale identification and its real practice in different sectarian studies in international context. The study is an attempt towards application of national and international construct with regard to QWL especially in sugar industry. This ultimately leads to more commitment to job and resultant increase in productivity which we desperately need in order to meet the basic requirement of our society. The present study has identified 18 independent variables adopted from Karla and Gosh (1984), Carlson

(1978), and Walton (1973). Practically, this study is different from earlier studies in Indian context since the perceptions of different cadre of employees of clerical, technical to managerial cadre have been considered. Moreover, essence of QWL for seasonal workers is equally important as permanent employees. The study follows the multi-dimensional comparison regarding effectiveness of quality of work life practices. Further, it is well-known fact that quality of work life problems is living and dynamic and there can be no final and permanent solution.

2.2 Objectives of the Study

The main objective of the study is **to assess the effectiveness of the various dimensions (working environment, relational, job and financial) of Quality of Working Life of Employees in Sugar Industry of Uttar Pradesh.** However, the sub-objectives of the study are as follows:

(I) To assess the existing QWL practices of employees with regard to various zones (Eastern, Central, and Western) of UP sugar mills;
(II) To investigate whether there is any significant difference between private and cooperative sugar mill employees perception regarding QWL issues;
(III) To compare perceived level of QWL between permanent and seasonal employees of sugar mills in UP;
(IV) To explore the influence of demographic variables (experience, income, education level and age) on QWL dimensions; and
(V) To investigate the impact of QWL on job satisfaction, workers participation in management, organisational loyalty, employees productivity, and motivation.

2.3 Hypotheses of the Study

On the basis of extensive literature survey and objectives, the present study is conducted under the broad framework of following research hypotheses:

(I) There is no significant difference of QWL practices in various zones of sugar mill employees;
(II) There is no significant difference between private and cooperative sugar mill employee's perception regarding QWL issues;
(III) Perceived level of QWL among permanent and seasonal employees is not significantly differing;
(IV) There is no significant influence of demographic variables (experience, income, education level and age) on dimensions of QWL; and

(V) There is no significant impact of QWL on job satisfaction, workers participation in management, organisational loyalty, employee productivity and motivation.

2.4 Identified Factors and Variables of the Study

Table 2.1: Quality of Work Life Variables Studied

S.No.	*Factors*	*Variables*
I.	**Demographic Factor (12)**	1. Geographical location, 2. Nature of organisation, 3. Nature of employment, 4. Position, 5. Experience 6.Income level, 7. Age, 8. Gender, 9. Marital status, 10. Number of family members, 11. Residential background, etc.
II.	**Working Environment Factor (10)**	1. Comfortable Workspace, 2. Lighting facilities, 3. Level of temperature, 4. Safety measure, 5. Health facilities, 6. Working conditions, 7. Type of welfare facilities,8. Quality of welfare facilities, 9. Supervisor Interference, 10. Workplace stress.
III.	**Relational Factor (09)**	1. Supervision quality, 2. Supervisory support, 3. Colleagues' relationship, 4. Supervisory relationship, 5. Superior's relationship, 6. Individual respect, 7. Industrial relations, 8. Role of trade union, 9. Management attitude.
IV.	**Job Factor (11)**	1. Job retention, 2. Technological support, 3. Adequate training, 4. Employees interest, 5. Additional responsibility, 6. Autonomy, 7. Work life balance, 8. Flexi-hours, 9. Work schedule, 10. Job security,11. Work dissatisfaction.
V.	**Financial Factor (06)**	1. Remuneration, 2. Regular compensation, 3. Adequate Bonus, 4. Social security benefits, 5. Fair promotion, 6. Performance-based promotion.
VI.	**Impact Factor (11)**	1. Job satisfaction, 2. Team spirit, 3. Workers participation, 4. Organisational loyalty, 5. Corporate communication, 6. Skill utilisation, 7. Confidence-building, 8. Sense of failure, 9. Productivity, 10. Motivation, 11. Supervisory style.

Sources: Karla and Gosh (1984), Carlson (1978), and Walton (1973).

2.5 Significance of QWL in Agro-based Industries

The sugar industry being the second largest organised industry next importance to textile industry plays eminent role in the economic life of India. It is an industry which affects agricultural fundamentally. The sugar industry has great significance which cannot be devalued in its relationship with agricultural and industrial economy of the rural region of India. The proposed research work is to highlight dimensions and status of QWL in sugar industry supposed to be contributing new insights in the field of social relevance and national importance in multiple ways. Preliminary study shows that Uttar Pradesh sugar industry suffers some basic problems, i.e., obsolete plant and machinery, poor physical condition and small size plants, etc. Thus, it is a great apprehension whether the industry follows the true sense of QWL or not. The scope of QWL movement which originally included only job redesign efforts based on the socio-technical systems approach has gradually widened very much so as to include a wide variety of improvements such as quality circles, employee participation, autonomous work groups, job security, equitable justice, empowerment, social relevance of work, balance between working life and personal life, career opportunities and social integration, etc.

In the case of Indian sugar industry QWL is of recent origin and has a long way to go. Individual as well as organised efforts are required to improve the quality of work life for millions of workers in the industry. The outcome of an effective QWL programme needs to be understood. The study originally address crucial issues as rampant sickness in the industry, the workers quality of life as well as performance of mills will be benefitted through redefining the structure of QWL.

The potential outcome of the study will be adding new outlook in national economy as well. Several high powered committee reported and survey have been conducted like as Bhargav Commission (1974), Mahajan Committee (1998), Tuteja Committee (2000), and KPMG Survey (2007) regarding status of the industry, technical issues, marketing and restructuring, statutory minimum price (SMP), procurement price, Levy Quota, promoter equity and privatisation, etc. Neither any study nor any committee has set-up till date towards improvement of the industry through effective QWL. In fact, the industry is a key driver of rural development, supporting over about 55 million sugarcane farmers, their dependents and a large mass of agricultural labourers involved in sugarcane cultivation, harvesting, machine manufacturing etc., of almost 527 sugar mills and ancillary activities, and constituting 7.5 per cent of the rural population (Sanyal *et. al.,* 2008), and the sector has been the focal point of socio-economic development of the rural India, but lesser attention on QWL. The scholar feels, as a result its contribution in GDP only one per cent and meager contribution in central and state exchequer and number of sick mills increasing year by year. The major findings of most of the studies attribute the causes of sickness either to raw material shortages or to defective government policies towards sugar industry or to efficient management. Not a single attempt has been made to diagnose the problem of sickness by means of QWL which has its applications in various other industry studies. In this context, the study is helpful for policy-makers, mill owners and employees by providing better working condition. Finally, the study is very helpful by introducing new perspective of QWL in national economy and quality of life of workers as well.

2.6 Research Design

Research design is the plan and structure of overall research work. It presents the operational plan, how the research work has been carried out. In short, it constitutes the blueprint for the collection, measurement and analysis of data (Cooper, 2010).

2.6.1. Scope of the Study

- **Type of Study:** The study falls under the category of descriptive research. The major purpose of this research is description of the state of affairs or problems as they exists and are faced at present by sugar mills employees of Uttar Pradesh.
- **Place of Study:** The study is conducted in entire Uttar Pradesh consisting three zones namely, Western, Central and Eastern.
- **Population:** The population under the study covers permanent and seasonal employees consisting managerial, supervisory, clerical, operative, skilled and semi-skilled of 135 (Sugar Year 2009-10) running sugar mills of Uttar Pradesh.
- **Period of the Study:** The study covers the policy issues and allied activities of QWL for the period of ten sugar years (October 1 to September 30), starting from 2000-01 to sugar year 2010-11. However, primary data has been collected during October 2010 to October 2012.

2.6.2 Method Design: A structured questionnaire was designed based on the literature review, **Karla and Gosh (1984), Carlson (1978),** and **Walton (1973).** For achieving the objectives of the study. The questionnaire used in the survey consisted of two sections. The first section was the 13 demographic information of respondents namely, name of organisation, nature of organisation, nature of employment, position, experience, income level, education level, age, gender, marital status, number of family members, residence background, etc. The last section, including 47 statements/questions, was designed to measure the perception by sugar mills employees on QWL issues. The questionnaire was used both in language English as well as Hindi. Beside this, personal interviews have been also conducted with the managerial employees at workplace for knowing the status and standard of QWL in sugar mills. The researcher has applied participatory observation technique to understand the prevailing working conditions of select sugar mills.

2.6.3 Measurement and Scaling Techniques: To judge the perception of QWL of sugar mills employees the scholar has uses three primary scales of measurement namely, nominal, ordinal and interval. Since the study mainly concerned with identification of perceived quality of work life and attitude of employees, therefore, the researcher has used Itemised Scale (Likert Scale) to indicate the agreement or disagreement with each of a series of statements about the stimulus objects.

2.6.4 Sampling Design

- **Target Population:** The target population is geographically stratified into three regions: western, central and eastern under nature of employment, i.e., seasonal and permanent workers. Hence, a

Table 2.2: Select Sugar Mills under Study

Zones	*Name of Mills (Factories)*	*Nature*
Eastern	1. Kisan Sahkari Chini Mill Ltd., Sultanpur.	Cooperative
	2. Triveni Engineering and Industry Ltd., Ramkola, Kushinagar.	Private
	3. The Kanoria Sugar and General Mft. Co. Ltd., Captainganj.	Private
	4. JHV Sugar Mills Ltd., Padrauna, Kushinagar.	Private
Central	5. Kisan Sahkari Chini Mill Ltd., Semikhera Bareilly.	Cooperative
	6. Kesar Enterprises Ltd., Baheri, Bareilly.	Private
	7. J.K. Sugar Ltd., Meerganj, Bareilly.	Private
	8. DSCL Sugar Ltd., Rupapur, Hardoi.	Private
Western	9. The Bagpat Co-operative Sugar Mill Ltd., Bagpat.	Cooperative
	10. Indian Potash Ltd., Saukoti Tanda, Meerut.	Private
	11. Bajaj Hindustan Ltd., Kinauni.	Private
	12. Indian Potash Ltd., Mohiuddinpur, Meerut.	Private

Source: Field Work Data Collection.

predominantly quantitative approach is adapted for this study. The Uttar Pradesh sugar industry is highly fragmented over 148 sugar mills in different districts and out of which 133 mills are in running condition. Sugar mills are selected randomly from eastern, western and central zone. A total of twelve sugar mills are identified. Each sugar mills/factory is contacted to gain permission to distribute the questionnaires.

- **Sampling Technique**: Stratified Random Sampling is adopted for the selection of respondent for the study.
- **Selected Sample Unit:** The spread over of sugar mills in Uttar Pradesh is mainly in three climatic zones. The following table represent selected sample unit.
- **Sampling Size:** A random sample of 360 permanent and seasonal employees in the executives, supervisory, clerical, operative, skilled and unskilled levels in various sugar mills received the questionnaire. The ratio of permanent and seasonal employees 1:1 and proportion of employees among private and co-operative sector was 3:1.

Table 2.3: Distribution of Sample Size

Unit	*Western*		*Central*		*Eastern*		*Total*
	Permanent	*Seasonal*	*Perman-ent*	*Season-al*	*Permanent*	*Seaso-nal*	
Coop-	15	15	15	15	15	15	**90**
Private	45	45	45	45	45	45	**270**
Total	**60**	**60**	**60**	**60**	**60**	**60**	**360**

2.6.5 Data Collection: Primary Data has been collected by visiting the private and co-operative sugar mills of Uttar Pradesh and distributing the questionnaires for obtaining the responses. In total, twelve mills were considered for the survey based on random sampling method, of which eight were private sugar mills and the rests four are cooperative sugar mills. The stratified random sampling method was, then, adopted for the selection of respondent for the study. In total, the sample consists of 360 respondents. The ratio of sample between private and co-operative was 3:1, i.e., 270 respondents were from private sector and 70 were co-operative sector sugar mills. The secondary data was collected from different books, journals, official statistics, annual reports, reports of individual sugar unit, economic survey, articles, publication and other documents, newsletters and websites.

2.7 Brief Profile of Select Sample Sugar Mills Under Study

2.7.1 The Kisan Sahkari Chini Mills Ltd. Sultanpur (Avadh):

Type of Organisation	Cooperative,
Year of Establishment	1976,
Distt.	Sultanpur, and
Region	Eastern UP

Table 2.4: Production Statistics of Kisan Sahkari Chini Mills Ltd. Sultanpur (Avadh)

Season	*Crushing Capacity (M.T.)*	*Cane Crushed (Lakh M.T.)*	*Sugar Produced (Lakh/Qtl.)*	*Sugar Recovery (%)*	*Molasses Produced (Lakh/Qtl.)*
2007-08	1250	1.39	1.30	9.11	0.75
2008-09	1250	0.65	0.57	8.48	0.34
2009-10	1250	0.61	4.90	8.00	2.88

2.7.2 Treveni Engineering and Industries Ltd., Ramkola

Type of Organisation	Private Ltd.
Distt.	Kushinagar.
Region	Eastern UP.

Table 2.5: Production Statistics of Triveni Engineering and Industries Ltd., Ramkola

Crushing Season	*Crushing Capacity (M.T.)*	*Cane Crushed (Lakh M.T.)*	*Sugar Produced (Lakh/Qtl.)*	*Sugar Recovery (%)*	*Molasses Produced (Lakh/Qtl.)*
2007-08	6500	6.36	6.49	10.22	3.32
2008-09	6500	4.54	4.31	9.50	2.25
2009-10	6500	4.62	4.68	10.12	2.13

2.7.3 The Kanoria Sugar and General Manufacturing Co. Ltd., Captaingang.

Type of Organisation	Private,

Table 2.6: Production Statistics of Kanoria Sugar and General Manufacturing Co. Ltd., Captainganj

Crushing Season	*Crushing Capacity (M.T.)*	*Cane Crushed (Lakh M.T.)*	*Sugar Produced (Lakh/Qtl.)*	*Sugar Recovery (%)*	*Molasses Produced (Lakh/Qtl.)*
2007-08	6000	4.76	4.68	9.76	2.61
2008-09	6000	2.38	2.07	8.72	1.20
2009-10	6000	3.01	2.88	9.55	1.58

Distt. Kushinagar,
Region Eastern UP.

2.7.4 J. H. V. Distillery and Sugar Mill, Paudrona

Type of Organisation Private,
Year of Establishment 2005,
Distt Kushinagar,
Region Eastern UP.

Table 2.7: Production Statistics of J.H.V. Distillery and Sugar Mill, Paudrona

Season	*Crushing Capacity (M.T.)*	*Cane Crushed (Lakh M.T.)*	*Sugar Produced (Lakh/Qtl.)*	*Sugar Recovery (%)*	*Molasses Produced (Lakh/ Qtl.)*
2007-08	4500	4.87	5.02	10.30	2.31
2008-09	4500	2.12	2.07	9.78	0.90
2009-10	4500	2.25	2.25	9.36	1.07

2.7.5 The Kisan Sahkari Chini Mills Ltd., Semikhera, Deoraniya, Bareilly

Type of Organisation Cooperative,
Year of Establishment 1984,
Distt. Bareilly,
Region Central UP.

Table 2.8: Production Statistics of Kisan Sahkari Chini Mills Ltd., Semikhera, Barailly

Season	*Crushing Capacity (M.T.)*	*Cane Crushed (Lakh M.T.)*	*Sugar Produced (Lakh/Qtl.)*	*Sugar Recovery (%)*	*Molasses Produced (Lakh/ Qtl.)*
2007-08	2750	9.78	10.43	9.78	4.27
2008-09	2750	5.61	5.25	7.87	2.48
2009-10	2750	6.94	6.52	9.70	3.13

2.7.6 Kesar Enterprises Ltd., Baheri, Bareilly

Type of Organisation Private,
Year of Establishment 1933,
Distt. Bareilly,
Region Central UP.

Table 2.9: Production Statistics of Kesar Enterprises Ltd., Baheri

Season	*Crushing Capacity (M.T.)*	*Cane Crushed (Lakh M.T.)*	*Sugar Produced (Lakh/Qtl.)*	*Sugar Recovery (%)*	*Molasses Produced (Lakh/ Qtl.)*
2007-08	7200	9.78	10.43	10.67	4.27
2008-09	7200	5.61	5.25	9.35	2.48
2009-10	7200	6.94	6.52	9.38	3.13

2.7.7 J.K. Sugar Ltd., Sindhauli Road, Meerganj

Type of Organisation Private,
Year of Establishment 1933,
Distt. Bareilly,
Region Central UP.

Table 2.10: Production Statistics of J.K. Sugar Ltd., Sindhauli Road, Meerganj

Season	*Crushing Capacity (M.T.)*	*Cane Crushed (Lakh M.T.)*	*Sugar Produced (Lakh/Qtl.)*	*Sugar Recovery (%)*	*Molasses Produced (Lakh/ Qtl.)*
2007-08	5000	6.01	6.30	10.48	3.10
2008-09	5000	2.96	2.62	8.86	1.44
2009-10	5000	4.51	3.98	8.81	2.40

2.7.8 DSCL Sugar Ltd., Rupapur, Hardoi

Type of Organisation Private,
Year of Estblishment ?
Distt. Hardoi,
Region Central UP.

Table 2.11: Production Statistics of DSCL Sugar Ltd., Rupapur Hardoi

Season	*Crushing Capacity (M.T.)*	*Cane Crushed (Lakh M.T.)*	*Sugar Produced (Lakh/Qtl.)*	*Sugar Recovery (%)*	*Molasses Produced (Lakh/ Qtl.)*
2007-08	6500	5.90	5.63	9.53	3.33
2008-09	6500	3.30	2.67	8.24	1.83
2009-10	6500	4.02	3.30	8.22	2.36

2.7.9 The Bagpat Co-operative Sugar Mills Ltd., Bagpat

Type of Organisation	Co-operative,
Year of Establishment	?
Distt.	Bagpat,
Region	West UP.

Table 2.12: Production Statistics of the Bagpat Co-operative Sugar Mills Ltd. Bagpat

Season	*Crushing Capacity (M.T.)*	*Cane Crushed (Lakh M.T.)*	*Sugar Produced (Lakh/Qtl.)*	*Sugar Recovery (%)*	*Molasses Produced (Lakh/ Qtl.)*
2007-08	2500	3.98	3.49	8.77	1.89
2008-09	2500	3.13	2.60	8.30	1.49
2009-10	2500	3.39	2.85	8.39	1.56

2.7.10 Indian Potash Ltd., Sakauti Tanda

Type of Organisation	Private,
Distt.	Meerut,
Region	West UP.

Table 2.13: Production Statistics of Indian Potash Ltd., Sakauti Tanda

Season	*Crushing Capacity (M.T.)*	*Cane Crushed (Lakh M.T.)*	*Sugar Produced (Lakh/Qtl.)*	*Sugar Recovery (%)*	*Molasses Produced (Lakh/ Qtl.)*
2007-08	1800	2.21	2.03	9.14	0.98
2008-09	1800	1.52	1.32	8.54	0.69
2009-10	1800	0.87	0.74	8.41	0.40

2.7.11 Bajaj Hindustan Ltd., Kinauni

Type of Organisation	Private,
Distt.	Meerut,
Region	West U.P.

Table 2.14: Production Statistics of Bajaj Hindustan Ltd., Kinauni

Season	*Crushing Capacity (M.T.)*	*Cane Crushed (Lakh M.T.)*	*Sugar Produced (Lakh/Qtl.)*	*Sugar Recovery (%)*	*Molasses Produced (Lakh/ Qtl.)*
2007-08	12000	14.94	14.89	9.97	7.08
2008-09	12000	7.88	6.86	8.72	3.65
2009-10	12000	12.24	11.01	9.00	6.18

2.7.12 Indian Potash Ltd., Mohiuddinpur

Type of Organisation Private,
Distt. Meerut,
Region West UP.

Table 2.15: Production Statistics of Indian Potash Ltd., *Mohiuddinpur*

Season	*Crushing Capacity (M.T.)*	*Cane Crushed (Lakh M.T.)*	*Sugar Produced (Lakh/Qtl.)*	*Sugar Recovery (%)*	*Molasses Produced (Lakh/ Qtl.)*
2007-08	2500	3.00	2.64	8.79	1.48
2008-09	2500	1.33	1.01	7.54	–
2009-10	2500	0.61	0.49	8.01	0.29

2.8 Personal Profile of Sugar Mills Employees

Table 2.16: Demographic Factor-wise Classification of Employees

S.N.	*Variable*	*Categories*	*No. of Employees*	*Percentage*
1.	Nature of Organisation	Private	270	75
		Cooperative	90	25
2.	Nature of Employment	Permanent	150	50
		Seasonal	150	50
3.	Designation	Clerical	93	25.8
		Accounting	51	14.2
		Administration	18	5.0
		Managerial	27	7.5
		Sales and Marketing	11	3.1
		Technical	152	42.5
		Other	08	2.2
4.	Work Experience	1-5 Years	21	5.8
		5-10 Years	60	16.7
		10-15 Years	86	23.9
		15-20 Years	97	26.9
		20 and above	96	26.7
5.	Monthly Income	Below Rs. 10,000	139	38.6
		10,000-20,000	177	49.2
		20,000 and above	44	12.2
6.	Education	Below High School	14	3.9
		High School Pass	35	9.7

(Contd.)

(Contd.. Table 2.16)

S.N.	*Variable*	*Categories*	*No. of Employees*	*Percentage*
		Intermediate	51	14.2
		Graduation	156	43.3
		Post-graduation	48	13.3
		Others	56	15.6
7.	Age	Below 30 Years	26	7.2
		30-40 Years	88	24.4
		40-50 Years	148	41.1
		50 and above	98	27.2
8.	Gender	Male	360	100
		Female	000	000
9.	Marital Status	Married	356	98.9
		Unmarried	04	1.1
10.	No. of Dependents	Up to 4	137	38.1
		5-6	155	43.1
		7 and above	68	18.9
11.	Residence	Rural Area	245	68.1
		Urban Area	115	31.9

Source: Primary Data.

It is discernible from the above table that the largest majority of the sample respondents (75 per cent) is belongs to private sector and rest of the (25 per cent) from co-operative sector. Further the ratio between permanent and seasonal employees was same. Out of 360 respondent majority of employees (42 per cent) were belongs to technical cadre followed by clerical and accounting cadre (40 per cent). As far as employees experience is concerned, it is found that the largest majority of the sample employees (26.9 per cent) had employee experience of 10-15 years followed by 26.7 per cent more than 20 years indicating that employees had longer attachment with their workplaces. The majority of the respondent's (49.2 per cent) monthly income is Rs. 10,000 to 20,000 and 12.2 per cent of them earnings above Rs. 20,000. Education-wise it is discernible that the largest majority of the employees are graduates (43.3 per cent) followed by intermediate and post-graduates. It is also apparent that the largest majority of the sample respondents, i.e., 41.1 per cent are between 40-50 age groups which was followed in by the age group of 50 and above years (27.2 per cent), 30-40 years (24.4 per cent), 21-30 and below 30 years (7.2 per cent). All the respondents (100 per cent) of the sample were male employees. A large number of employees (99 per cent) are married and one per cent respondents were unmarried. It can be seen from the table that 52 per cent of employees have more than five dependents. Only a very small number of respondents (38 per cent) have four or less than four dependants. The last column of the table shows that 68 per cent of the sample employees were belongs to rural area and rest were (32 per cent) residing in urban areas. It shows that most of the rural people are primarily dependent on sugar mills of Uttar Pradesh.

2.9 Analysis Design

- **Descriptive Analysis:** Summarisation of data, frequency distribution, graphical display, measures of location, measures of dispersion and crosstabs.
- **Associational Analysis:** Measures of Correlation and Association, and Multiple Correlations.
- **Inferential Analysis:** Hypothesis testing (ANOVA, Chi-square test, Mann-Whitney U-test, ANOVA, Kruskal-Wallis (H) Test, and Regression Analysis (linear regression, binary logistic regression and ordinal regression).

2.10 Chapter Scheme: The Entire Study has been Divided into Nine Chapters

Chapter 1: Quality of Work Life: An Introduction- Introductory in nature and provides the necessary background for the study.

Chapter 2: Review of Literature and Research Strategy is presented in this chapter.

Chapter 3: Indian Sugar Industry - An Overview- It Covers Evolution, growth and development of Sugar Industry in India, vis-a-vis Uttar Pradesh. It also focusses on global sugar industry scenario.

Chapter 4: Working Environment Factor - An Analysis- It deals with the analysis Working Environment Factor.

Chapter 5: Relational Factor- An Evaluation- This chapter deals with evaluation of Relational Factor.

Chapter 6: Job Factor- An Appraisal- It deals with appraisal of Job Factor.

Chapter 7: Financial Factor- An Assessment- It covers the analysis of Financial Factor.

Chapter 8: Factors of QWL- An Effectiveness and Impact Analysis- It deals with Impact Factor and overall analysis of QWL.

Chapter 9: Summary of Findings, Conclusion and Suggestions- The last and concluding chapter consists of findings and conclusions, some useful suggestions have been made in order to fulfill the objectives of Quality of Work Life.

References

Baba, V.V. and Jamal, M. (1991). Reutilisation of job context and job content as related employees Quality of working life: A study of psychiatric nurses, *Journal of Organisational Behaviour, 12*, 379-386.

Chander, Subash and Singh, Prampal (1993). Quality of work-life in a university: An Empirical Investigation, *Management and Labour Studies,* 18 (2), 97-107.

Che Rose, R.; Beh L.S., Uli, J., and Idris K. (2006). An Analysis of Quality of Work Life (QWL) and Career-Related Variables, *American Journal of Applied Science*, 3 (12), 2151-2159.

Carlson, C. (1978). General Motor's Quality of work life efforts, 55(4):11-23.

Cunningham, J.B. and T. Eberle, (1990). A guide to job enrichment and redesign. *Personnel,* 67, 56-61.

De, Nitish, R. (1982) Inter-linkage between Quality of work life and Quality of life, *Productivity*, 22(4), 89-91.

De, N.R. (1984). 'Towards an appreciation of quality of life and quality of work life'. *Economic and Political Weekly,* 19 (20-21): M-46-M-57.

Delamotte, Y. and Walker, K.F., (1974). Humanisation of Work and the Quality of Working Life Trends and Issues, *International Institute for Labour Studies Bulletin,* 11, 3-14.

D'souza, and Keith C. (1984). QWL: An Evolutionary Perspective, *Abhigyan,* Vol. Autumn 1-15.

Ganguli, O.N. and Joseph, J.S. (1976). *Quality of working life: work prospects and aspiration of young workers in Air India,* Central Labour Institute: Bombay.

Gani, A. (1993). Quality of work life in a state setting: Findings of an empirical study, *The Indian Journal of Labour Economics,* 36 (4), 817-823.

Glasier, E. (1976). State of the Art, Questions about Quality of Work Life, Personnel.

Ghosh, and Subratesh (1992). Quality of Work Life in Two Indian Organisations, *Decisions,* 19(2), 89-102.

Gupta P. and Khandelwal, P. (1988). Quality of Work Life in Relation to Role Efficiency, *Psychological Studies,* 33 (1), 34-38, p. 73.

Hackman, J.R. and G.R. Oldham, (1980). *Work Redesign*. Reading, M.A: Addison-Wesley.

Haque, A.B.M.Z. (1992). Quality of Working Life and Job Satisfaction of Industrial workers in relation to size of organisation, Bangladesh. *Journal of Psychological Studies,* 2 (1), 43-55.

Hossain, J.A. (1997). Quality of Working Life of Industrial Worker in Bangladesh: A case study in Greeter Kush.

Hossain Md. Mosharraf and Islam Md. Tariqual (1999). Quality of Working Life and Job Satisfaction of Conventional Hospital Nurses in Bangladesh, *Indian Journal of Industrial Relations,* 34 (3).

Huang, T.C., Lawler, J., and Lei, C.Y. (2007). The effects of quality of work life on commitment and turnover intention. *Social Behaviour and Personality*, 35, 735-750.

Igbaria, M., and Greenhaus, J.H. (1992). Determinants of MIS employees' turnover intentions: A structural equation model. *Communications of the ACM,* 35 (2), 34-51.

Jonston, R. (1975). Pay and job satisfaction: A study of sum research finding. *International Labour Review,* 111 (5), 441-49.

Johnsrud, L. 2002. Measuring the quality of faculty and administrative work life: implications for college and university campuses, *Research in Higher Education,* 43(2), 379 -395.

Joseph, J.S. (1978). Quality of working life (QWL) and job attitudes of Indian Craftmen, *Bombay Psychologists,* 11 (1), 28-34.

Kalbers, L.P., and Cenker, W.J. (2007). Organisational commitment and auditors in public accounting. *Managerial Auditing Journal,* 22, 34-36.

Ghosh , S. and Kalra, S.K. (1982). Perceptual Differences in Quality of Work Life Factors. *Indian Journal of Training and Development,* 12 (374), 10-12.

Katzell, R.A., Yankelovich D., Fein M., Ornate, D.A. and Nash A. (1975). Work productivity and job satisfaction. The psychological corporation: New York.

Kalra, S. and Ghosh, S. (1984). Quality of work life: A study of associated factors. *The Indian Journal of Social Work,* 45-54.

Khalique, A. and Rehman, M.A. (1987). Perceived importance of job facets and overall job satisfaction of industrial workers, *Human Relation,* 40(7), 401-416.

Lau, T.,Y.H., Wong, K.F., Chan, and M., Law, (2001). Information Technology and the work environment — Does it Change the Way People Interact at Work, *Human Systems Management,* 20 (3), 267-280.

Loscocco, K.A. and Roschelle, A.R. (1991). Influences on the quality of work and non-work life: two decades in review, *Journal of Vocational Behaviour,* 39 (2), 182–225.

Livneh, A. (1978). Life cycle approach to the Quality of work experience. Dissertation Abstracts International, 39, 2578-A.

Majumdar, N. (1978). Industrial pollution in proceedings of the national seminar on Quality of working life, Organised jointly by central labour institute Bombay and National Labour Institute: New Delhi.

May, B.E., Lau, R.S.M., and Johnson, S.K. (1999). A longitudinal study of quality of work life and business performance. *South Dakota Business Review*, 58, 3-7.

Mehta, P. (1987). Administrative Organisation Structure, Perceived Quality of Work Life and Development Related Bureaucratic Behaviour, New Delhi: Participation and Development Center Mimeographed.

Mirvilis and Mehta, P. (1977). 'The role of workers participation' *Vikapla* 1976, 1 (4), 39-46 and Employee motivation and work satisfaction in Public Enterprises, *Vikapla* 2(3), 236.

Mirvis, P.H. and Lawler, E.E. (1984). Accounting for the Quality of Work Life. *Journal of Occupational Behaviour.* 5. 197-212.

Rahman, A. (1984). QWL as perceived by industrial shift worker' thesis, Osmania University: Hyderabad.

Rainaye, R. (2005). Quality of Work Life in Banks: A micro-level Comparative Analysis, *The Indian Journal of Commerce*, 58 (4), 113-121.

Rao, M.G. (1993). Quality of working life and Quality circle, *Human Behaviour at Work*, (1), 43-54.

Rao, Rukmini V. (1986), A Study of Quality of Work Life, Self-concept, Aspiration and Family Life of Working Women, Ph.D, thesis submitted to University of Delhi, Delhi.

Razali, M.Z. (2004). Perception of professional engineers toward quality of work life and organisational commitment, a case study. *International Journal of Business,* 6, 323-334.

Rhoades, L. and Eisenberger, R. (2002). Perceived Organisational Support: A Review of the Literature, *Journal of Applied Psychology*, 87 (4), 698-714.

Robert, H. Guest. (1979). Quality of work life Learning from Tarrytown, *Harvard Business Review,* 28-39.

Runcie, J.F. (1980). Dynamic Systems and the Quality of Work Life, *Personnel,* 57(6), 13–24.

Saklani, D.R. (2004). Quality of work life in the Indian context: An empirical investigation. *Decision*, 31.

Sandrick, K. (2003). Putting the emphasis on employees as an award winning employer, Baptist health-care has distant memories of the work force shortage, *Trustee*, 6-10.

Sanyal, A. and Singh, B.R. (1982). Improving the quality of work-life, *Lok Udyog,* 27-35.

Sayeed, O.B. and Sinha, P. (1981). QWL in relation to Job Satisfaction and performance in two organisations, *Managerial Psychology*, 2(1), 15-30.

Sekaran, Uma (1985). The Perceived Quality of Working Life in Banks in Major Cities in India, *Prajan,* 14 (3), 273-284.

Sengupta and Sidique (2001). The effect of Quality of work life on Group Cohesiveness: An Empirical Analysis, *Labour and Development,* 7(2), 126-36.

Singh, A. (1992). Collective Bargaining in Sugar Industry in UP, Unpublished Thesis, Banaras Hindu University, UP, India.

Singh, B.K. (2001) Industrial Relation Practices in Sugar Industry in UP: Sectoral Differences, Banaras Hindu University, UP, India.

Singhal, Sushila. (1983). Quality of work life: A re-examination of assumption, Hyderabad, *National Symposium on Quality of Working Life,* 25-26.

Singh, J.P. (1982). Improving Quality of working life in the Indian context, *Productivity*, 22 (4), 13-20.

Singh, J.P. (1983). QWL experiments in India — Trails and Triumphs, *Abhigyan*, Vol. Autumn, 23-37.

Sinha, Prakash. (1982). Quality of working life and quality of life, *Indian Journal of Industrial Relation,* 17 (3), 373-94.

Sirgy, M.J., Efraty, D., Siegel, P. and Lee, D. (2001). A new measure of quality of work life based on need satisfaction and spillover theories. *Social Indicators Research*, 55, 241-302.

Sirota, D. (1973). Production and services personnel and job enrichment, *Work Study,* 22(1) January, 9-15.

Straw, R.J. and C.C. Heckscher, (1984). QWL: New working relationships in the communication industry. *Labour Studies J.* (9), 261-274.

Tomar, A.S. (1993). Problems of Sugar Industries in India with special reference to Units Located in Eastern UP. Unpublished Ph.D Thesis, Banaras Hindu University, UP.

Tandon, Rajesh and Dhawan, K. Sunil (1987), Variations in Job Satisfaction with age Among Blast White Collor Indian Workers, *Indian Journal of Industrial Relations*, 16(4), 615-622.

Varadaraj S. and Sellappan, R. (2008). Quality of Work Life of Employees in Engineering Industry, *The Management Accountant,* 711-715.

Walton, R. (1973). Quality of Work life Indicators — Prospects and Problems - A Portugal Measuring the Quality of Working Life, 57-70, Ottawa.

Walton, R.E. (1975). Criteria for Quality of Working Life. In L.E. Davis, A.B. Cherns and Associates (Eds). The Quality of Working. New York: The Free Press, Life, 1: 91-104.

Wyatt, T.A. and Wah, C.Y. (2001). Perceptions of QWL: A study of Singaporean Employees Development, *Research and Practice in Human Resource Management,* 9(2), 59-76.

Wadud, N. (1996). Job stress and QWL among working women, *Bangladesh Psychological Studies,* 6, 31-37.

Worrall, L. and Cooper, C.L. (2006). The Quality of Working Life: Managers' Health and Well-being. Executive Report, Chartered Management Institute.

Winter, R.T. Taylor and J. Sarros, (2000). Trouble at Mill: Quality of academic work life issues within a comprehensive Australian university. *Studies in Higher Education*, 25: 279-294.

3

Indian Sugar Industry – An Overview

3.1 Overview of Indian Sugar Industry

India is known as the original home of sugar and sugarcane. In global sugar economy, the Indian sugar industry has achieved a number of milestones. India is the second largest producer of sugarcane next to Brazil (accounting 15 per cent of the world's sugar production). The sub-tropical region (Uttar Pradesh) contributes almost 60 per cent of India's total sugar production, while the balance comes from the tropical region, mainly from Tamil Nadu, Karnataka, Maharashtra and Madhya Pradesh. The sugar industry is one of the world's major agro-based industries. Around 75 per cent of the global sugar production comes from the top ten producers, of which the top three (Brazil, India and the European Union) contribute 40 per cent of the total. The production of sugar is spread across the country. Maharashtra, Uttar Pradesh, Karnataka, Tamil Nadu, Gujarat and Andhra Pradesh are the major sugar producing states in the country. In SY 2009-10, these six states together accounted for almost 94 per cent of the total sugar produced in India. In SY 2009-10, the State of Maharashtra produced the highest sugar at 7.0 million tonnes followed by UP with 5.1 million tonnes. These two states together account for almost 64.5 per cent of the total sugar produced in India. Sugarcane is the primary raw material for the sugar industry. It accounts for almost 80-85 per cent of the total operating cost of the sugar industry. UP is the largest sugarcane producing state in the country and accounted for about 36.2 per cent of the total sugarcane output in SY 2010-11 followed by Maharashtra with 23.6 per cent. Even though, UP is the largest sugarcane-producing state in the country and it is the second-largest sugar producer in India as drawl and recovery rates in UP are one of the lowest in India. (www.careratings.com). Among six major sugar producing states, the sugar firms of Uttar-Pradesh (UP) and Maharashtra are contributing about 27.06 per cent and 30.12 per cent, respectively to the total sugar production of India (Ray, 2012). The Indian sugar industry is marked by co-existence of different ownership and management structures since the beginning of the 20th century. At one extreme, there are privately owned sugar mills in Uttar Pradesh that procure sugarcane from nearby cane growers. At the other extreme, there are co-operative factories owned and managed jointly by farmers, especially in the western state of Gujarat and Maharashtra. There are state owned factories in both the states and state-managed co-operatives in Uttar Pradesh. Sugar is the India's second largest agro-processing industry, with around 527 operating mills as of SY 2011-11. Presently, about four million hectares of land is under sugarcane with an average yield of 70 tonnes per hectare (USDA Foreign Agricultural Service). The Indian sugar industry is the second largest agro-based industry after textile located in rural India. In an era where there is a need for inclusive growth, the sugar industry is amongst the few industries that have successfully contributed to the rural economy. It has done so by commercially utilising the rural resources to meet the large domestic demand for sugar and by generating surplus energy to meet the increasing energy needs of India. The industry is a key driver of rural development, supporting over about 55 million sugarcane farmers, their dependents and a large mass of agricultural labourers involved in sugarcane cultivation, harvesting, machine manufacturing etc., of almost 527 sugar mills and ancillary activities, and constituting 7.5 per cent of the rural population (Sanyal *et. al.*, 2008). It is worth mentioning that the industry employs over five lakh skilled and unskilled workers mainly from the rural areas (ISMA 2005). The total value of sugarcane produced in the country is estimated at Rs. 24000 crore per year (Department of Economic Analysis and Research, 2010). Sugar production in India is likely to be about 26 million tonnes in the current season (SY: 2011-12) while domestic consumption is estimated at about 22 million tonnes. Thus, the sugar industry has been a focal point for socio-economic development in the rural areas by mobilising rural resources, generating employment and higher income, besides giving a fillip to transport and communication facilities (Government of India, 2002).

The Indian sugar industry comprises about 20 per cent of sugar mills and 15 per cent of sugar production of the world. The sugar industry's contribution to the Indian economy is presently enormous with its total turnover of over Rupees fifty-five thousand crore or 12 billion US Dollars per year. The Indian sugar industry is amongst the largest tax payers to the Central exchequer contributing Rupees two thousand six hundred crores per annum or 0.568 billion US Dollars as tax, cess, and excise duty every year (Ministry of Food, Government of India, 2006). The Indian sugar industry has been accounting for around one per cent GDP of the country in the recent past.

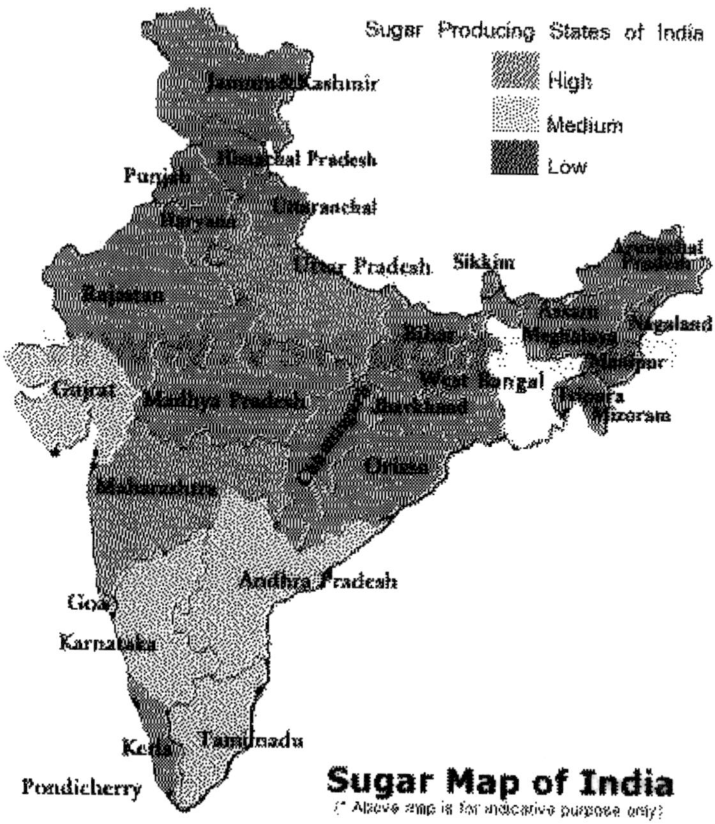

Fig. 3.1: Sugar Map of India.

Source: www.upfed.org

Besides sugar production, the industry has also diversified into manufacturing of by-products like molasses for alcohol, ethanol and chemical industries, bagasse for paper industry and also has the potential to generate over 9700 MW of power from bagasse. Every 100 tonnes of sugarcane crushed on an average gives 11 tonnes of sugar, four tonnes of molasses, 28 tonnes of bagasse and 3 tonnes of Press Mud. Combinations of all these ancillary ventures/activities immensely contribute towards the productivity and profitability for the industry thereby presenting a highly prospective opportunity for investments in this promising field. The industry does not depend on fossil fuel but generates its own renewable source of energy. Not only has that it generated surplus power through cogeneration for use by consumers in interior rural areas. The sugar industry has the potential to generate 5000 MW surplus power. With such larger expense and wide horizon of associated economic activities which can transform rural India, the sugar industry has indeed carved for itself a very important place in the Indian economy.

In sugar year 2010-11, there were 651 installed sugar mill in the country with a production capacity of 24,390 thousand tonnes of sugar of which only 490 are working. Over the years, the sugarcane and sugar production fluctuated noticeably (Table: 3.1). The production of sugar in India increased substantially from 185.19 lakh tonnes in sugar year SY: 2000-01 to 283.64 lakh tonnes in SY: 2006-07 and decreased to 243.94 lakh tonnes in SY: 2010-11 particularly due to the onslaught of drought and white woolly aphid in major sugar producing states like Maharashtra, Tamil Nadu and Karnataka resulting in a fall in sugarcane production, delayed payment of cane price and closure of some sugar mills. Sugar productions increased substantially from 2959.56 lakh tonnes in SY: 2000-01 to 3555.20 lakh tonnes in SY: 2006-07 and again decrease to 3366.98 lakh tonnes in SY 2010-11. The number of sugar factories in operation in India increased from 412 in 2000-01 to 409 in 2010-11. As regards the productivity of sugarcane in India, it may be observed that the yield per hectare marginally decreased from 66.6 tonnes during the SY: 2000-01 to 59.4 tonnes during the SY 2003-04 and marginally increased to 68.6 tonnes during the SY: 2010-11(Table: 02-03-04). Thus, much variation was not observed in the yield per hectare of sugarcane in India over a decade. While the countries like Brazil, Australia, USA, etc., have recorded sugar recovery percentage of around 14, the sugar recovery in India has remained stagnant at around 10 per cent for the last few years. Although climatic suitability determines the sugar recovery to a great extent, there is a need on the part of sugarcane breeding institutes to take steps towards evolving improved technology for improving sugar recovery.

Table 3.1: Indian Sugar Industry: At a Glance

Year	*Sugar-cane Production (Lakh Tonnes)*	*Sugarcane crushed Lakh Tonnes*	*Sugar production (Lakh Tonnes)*	*Recovery (%)*	*Yield (%)*	*Sugar Mills in operation*
2000-01	2959.56	1767.42	185.19	10.48	66.6	412
2001-02	2972.08	1803.21	185.27	10.27	67.4	416
2002-03	2873.83	1943.24	201.40	10.36	63.6	453
2003-04	2338.62	1326.70	135.60	10.22	59.4	423
2004-05	2370.88	1247.71	126.91	10.17	64.7	400
2005-06	2811.72	1886.72	192.67	10.22	66.9	455
2006-07	3555.20	2792.95	283.64	10.17	69.0	504
2007-08	3481.88	2499.06	263.57	10.55	67.5	516
2008-09	2850.29	4449.83	145.39	10.03	70.0	489
2009-10	2923.02	1855.48	189.12	10.19	67.9	490
2010-11	3366.98	2398.07	243.94	10.17	68.6	490

Source: Indian Sugar Year Book 2011, Indian Sugar Mills Association, New Delhi.

Table 3.2: State-wise Sugar Production in India (1000 Tonnes)

States	*2005-06*	*2006-07*	*2007-08*	*2008-09*	*2009-10*
Andhra Pradesh	1236	1680	1335	593	515
Bihar	422	451	336	214	258
Chhattisgarh	18	24	38	13	9
Gujarat	1168	1425	1366	1012	1189
Haryana	409	652	599	229	248
Karnataka	1943	2662	2900	1651	2558
Goa	11	19	15	9	8
Madhya Pradesh	94	180	174	60	80
Maharashtra	5197	9100	9075	4578	7067
Punjab	338	486	534	242	181
Rajasthan	6	7	6	4	4
T.N. and Pondy.	2170	2599	2192	1614	1299
UP Central	1778	2908	2473	1373	1820
UP East	2093	2823	2414	1291	1578
UP West	1913	2744	2432	1400	1781

Source: Annual Report of Ministry of Agriculture, Government of India.

Table 3.3: State-wise Cane Crushed by Sugar Factories in India (1000 Tonnes)

States	*2000-01*	*2001-02*	*2002-03*	*2003-04*	*2004-05*	*2005-06*	*2006-07*	*2007-08*	*2008-09*	*2009-10*
Andhra Pradesh	9867	10467	11980	8597	9217	12303	17323	13201	5993	5547
Bihar	3161	3898	4537	2932	2649	4455	5204	3639	2370	2724
Chattisgarh	....	......	39	175	102	185	310	424	150	110
Gujarat	10249	9783	11828	9753	7405	10787	13390	12801	9445	11295
Haryana	5976	6268	6276	5560	3938	4188	6695	6065	2528	2648
Karnataka	15020	14450	17299	10942	10283	17953	25151	26685	16065	23977
Goa	249	146	160	112	89	121	201	148	108	100
Madhya Pradesh	1012	718	717	1018	732	959	1931	1822	625	853
Maharashtra	57640	48387	53404	29077	19456	44578	79884	76144	40023	61390
Punjab	5113	6281	6035	4065	3220	3676	5092	5760	2603	2112
Rajasthan	66	54	24	99	52	83	79	84	42	48
T.N. and Pondy.	18944	19603	16999	9488	11677	23555	28167	23546	16772	14552
UP Central	17166	21111	19659	15185	16719	19117	30895	25211	15265	20103
UP East	11590	15618	20764	14086	16242	21027	29429	24380	14353	17124
UP West	16381	18480	18848	17081	18511	20665	29170	25148	15864	19507
Uttrakhand	3824	4717	5238	3973	3955	4519	5608	4110	2421	3174
Others- Orissa/ W.B.	439	340	517	527	524	501	720	738	356	280
All India	**176742**	**180321**	**194324**	**132670**	**124771**	**188672**	**279249**	**249906**	**144983**	**185544**

Table 3.4: State-wise Average Recovery of Sugarcane

States	*2000-01*	*2001-02*	*2002-03*	*2003-04*	*2004-05*	*2005-06*	*2006-07*	*2007-08*	*2008-09*	*2009-10*
Andhra Pradesh	10.36	10.01	10.32	10.32	10.65	10.56	9.70	10.12	9.89	9.29
Bihar	9.11	8.78	9.00	9.33	9.48	9.48	8.67	9.24	9.04	9.49
Chhattisgarh	-	-	9.15	9.90	10.15	9.70	7.62	9.00	8.43	7.82
Gujarat	10.42	10.79	10.58	10.93	10.76	10.82	10.64	10.67	10.72	10.53
Haryana	9.80	9.97	10.13	10.47	10.16	9.78	9.75	9.87	9.05	9.37
Karnataka	10.76	10.73	10.82	10.21	10.11	10.82	10.57	10.87	10.2	10.67
Goa	9.04	8.58	8.95	8.89	8.51	9.28	9.57	9.87	8.72	8.17
Madhya Pradesh	9.26	9.89	9.90	10.15	9.80	9.76	9.29	9.54	9.62	9.40
Maharashtra	11.64	11.61	11.65	10.93	11.39	11.68	11.39	11.92	11.44	11.51
Punjab	9.70	9.45	9.72	9.72	9.79	9.19	9.55	9.26	9.29	8.59
Rajasthan	8.76	9.45	8.43	9.53	7.63	6.85	9.04	7.05	8.82	7.80
T.N. and Pondy.	9.60	9.58	9.87	9.91	9.64	9.24	9.25	9.32	9.62	8.94
UP Central	9.42	9.34	9.29	9.56	9.58	9.3	9.41	9.81	8.99	9.06
UP East	9.61	9.36	9.53	9.93	9.86	9.95	9.49	9.9	8.99	9.22
UP West	10.15	9.88	9.79	9.95	9.92	9.26	9.41	9.67	8.83	9.13
Uttarakhand	9.40	9.42	9.51	9.75	9.63	9.42	9.54	9.74	9.20	9.19
Orissa/ WB	9.18	8.92	9.16	9.12	9.26	8.96	9.74	9.51	9.44	9.01
All India	**10.48**	**10.27**	**10.36**	**10.22**	**10.17**	**10.21**	**10.16**	**10.55**	**10.03**	**10.19**

Source: Sugar India Year Book (2011).

3.1.1 Structure of Indian Sugar Industry

Regarding the structure of sugar industry in India, data for the year 2010 show that there are 20 sugar producing states in India but the combined share of 10 major states is about 97 per cent. Table (3.5) provides the following stylised facts of sugar industry in India: (i) Among 10 major sugar producing states, the sugar firms of Uttar Pradesh (UP), and Maharashtra are contributing about 27.40 per cent and 37 per cent, respectively to the total sugar production of India.

In addition, the contributions of sugar firms of Tamil Nadu and Karnataka are 6.80 and 13.5 per cent respectively. On the whole, four states, namely, UP, Maharashtra, Tamil Nadu and Karnataka are contributing about 84.7 per cent to the national output of sugar. In the remaining eight major sugar producing states, the contribution is in single digit (Table: 3.5).

About 25 per cent of sugar firms in India are sick or have shut down their operations. Thus, the installed capacity of one-fifth sugar firms is remained underutilised. According to the High Powered Committee on Sugar Industry (Mahajan Committee) in its report submitted to the Government in April 1998, mentioned that "half of the sugar factories are more than 25 years old. The physical condition of many of these sugar factories is poor, resulting in high down time and loss of capacity." In India, it has been observed that out of 490 running sugar mills 40 per cent factories are still below the minimum economic size of 2500 TCD. Still only 25 per cent of sugar factories out of 490 running sugar factories have crushing capacity more than 2500 TCD, thus leaving adequate scope for modernisation and expansion. In Brazil and Thailand, some of India's competitors in the world market, the sugar factories have higher capacity plants. Therefore, increasing the size of sugar factory and replacing the old plant and machinery of Indian industry offers a challenging task.

Sugar firms in India are operating under three types of ownership structures viz., public, private and co-operative sectors. Recently, in the country there are 651 licensed sugar factories with an average installed capacity of 18 million tonnes have been spread among large sugarcane growing states like Uttar Pradesh, Maharashtra, Karnataka, Gujarat, Tamil Nadu, and Andhra Pradesh. The co-operative sector dominates with the 320 co-operative sugar firms. It is apparent from the data that 49 per cent of sugar firms are installed under the co-operative sector as compared to the 40.55 per cent under private ownership and 9.50 per cent under public ownership.

Table 3.5: Structure of Sugar Industry in India (as on 30-09-2010)

States	*Output (000 tonnes)*	*Percentage share (%)*	*No. of Sugar Factories Installed*				*Sugar Factories in Operation*	*Sick Sugar firms*
			Public	*Private*	*Cooperative*	*Total*		
(1)	**(2)**	**(3)**	**(4)**	**(5)**	**(6)**	**(7)**	**(8)**	**(9)=(7-8)**
Andhra Pradesh	515	2.70	1	27	15	43	35	8
Bihar	258	1.40	15	13	-	28	9	19
Gujarat	1189	6.30	-	1	22	23	18	5
Haryana	248	1.30	-	3	13	16	14	2
Karnataka	2558	13.50	3	37	24	64	54	10
Madhya Pradesh	80	.04	2	11	5	18	11	7
Maharashtra	7067	37.00	-	35	166	201	143	58
Orissa	25	.01	-	4	4	8	5	3
Tamil Nadu	1299	6.80	3	26	16	45	42	3
Uttar Pradesh	5179	27.40	33	95	28	156	128	28
Others	494	2.60	5	17	27	49	31	18
All India	**18912**	**100**	**62**	**269**	**320**	**651**	**490**	**161**

Source: Indian Sugar Year Book 2011, Indian Sugar Mills Association, New Delhi.

3.1.2 Progress of Sugar Industry in India during Five Year Plans

(A) First Five Year Planning (1951-1956)

The planning period boosted up the regulated growth of sugar industry in India. Such a planned growth was not discernible before the first five year planning. In 1951, the target of sugar production was fixed at 15 lakh tonnes compare to 11.16 lakh tonnes in 1949-51. As the consumption and demand increased the target for the production was raised to 18 lakh tonnes during the mid-plan and to 17.77 lakh tonnes by the end of the first plan period. Naturally beyond expectation the sugar production increased to 19.34 lakh tonnes crossing the first five year planning. During the first five year planning, the total number of factories in India was 138 including two cooperative factories.

Table 3.6: Sugar Industry in Five Year Plan

Plan Period	*Production Targets (Lakh tonnes)*	*Actual production (Lakh tonnes)*	*Number of Sugar mills*
First Plan (1951-1956)	18	19.34	138
Second Plan (1956-1961)	25	30.29	175
Third Plan (1961-1966)	35	35.32	200
Fourth Plan (1969-1974)	47	39.5	229
Fifth Plan (1974-1978)	54	58..42	298
Sixth Plan (1980-1985)	76	61.78	356
Seventh Plan (1985-1990)	102	109.9	414
Eigth Plan (1992-1997)	143	139.56	412
Ninth Plan (1997-2002)	148	185	434
Tenth Plan (2002-2007)	156	170	461
Eleventh plan (2007-12)			
2007-08	NA	263.57	516
2008-09	NA	145.39	489
2009-10	NA	189.12	490

Source: Yojana, November 1999, ISMA Report 2004, 2005 and 2006 (T.S. Devraja p. 41).

(B) Second Five Year Planning (1956-1961)

During the second plan it was proposed to raise the production of sugar to 22.5 lakh tonnes with an installed capacity of about 25 lakh tonnes by the end of 1960-61. For this purpose sugarcane was made available to the factories in the increased quantities so that the total production was increased from 5.8 million tonnes in 1955-56 to 17.1 million tonnes in 1960-61. Hence, much care was taken for extensive cultivation of sugarcane providing irrigation facilities, establishment of seed miseries, distribution of disease-free varieties of improved seeds, distribution of manures and fertiliser and control of pests and diseases. Thirty mills were established during the second plan as against the target of 35 mills by the co-operative society. These measures brought a record production of 30.29 lakh tonnes with installed capacity of about 25 lakh tonnes by the end of 1960-61.

(C) Third Five Year Planning (1961-1966)

During the third five year planning period, the installed capacity in the industry recorded a further rise to about 32.1 lakh tonnes in 1965-66. The last year of planning period industry recorded a production of 35.32 lakh tonnes against a target of 35 lakh tonnes. There was a gap of three years after1966 because of Fourth Five Year Plan lately commenced from first April 1969. Chiefly because of the drought and reduction in cane acreage by about 22 per cent in factory area as compare to 1965-66, the production of sugarcane sharply declined to 21.3 lakh tonnes in 1966-67.

(D) Fourth Five Year Planning (1969-1974)

In the Fourth Five Year planning period, the Government fixed the target on 47 lakh tonnes to be achieved by 1974. For the execution of target production the licensed capacity was raised from 40 lakh tonnes in the beginning of 1969 to 48.65 lakh tones, but because of slow progress in the establishment of capacity, the government had to revise the target of licensed capacity to 53 lakh tonnes. However, as the progress was not up to the mark rather very slow. The planning commission decided to further raised the license capacity to 56 lakh tonnes. Thus, the government issued licensed and letters of intents to bring the total licensed capacity to 56 lakh tonnes in the industry.

These measures helped in the achievement of all time record of 4.6 lakh tonnes in 1969-70, the first year of the fourth planning. This ratio was not maintained at this level in 1970-71 and declined to 37.4 lakh tonnes. It was another fact that with larger carry forward stock about 22 lakh tonnes from the previous season, the total availability of sugar was higher, i.e., 51 lakh tonnes. Owing to larger availability of stock the government decontrolled sugar with effect from the 25th day, 1971 but the policy at decontrol could not continue as the production declined to 31.1 lakh tonnes in 1971-72. The sugar price increased and showed an upward trend. During the fourth five year planning the total number of sugar factories in India reached to 229 including 84 co-operative factories during the third planning as it was 200.

(E) Fifth Five Year Planning (1974-1978)

In the fifth planning period the development programmes of the sugar industry was estimated by the planning commission keeping in view the per capita domestic requirement of sugar at 8.68 kg. In 1978-79, taking into account the population at the end of the fifth plan at 673 million and thus the total requirement for domestic consumption was estimated at 55 lakh tonnes. On the other hand, the requirement for export and buffer stock was estimated at five lakh tonnes on the basis of these estimates, the task force of the planning commission recommended 60 lakh tonnes sugar production at the larger for the period. For achieving the production target of 57 lakh tonnes in 1978-79, licenses were issued to 62 new sugar factories and expansions in 32 existing units in sugar producing states for an additional capacity of 15.70 lakh tonnes.

(F) Sixth Five Year Planning (1980-1985)

During the sixth planning period the government estimated the requirement of sugar 76 lakh tonnes by the end of the 1984-85. The targets of installed capacity and licensed capacity were put at 80.4 and 86.2 lakh tonnes respectively. Thus, the sugar industry again achieved a record production of eight million tonnes during 1982-83 which crossed even the world record. The Government instituted an enquiry into cost structure of the industry and other relevant matters through a high-level committee in 1980 under L. Kumar as its chairman which recommended the policy of restoring the partial control for the season 1981-82 along with levy and free sugar production at 65.35 lakh tonnes respectively which came into effect from 30th November 1930. The statutory cane price was maintained at the level of Rs. 13. 00 per quintal linked to basic recovery of 8.5 per cent for three consecutive years, i.e., from 1980 to 1983 and the price of levy sugar was determined accordingly. The Government had to import about five lakh tonnes of sugar in last quarter of the year 1984, because of the depletion of stock. In the sixth plan period the total number of factories in India came to 356 including 178 co-operative factories.

(G) Seventh Five Year Planning (1985-1990)

On the basis of an annual growth rate of five per cent per annum, the planning commission had estimated the requirement of sugar at 98 lakh tonnes during the seventh plan period ending 1989-90. The installed and licensed capacity targets were put at 114.6 and 132.6 lakh tonnes respectively. The government had issued licenses for 162.1 lakh tonnes by the end of 1989-90, exceeding the target by as much as 30 lakh tonnes. The installed capacity, however, was only 93.4 lakh tonnes leaving the unimplemented capacity of about 70 lakh tonnes. The Government of India had announced a pragmatic sugar policy with increase in the statutory Minimum Price of sugarcane on the basis of the recommendations of the commission for Agricultural Costs and Prices and change in the levy ratio in the year 1984-85. This had enabled the industry to increase sugar production substantially in the shortest period. In the 7th plan period the total number of factories in India came to 414.

(H) Eighth Five Year Planning (1992-1997)

A task force was constituted to project the requirement of sugar during the eighth plan period. The task force after detailed deliberation of various aspects projected the requirement of sugar the eighth plan period ending 1994-95 at 134.13 lakh tonnes. The installed and licensed capacity targets were put at 141.19 lakh tonnes and 180.20 lakh tonnes respectively. The eighth plan was delayed by two years and the Government had projected the requirement of sugar, installed and licensed capacity on the basis of parameters, adopted for working out the targets at the end of 1994-95. The Government had re-assessed the installed capacity in the industry on the basis of the average 10 years' working during the period 1978-79 to 1987-88. The installed capacity in the industry during the 1988-89 which was assessed at 85.03 lakh tonnes was revised to 90.81 lakh tonnes. The licensed capacity in the industry, stood at 175.56 lakh tonnes as against the target of 180 lakh tonnes at the end of 1994-95. On this basis of the installed and licensed capacities at the end of the eighth plan were 148 and 200 lakh tonnes respectively.

(I) Ninth Five Year Planning (1997-2002)

During the ninth planning period the government estimated the requirement of sugar 15.5 million tonnes by the end of the 1997-98. The targets of installed capacity and licensed capacity were put at 16.4 and 20.1 million tonnes respectively. Thus, the sugar industry again achieved a record production of 16.4 million tonnes during 1998-99. During the period of 2000-01 the targets of installed capacity and licensed capacity were put at 19.1 and 23.5 million tonnes. The production and consumption is estimated to 18.2 million tonnes and 16.5 million tonnes respectively.

However, at the end of ninth planning period (2001-02), the target licensing and installed capacity successfully achieved as 24.4 and 20.2 million tonnes respectively. Naturally, as per expectation the sugar production increased to 19.1 million tonnes at the end of the ninth plan.

(J) Tenth Five Year Planning (2002-2007)

Sugar production in India has been generally higher than the rate of growth of sugar consumption. Consequently, there are huge inventories. The projection for internal consumption of sugar during the Tenth Plan period (taking the base internal consumption figure of 15.5 mmt for the 1999-2000 sugar season) has been calculated at 21.3 mmt in 2006-07. This assumes a 6.5 per cent GDP growth and a compound growth rate of 4.9 per cent. The internal consumption has been projected at 23.8 mmt in 2006-07, when an eighth per cent GDP and compound growth rate of 6.14 per cent is assumed. The carry forward of stocks is estimated at 2.65 mmt in 2006-07. The likely scenario of sugar production is projected as 21.3 mmt during 2006-07 and it is estimated that 1.5 mmt of sugar could be exported every year during the Tenth Plan period (Planning Commission, Government of India).

(K) Eleventh Five Year Planning (2007-2012)

While international prices have been fluctuating, the SMP fixed by the Central Government has been raised gradually from Rs. 62.05 per quintal in 2001–002 to Rs. 81.18 per quintal in 2007–08. Additionally some of the State Governments have been advising sugar factories to pay cane price at a higher level than the SMP. The sugar industry thus faces a predicament in which it is asked to pay more for the raw materials even as it gets less for its produce in the market. Indian sugar industry is amongst the most diversified industry in the world, with an installed capacity to produce 1000 MW co-generated power against a potential of 7500 MW. An addition of 1000 MW is under implementation. Despite emphasis laid by the GOI to harness the growth potential further, the progress as co-generation of power is sapped by problems with regard to tariff fixation, third-party sale, and timely payments by State Electricity Boards (SEBs).

3.1.3 SWOT Analysis of the Sugar Industry

SWOT analysis is a strategic planning method used to evaluate the Strengths, Weaknesses, Opportunities, and Threats involved in a project or in a business venture. It is undertaken by combining organisational capability profile (OCP) and environmental threat and opportunity profile

(ETOP). The basic objective of SWOT analysis is to provide a framework to reflect on the organisational capability to avail opportunity or to overcome threats presented by the environment. In fact, the dimension of organisational capabilities has relevance in so far as they relate to the environmental condition. Hence, organisational analysis and environmental analysis should be inter-linked. Based on the industry analysis, SWOT analysis of Indian sugar industry can be presented as follow:

(A) STRENGTH

- India is the second largest producer of sugar in the world after Brazil and it is the largest consumer of sweetener with about 20 million tonnes p.a. In global sugar economy, the Indian sugar industry has achieved a number of milestones. The sector has a potential to make the country to be self-reliant in this highly sensitive essential commodity of mass consumption.
- Besides being the second largest producer, it has also the second largest area under sugar cane cultivation. Presently, about 4.3 million hectors of land under sugarcane with the average yield of 70 tonnes per hectares.
- The sugar industry paid well over Rs. 122.69 billion to the sugarcane growers in the financial year, 2006. In the last sugar season 2009-10, approximately Rs. 45,000 crore was paid to farmers as cane price. This year, it is expected to rise to about Rs. 51,000 crore.
- This sector plays a key role of socio-economic development of the rural India. It provides direct employment including ancillary activities to near about 0.5 million workers.
- It also supports the other industries by providing the raw materials.
- The industry has vast domestic market.
- It contributes about Rs. 2500 crore annually to the Centre and the State exchequers in the form taxes (ISMA, 2004).
- Sugarcane farming is more profitable than any other cash crop in India.
- Most of the sugar factories are situated near to the fields hence easily availability of raw materials promote the industry.

(B) WEAKNESSES

- Indian sugar industry has been facing crunch of raw material and resources as well as infrastructure problems.
- Most of the sugar factories are more than 40 years old and still using old technology.

- The industry produces during the period 4-5 months in a year but it has to maintain the sugar stock over whole year.
- The industry runs only seasons based. Hence, it creates hidden unemployment in seasonal workers.
- Most of the sugar factories of public sectors are facing financial problems and generating losses. Hence, they need high working capital.
- A large number of sugar units in India utilise production capacity below 50 per cent. Low capacity utilisation and inadequacy of raw materials led to closer of many sugar factories in India.
- Lack of adequate automation and information management.
- Lack of Research and Development department in the industry.
- Most of the sugar factories faced low installs production capacity; hence it leads to decrease in production. There is inadequate production capacity utilisation.
- Sugar recovery is also lower in comparison with other sugar manufacturing countries. This leads to escalation of production costs and weakness in giving competitive edge to the industry.
- The industry is not able to attract the talented and skilled employees due to less pay package.
- Lack of modernisation and professionalism.

(C) OPPURTUNITY

- Due to increasing per capita consumption of sugar. There is increasing demand of sugar in India.
- India is known as the agro-based country; hence it offers huge potential to agro-based activity.
- Integration of development in contemporary technologies such as electronics, material science, computers, bio-technology, etc., offer, vast scope for rapid improvement and progress.
- There is no immediate threat of entry by any technically superior company in this industry sector.
- High value of by-product for downstream industries.
- The industry has huge potential to increase the productivity of cane and sugar recovery rate.

(D) THREATS

- India ranks first in sugar consumption and second in sugar production in world but its share in global sugar trade is below three per cent. Indian sugar industry has been facing raw material, and resource as well as infrastructural problems. Globalisation has brought a number of opportunities but at the same time posed certain challenges before sugar industry. Most of sugar units in India utilise production capacity below 50 per cent.

- The industry growth rate is not very attractive.
- Sugar sector is vulnerable to political interest and it has also suffers from the Government control and regulation policies.
- In recent years, sugarcane production in India has decelerated to a great extent due to water and power shortage. Hence, special attention is needed to given on water resource management. All the area under sugar cultivation should be brought under drip irrigation to conserve water as well as fertilisers.
- Adequate and regular power supply to sugarcane growers and sugar factories would increase production and productivity.
- Unhealthy competition between members of the society.
- Rapid development in contemporary and requirement of the industry may lead to fast obsolescence.
- To enhance share of Indian sugar industry in global trade, quality and quantity of sugar needs to be enhanced.
- Due to unhealthy working condition there is lack of trained and professional manpower.

3.1.4 Sugar Export and Import

Indian domestic sugar market is one of the largest markets in the world; in volume terms. It remains a key growth driver for world sugar, growing above the Asian and world consumption growth average. Sugar is one of the most important cash crops in the world and hence there is always a wrestle to control its imports/export. The sugar export from India decreased substantially from 338.691 metric tonnes in SY 2000-01 to 44.045 metric tonnes in SY 2009-10 due to decreased sugar production and uncompetitive sugar prices (Table: 07). The sugar import into India increased substantially from 30.404 metric tonnes in SY 2000-01 to 386.099 metric tonnes, 2424.045 metric tonnes and 528.732 metric tonnes in SY 2008-09, 2009-10 and 2010-11 respectively. Thus, during the SY 2000-01 to SY 2010-11, the quantity of sugar exported was substantially lower than what was imported. There is a need on the part of the government to take suitable steps towards encouraging export of sugar and jaggery, after meeting the domestic requirement.

Table 3.7: Export and Import of Sugar in India

Financial Year	*Export ('000 Metric Tonnes)*	*Export Value (in Rs crore)*	*Import ('000 Metric Tonnes)*	*Import Value (in Rs crore)*
2000-01	338.691	430.98	30.404	31.11
2001-02	1456.448	1720.29	26.578	32.60
2002-03	1662.370	1769.49	41.430	32.83
2003-04	1200.600	1216.59	74.400	62.70
2004-05	108.587	149.52	933.00	976.17
2005-06	316.850	557.09	558.77	651.80
2006-07	1643.403	3127.47	1.052	3.49
2007-08	4684.554	5412.16	0.494	2.24
2008-09	3331.997	4448.74	386.099	583.11
2009-10	44.045	110.23	2424.045	5961.24
2010-11	....	....	528.732	1365.13

Source: DGCI and S. Kolkata (Co-operative Sugar, Vol. 43 (4), Dec 2011.

3.1.5 Policies and Issues Relating to Indian Sugar Industry

(a) Licensing Policy

Since 1952, the development of the sugar industry was being regulated by Government of India under the provisions of the Industries (Development and Regulation) Act 1951. The advantage under this system was that the sugar factories had their cane supply area reserved and they had the freedom to develop their areas for the best return without fear of anyone else usurping it. The main feature of Industrial Development Regulation Act, 1951 are as follow:

- Sugar Industry is a schedule industry under Industrial Development Regulation Act requiring license to manufacturer.
- Gestation period has been reduced from three years to one.
- Minimum capacity of a new sugar mill is 2500 TCD and expandable up to 5000 TCD.
- Minimum distance between two sugar mills is now 15-km which used to be 40-km.
- Cane availability is now not so critical requirement.
- Government gives incentives where in new mills can sell up to 100 per cent of the sugar in free market against 60 per cent of existing mills -- Government has also announced such incentive for expansion up to 5000 TCD.

- The impact has been horizontal growth-causing cane shortage-higher per unit processing cost, etc.

(b) Domestic Policy

The Sugar Policy of the Government of India has been seriously lacking a long-term perspective. Controls, Decontrols, Partial Controls have been used in a most ad hoc manner. Under the Essential Commodities Act of 1955, the sugar industry has always been subjected to various controls as per the Act and Rules there under, viz., the Sugar (Control) Order, 1966, Sugarcane (Control) Order 1966, the Levy Sugar Supply Order, 1979, Sugar (Packing and Marking) Order,1977, Sugar Cess Act, 1982, etc., sugar was a controlled commodity in India. The controls on the sugar industry have caused more harm than benefits. These controls were introduced at a time when India was mainly dependent on imported sugar. Most of these controls have outlived their utility if they ever had any. But now with the changed scenario of India being the second largest producer of sugar, and with all other commodities freed from Government regulations, the control on sugar industry has been stifling its growth. The levy sugar percentage was reduced from 70 per cent to 10 per cent in ten steps from 1972. Now the Government has been taking a percentage of sugar production (currently 20 per cent) as levy sugar for distribution to below poverty line (BPL) population under Public Distribution System (PDS). This is procured by the Government at a price which is much below cost of production of sugar. But still whenever the price of free sale sugar goes below levy sugar price, the Government nominees to whom levy sugar is allotted do not lift the sugar, but the sugar factories have to keep the levy quota for them for long periods by replacing the stock with New Year's production. On the other hand, the Government in their enthusiasm to contain price of free sale sugar make additional free sale release. Consequently, the price of free sale sugar very often goes below cost of production but the sugar factories per force have to sell the sugar to avoid the penalty of conversion of lapsed free sale sugar to levy. This is one of the reasons for the sugar factories being perennially in liquidity crisis and burdened with cane price arrears. Government of India initiated delicensing policy in sugar industry on 11th September, 1998 in view of globalisation process, and since then industry has experienced significant changes. Delicensing of sugar industry has led to mushrooming growth of sugar mills. Since then, the industry has experienced significant changes. As a result, the entrepreneurs are free to start sugar mills without license with a minimum economic capacity of 2500 TCD (Tonnes of Cane Crushed per Day), with no maximum limit on capacity, but at a distance of 15km away from existing sugar mills. However, in industrially backward areas, cooperative and public sector are allowed with an initial capacity of 1750 TCD subject to the condition that the units would expand their capacities to 2500 TCD within a period of five years of going into production. Preference is given to proposals from the co-operative sector, public sector, private sector, etc., in that order in licensing. Sugar mills in India have capacities ranging from 1250 TCD to 10000 TCD. The government has now established the minimum capacity criteria for new sugar mills at 2500 TCD. The report of the Task Force on Sugar Industry for the Tenth Five Year Plan had noted that nearly 84 per cent of sugar mills had a capacity of below 2500 TCD.

A high powered committee under the Chairmanship of B.B. Mahajan was set up to review the various facets of the sugar industry. The Committee made the following recommendations: (i) The Decontrol of sugar prices in a phased manner, achieving full decontrol by 1999-2000; (ii) Discontinuation of sugar supply through PDS as there are large scale leakages of levy sugar into open market; (iii) To exclude expansion projects from licensing. However, the licensing of the new mills to be continued with little modifications; (iv) Monthly issue of sugar quota to be continued even during the era of decontrolled prices; (v) The Statutory Minimum Price (SMP) to be continued mainly based on the cost of production of sugarcane and not on sugar price in the market; (vi) To set-up Cane Pricing Board which will announce sugarcane prices in the beginning of every season. The Board will be represented by all the players of the industry; (vii) Sugar exports should be at least one million ton; and (viii) To abolish licensing of wholesale dealers and the stock restrictions. The government accepted all the recommendations of the Mahajan Committee and declared a new Sugar Policy in November 2001. At the same time, S.K. Tutleja Committee recommended complete decontrol of sugar trade by October, 2005. The sugar pricing policy in India is complex and cumbersome. The Central Government announces the statutory minimum prices (SMP) of the sugarcane mainly based on the recommendations of the Bhargava Committee. And on this basis the state governments fix State Advised Prices (SAP). Unfortunately, SAP is being used as a political tool causing severe damage to the economics of the sugar industry. In some of the states, the difference between the SMP and SAP has been substantial (20-25 per cent above SMP). The government controls the supply of sugar in the open market through monthly sugar release notifications based on market conditions and thus influence the open market prices to a great extent.

The latest sugar policy has the following contents: (i) The government has reduced the levy sugar ratio to 20:80 by 2010; (ii) The government is announcing the SMP of sugarcane linked to basic recovery, a premium for every 0.1 per cent increase in the recovery above that level; (iii) Announcing of the levy-sugar price for each sugar zone; (iv) Restructuring the PDS for sugar-limiting only to BPL families and excluding income tax assesses; and (v) To introduce futures trading in sugar – approval to three exchanges to conduct futures trading in sugar - e-Commodities Ltd., Mumbai; NCS InfoTech Ltd, Hyderabad; and e-Sugar India, Mumbai. The government controls all the aspects of the production and sale of sugar. The wholesale traders need to obtain a license and conform to the government notifications of their inventories.

(c) Trade Policy

Exports: The exports of sugar were governed by the Sugar Export Promotion Act 1958, according to which the government can use 20 per cent of the country's total production for sale abroad. The imports and exports were routed through Indian Sugar and General Industry Export-Import Corporation Ltd. (ISGIEC), a consortium of apex organisations of private and co-operative sugar mills and government agencies. The government de-canalised the exports in 1997 allowing private parties to export sugar. The government has also put the sugar imports on Open General License (OGL) allowing private parties to import sugar. The imported sugar has been subjected to a customs duty of 20 per cent from January 1999, so as to provide a level playing field to the domestic industry, which supplies sugar at levy prices to Gal, for PDS supply. India's competitiveness has been hampered by the low sugar recovery of 10.2 per cent as compared with12-13 per cent in some other major producing countries and around 14.6 per cent in Brazil. However, the prevailing cane price system provides little incentive to improve quality (in terms of sucrose content), the sugar recovery content of cane has remained stagnant at around 10 per cent at the last two decades. To facilitate exports, the government removed the quantitative ceiling on sugar exports in April, 01. Export of sugar can now be undertaken by the various sugar mills/exporters after obtaining the export Release Order from the Directorate of Sugar under the Ministry of Consumer Affairs, Food and Public Distribution. As a result, India's sugar exports have increased from 0.34 mt in 2001 to 1.18 mt in 2004. However, lower domestic production during 2005 resulted in lower sugar exports during 2005-06. In July 2006, the Government of India banned sugar exports till March, 2007, because of the lower domestic sugar stocks and rising sugar prices. However, this ban is not applicable to sugar exports on preferential quota to the US and the EU permitted only through the Indian Sugar Exim Corporation Ltd. (ISEC), up to a quantitative ceiling notified by the Directorate General of Foreign Trade (DGFT).

Imports: Import of sugar which was under Open General License (OGL) with zero duty in March 1994, continued up to April 27, 1998. The government imposed a basic customs duty of five per cent and a counter-veiling duty of Rs. 850 per tonne on imported sugar from April 28, 1998. India's import duties on sugar are generally modified in response to domestic demand-supply conditions. Because of the rising domestic production in 1999, the basic customs duty was increased to 20 per cent in January 1999. In 2000, the duty was further increased to 25 per cent with a surcharge of 10 per cent. India's sugar imports decreased in 2001-02, because of rising domestic availability and increase in customs duties. However, imports increased during 2004-05 because of lower domestic supply. To enable the Government to meet the normative three months consumption requirement of the country, the Advance License (AL) Scheme was liberalised for raw sugar import. India's raw sugar imports have increased from 0.07 mt in 2004 to 0.93 mt in 2005.

3.2 Global Sugar Industry Scenario

Historically, sugar has been regarded as one of the most regulated agro industries in the world. At present Sugar is produced in 122 countries or territories either from sugar cane or from sugar beets. The leading sugarcane producing countries are Brazil, India, Australia, Thailand, China and Cuba. The world's major sugar producers are Brazil, India and the EU, which together represented around 42 per cent of the world's total production in 2009-10. These countries are followed by China, the US, Thailand, Mexico, Australia, and Pakistan, which together account for another 30 per cent of the world's total production. The choice of sugarcane and sugar beet for sugar production is influenced by weather condition, crop diseases, soil quality, international trade agreements and domestic price support programmers. The sugar beet, which is an annual root crop, is grown in temperate regions which accounts one-third of world production. India has 20 per cent of the total sugar mills in the world and accounts for about 16 per cent of the global production.

Table 3.8: World Raw Sugar Production (Million Tonnes)

Country	*2002*	*2004*	*2006*	*2008*	*2010*
Brazil	23.50	27.30	31.6	32.3	36.40
India	19.5	14.4	22.3	25.9	20.63
EU	18.3	21.9	18.1	16.4	16.68
USA	6.8	7.6	7.1	6.9	7.2
China	9.8	10.9	10.7	15.4	11.42
Thailand	6.4	7.5	5.6	7.8	6.9
Mexico	5.1	5.7	5.4	5.9	5.11
Austria	5.6	5.5	4.7	4.6	4.7
Cuba	3.5	2.6	1.3	1.4	1.6
South Africa	2.8	2.2	2.3	2.4	2.7
Sub total	101.3	105.7	109.1	119.4	----
Percentage of the World	71%	72%	72%	73%	----
Percentage of Other World	29%	28%	28%	27%	----
Total	142.1	147.3	152.1	162.5	----

Source: Indian Sugar Year Book (2009), Indian Sugar Mills Association, New Delhi.

The world sugar trade accounts for around 36 per cent of the global sugar production. India is a marginal player in the world sugar trade market.

Table 3.9: India's Share of Sugar Production at Global Level

(Figures in Million Tonnes)

Period	*Global Production*	*India's*	*India's Production as percentage to Global production*
2000-01	130.00	20.10	15.50
2001-02	135.20	20.10	14.80
2002-03	143.00	21.60	15.10
2003-04	148.13	21.70	14.64
2004-05	147.26	14.43	09.80
2005-06	141.35	15.21	10.76
2006-07	152.15	22.34	14.68
2007-08	166.34	29.10	17.50
2008-09	162.50	25.94	15.96
2009-10	174.30	28.50	16.35

Source: Food and Agricultural Organisation of United Nations: Economic and Social Department: The Statistical Division and Indian Sugar Year Book (ISMA).

The average volume of preferential trade is around 10 million MT of sugar annually. Brazil and EU dominate the world sugar trade. Australia and Thailand are other major sugar exporting country. Sugar is widely-traded commodity. On an average, about 70 per cent of world sugar production is consumed in the country of origin, and the balance 30 per cent is traded in international markets. The forthcoming table (8 and 9) is showing the raw sugar production, India's share of sugar production and per capita consumption of sugar of leading countries.

3.3 Origin and Development of Sugar Industry in Uttar Pradesh

Uttar Pradesh is the foremost state in production of sugar and sugarcane in the country. The state tops the list of sugarcane producing states, whereas, it ranks second in sugar production. Sugar industry of the state has a symbiotic relationship with the rural masses and serves as a nerve centre for the rural development. It contributes almost 50 per cent of the total production of the country. The state had 21.25 lakh hectare areas under sugarcane out of the total 49.62 lakh hectare area under sugarcane cultivation in the country in 2010-11 (Sugar India, 2011). The sugar industry in Uttar Pradesh is able to manufacture sugar in such a huge quantity due to fact that the agro-climatic condition and the condition of soil are favourable to the sugarcane production. The region of India where the state of Uttar Pradesh lies is one of the most fertile lands in India called the "DOAB". This is an extremely fertile belt of lands between the rivers of Ganga and Yamuna. The geographical position of the state of Uttar Pradesh is one of the key advantages as it is very easy to access. All the sugar factories are set up near to the sugarcane field (area). The manpower required in sugar industries is easily available in the region. All means of transport and communication facility is available here. In Uttar Pradesh, there is only one sugarcane-crushing season, i.e., September to May every year.

The sugarcane is produced in 44 districts of the state and of these districts 28 districts are the major sugarcane producing districts. There are 128 operational sugar mills running in the State at the end of crushing season 2010-11. A total of about 29 lakh sugarcane farmers are members of the 168 UP Cooperative Cane Development Societies and the sugarcane is supplied to mills through these societies (www.upcane.org). The entire sugar industry consist of Public, Private and Cooperative sector mills that spread over three zones, i.e., Eastern, Central and Western Uttar Pradesh. Almost 50 per cent of sugar mills are in private sector and rest of the mills are in other sectors.

Table 3.10: Profile of Uttar Pradesh Sugar Industry

Crushing season	*Sugarcane area (000 Hec.)*	*Sugarcane Production (million tonnes)*	*Yield of Sugarcane (tonnes/ha)*	*No. of mills in operation*	*Sugarcane Crushed (million tonnes)*	*Sugar Recovery (per cent)*	*Sugar Production (million tonnes)*
2000-01	1938	106.068	54.7	110	45.137	9.73	4.39
2001-02	2035	117.982	58.0	112	55.209	9.53	5.26
2002-03	2149	120.948	56.3	111	59.271	9.53	5.65
2003-04	2030	112.754	55.5	----	46.352	9.82	4.55
2004-05	1955	118.716	60.7	----	51.472	9.79	5.03
2005-06	2156	125.470	58.2	116	60.809	9.49	5.78
2006-07	2247	133.949	59.6	133	89.494	9.47	8.48
2007-08	2179	124.665	57.2	133	74.739	9.79	7.32
2008-09	2048	109.048	52.3	132	45.482	9.72	4.06
2009-10	1977	117.140	59.3	126	56.734	9.63	5.18
2010-11	2125	121.998	57.4	128	-----	9.72	----

Source: Sugar Year Book 2011 and ISMA Publication.

Source: www.upfed.org

Fig. 3.2: Map Showing the Location of Sugar Factories in Uttar Pradesh.

Uttar Pradesh is the largest sugarcane producing State in India. Production of sugarcane is highly volatile, creating cyclical trend in the sugar production during 2000-01, 110 sugar mills were in operation and crushed 45.137 million tonnes of sugarcane which was almost 50 per cent of the total production of the country. In crushing season 2009-10, there were 128 sugar mills in operation and produced 5.18 million tonnes of white sugar in the state (Table 3.10). The sugar industry consists of private, co-operative and public sector mills that spread over the western, central and eastern regions of the State. Over 50 per cent of these mills are in the private sector and the remaining mills are in the other sectors. The above table shows that the area and production of sugarcane have significantly increased between the period 2000-01 and 2009-10. As it is evident from the Table 10, there has been remarkable increase in sugarcane crushed by the mills, albeit with wide fluctuations across years. The figure rose from 45.137 million tonnes (MT) in 2000-01 to 56.734 MT in 2009-10. However, the most disquieting situation in the industry is regarding low percentage of net sugar recovery. In Uttar Pradesh, the sugar recovery percentage varied from 9.82 in 2003-04 to 9.72 in 2010-11 as against the higher all India average of 10.22 and 10.17 in 2003-04 and 2010-11 respectively. The recovery percentage has remained less than 10 per cent throughout the period. During 2010-11, the area under sugarcane was maximum in Uttar Pradesh (2,125 thousand hectare).

3.3.1 Zone-wise Performance of UP Sugar Industry

The spread over of sugar mills in UP is mainly three climatic zones namely, Central, Eastern and Western shows important statistics (Table 3.11) regarding cane crushed, sugar recovery and sugar production, etc. It has been observed that there is no any categorical difference in terms of cane, sugar production in different zones. Ten years data projects that after 2006-07 there has been drastic downfall of cane, sugar production, sugar recovery and average crushing days.

3.3.2 Uttar Pradesh State Sugar Corporation Ltd., (UPSSCL)

The Uttar Pradesh Sugar Corporation Limited was incorporated on 26 March, 1971 under the Companies Act 1956 as a fully owned by Government to run the 28 'sick' sugar mills acquired by the state Government under the Uttar Pradesh sugar undertakings (Acquisition) Act, 1971. The Board for Industrial and Financial Reconstruction (BIFR) declared the company as a sick industrial company from 21st August 1995. The company was controlling 30 sugar mills (acquiring during 1971-1989) up to 1997-98. Out of these 10 mills were closed (four mills from crushing season 1998-99 and six mills from crushing season 1999-2000) as these mills/units became unviable due to continued losses. Moreover, one mill was transferred in January, 2002 to the state of Uttaranchal (Doiwala Unit).

According to the condition of BIFR (July, 2002) and the decision taken by the Government 18 Sugar mills (ten closed mills and eight working mills) were transferred to the new subsidiary company, i.e., Uttar Pradesh State Sugar and Cane Development Corporation Ltd., in September, 2002.

Table 3.11: Zone-wise Performance of UP Sugar Industry

Crushing Season	*Sugar Cane Crushed (000 tonnes)*				*Sugar Production (000 tonnes)*				*Sugar Recovery (%)*				*Average Crushing Days*			
	Central (C)	*Eastern (E)*	*Western (W)*	*All UP*	*Central (C)*	*Eastern (E)*	*Western (W)*	*All UP*	*(C)*	*(E)*	*(W)*	*All UP*	*(C)*	*(E)*	*(W)*	*All UP*
2000-01	17166	11590	16381	**45137**	1617	1114	1663	**4394**	9.42	9.61	10.15	9.73	---	-----	---	----
2001-02	21111	15618	18480	**55209**	1973	1462	1825	**5260**	9.34	9.36	9.88	9.53	----	----		
2002-03	19659	20764	18848	**59271**	1826	1980	1845	**5651**	9.29	9.53	9.79	9.53	156	144	183	**158**
2003-04	15185	14086	17081	**46352**	1452	1399	1700	**4551**	9.56	9.93	9.95	9.82	115	84	157	**113**
2004-05	16719	16242	18511	**51472**	1601	1601	1835	**5037**	9.58	9.86	9.92	9.79	120	90	154	**117**
2005-06	19117	21027	20665	**60809**	1778	2093	1913	**5784**	9.24	9.93	9.49	9.49	123	113	142	**124**
2006-07	30895	29429	29170	**89494**	2908	2823	2744	**8475**	9.42	9.59	9.47	9.47	166	139	173	**158**
2007-08	25211	24380	25148	**74739**	2473	2414	2432	**7319**	9.81	9.90	9.79	9.79	114	111	139	**120**
2008-09	15265	14353	15864	**45482**	1337	1291	1400	**4064**	8.99	8.99	8.83	9.83	87	64	89	**67**
2009-10	20103	17124	19507	**56734**	1820	1578	1781	**5179**	9.06	9.22	9.13	9.43	83	74	99	**83**

Source: Sugar India Year Book (2011).

Thus, the company is left with only 11 working sugar mills with install crushing capacity of 25,200 tonnes per day (TCD) in crushing season 2003-04 onwards. In July, 2003 the company decided to lease out of these 11 sugar mills at the direction of the State Government. However, the company/State governent had not transferred these sugar mills on lease because the approval of BIFR was awaited (August 2004).

Although the sugar production in the state varied from 45.56 lakh tonnes in the crushing year 1999-2000 to 45.51 lakh tonnes in the crushing year 2003-04. The share of companies varied during the period from 3.64 lakh tonnes (7.9 per cent) to 2.98 lakh tonnes (6.55 per cent). The company would not grow because the sugar mills acquired by the company were sick at the time of their acquisition itself, having old/obsolete plant and machinery and very low crushing capacity. Consequently, the cost of production in most of the mills of the company was higher than its sales realisation.

The winds of privatisation have finally blown in UPSSL in a major development, ten out of the 11 operational sugar factories of the UPSSL have found private buyers. More importantly, the sale helped plug the loss of almost Rs.200-400 crore every year that UP government was incurring

Table 3.12: Privatisation Movement of UPSSCL

S. No.	*Unit (District)*	*Capacity (TCD)*	*Buyer*	*Amount paid (Rs in crore)*
1.	Amroha (J.P. Nagar)	3000	-	NA
2.	Bijnor (Bijnor)	2500	Waves Industries	101.25
3.	Chandpur (Bijnor)	2500	--	NA
4.	Bulandsaha (Bulandsahar)	2500	Waves Industries	29.75
5.	Jarwal Road (Behraich)	2500	Indian Potash Ltd.	NA
6.	Khadda (Kushinagar)	1600	Indian Potash Ltd.	22.05
7.	Siswabazar (Maharajganj)	2500	Indian Potash Ltd	NA
8.	Mohhiddinpur (Meerut)	2500	Indian Potash Ltd.	NA
9.	Sakauti Tanda (Meerut)	1800	Indian Potash Ltd.	43.15
10.	Rohankala (Muzaffarnagar)	1300	Indian Potash Ltd.	50.4
11.	Saharanpur (Saharanpur)	2500	Waves Industries	35.85

over the last several years as subsidy to run these mills. It may be mentioned that the government had earlier tried to sell all the 33 mills of the UP Sugar Corp together but there were no takers for the purpose. Apart from successfully selling 11 operational mills (Table 3.12), the state government's effort to sell the closed mills, too, is in a very advanced stage. Of the 15 closed mills on the block, bids have been invited for 13 under the Swiss Challenge Method as they have had all received single bids and the date for submitting bid for the remaining two has been extended as they did not get any buyers. The remaining seven out of the 33 mills are not going to be sold as of now, as they are mired in legal hurdles.

3.3.3 Uttar Pradesh Co-operative Sugar Factories Federation Ltd. (UPCSFFL)

Learning from the experience of Maharashtra, the other states also started setting up of co-operative sugar mills and as a result, organisation of sugar companies on co-operative basis became a common feature in most of the states in India. In comparison to Maharashtra, conditions in Uttar Pradesh were quite different. Firstly, there was no much scope for establishment of many more factories in one spurt as Uttar Pradesh had already reached a saturation point. Secondly, except a few, all the mills were in the private sector. Therefore, there was no possibility of establishing a pre-eminent position for the co-operative sector in the sugar industry of Uttar Pradesh. The interest of sugar industry in UP had always been construed as the interest of mills owner only, while the interest of sugar industry in Maharashtra had always been seen as the interest of cane growers as well. Thirdly, since sugar industry of UP was already facing shrinkage of its market, search for new markets would have posed problems to factories to be established in the co-operative sector.

For planned development of co-operative sugar factories and guidance for efficient working of the existing co-operatives units, Uttar Pradesh Co-operative Sugar Factories Federation Limited was established at Lucknow in 1963, as an apex body of co-operative sugar factories of the state. The sugar federation since its inception has been playing active role in establishment of new sugar factories, expansion and modernisation of existing sugar factories, establishment of distilleries for use of by-products and giving financial, technical and administrative advices and guidelines. Due to sustained efforts of the federation, the number of working co-operative sugar factories has now gone up to thirty. At present, there are 28 co-operative units in Uttar Pradesh in which six in Western Zone, 14 in Central Zone and rest eight in the Eastern Zone. Thus, a total 27 sugar factories are functioning in UP in Co-operative sector with total crushing capacity 69125 TCD.

Sources: (www.upsugarfed.org).

3.3.4 Private Sector Sugar Mills in Uttar Pradesh

In Uttar Pradesh private sugar mills covers almost 50 per cent shares of the industry. The major private sugar players included big names like Birla Sugar, Dalmia group, Simbholi Sugar, Dhampur Sugar, Dwarikesh Sugar, Uttam Sugar, Treveni Engineering and Industries Ltd., Bajaj Hindustan, Modi Sugar, JK Sugar, Kanoria Sugar, Parle, Shri Renuka Sugars Ltd., Mawana Sugar, Dalmia Cement, Indian Oil Corp, Indian Potash Ltd. Indian Sucrose, Anjani Steel and Wave Industries, etc. After delicensing of the industry, private entrepreneurs get incentives to expand their plant sizes.

3.4 Problems of the Sugar Industry in Uttar Pradesh

The sugar industry in Uttar Pradesh finds itself entangled in a complex web of problems leading to "declining profitability to the cane growers as well as sugar industries". The reasons for the same are to be traced and suitably addressed to give a boost to this sector in the country. Over a last decade the sugar industry of Uttar Pradesh has been facing some grave problems. The problems faced by sugar producing units are mainly technological which are reflected in the rate of recovery, duration of the crushing season and ultimately in sugar production. The industry that has transformed the life of millions of farmers and societal development, has been striving hard for its very existence. Gone are the days when the industry has royal patronage, now it begging for the government aid for its survival. In this context of recent globalisation and privatisation era the Uttar Pradesh sugar industry currently facing the following obstacles: Practically more than half of the sugar factories are 30-year-old. The physical condition of many of these sugar factories is poor, resulting in high down time and loss of capacity. The other main problems of the Uttar Pradesh sugar industry are the small size of sugar plants, lack of professional management, need of modernisation, shortage of sugarcane, threat of privatisation, old and outdated machineries, financial problems, weak transport system, personnel problems, problems of proper utilisation of by-product etc.

The performance of the Uttar Pradesh sugar industry is marked by exceptionally high cost of production caused due to payment of higher cost of sugarcane, excessive loss of sugar in production, wastage of energy leading to higher consumption of bagasse and excess manpower. The sales are declining and inventory of sugar reached an alarming level leading to storage problem. In order to improve the performance of the industry, the Government and Management needs to make concerted efforts to improve the operation of the mills by minimising the stoppages, improving recovery of sugar, timely payment to cane growers for ensuring steady supply of sugarcane. Further, efforts are required to be made for liquidation of inventory and rationalisation of manpower. The UP sugar industry needs a pragmatic policy. Sugarcane cultivation should be made economically viable. Then only it is possible to boost sugar industry.

3.5 Critical Assessment and Conclusion

The share of India in the total production of sugarcane in the world is 37 per cent. But the production of sugarcane is only 15 tonnes per acre whereas in Java it is 56 tonnes and in Hawaii it is 52 tonnes, i.e., almost four times than India. The production cost of sugar is also high due to inferior quality of Indian sugarcane. Since sugar mills are running to loss so they are unable to pay the cane growers timely. So, the quality improvement in cane grower is the need of the time.

The Indian sugar industry is the second largest agro-processing industry in India, accounting for 15 per cent of the total world consumption. India's average recovery rate at 10.27 per cent is quite low in comparison with the international average. Uttar Pradesh, Maharashtra, Tamil Nadu, Karnataka, Punjab and Gujarat contribute more than 90 per cent of the total domestic sugarcane production, while UP and Maharashtra each contributes 30 per cent to total production. The Indian sugar industry is divided into the organised and unorganised sectors with the former accounting for 20 per cent of the total production. Sugar industry is a cyclical industry with two years of deficit followed by two years of surplus, influenced by the production of sugarcane. The Indian domestic sugar industry has entered into severe shortage phase due to sharp decline in production over the last two years. Indian sugar mills faced a cane shortage in the 2010-11 sugar season (October 2010 to September 2011), and suspended their crushing operation to two-three months ahead of schedule. The shortage emerged from farmers switching their crop pattern owing to lower realisations during the previous sugar season and a yield decline from around 40 tonnes per acre to 25-30 tonnes. As a result, India's sugar production is likely to decline to 16.5 million tonnes while consumption is expected to remain steady at 22–23 million tonnes. Per hectare production of sugarcane is also not improving which is a matter of great concern. It is probably due to lack of land facility and lack of irrigation facilities. In comparison to other countries of the world such as Cuba, Fizzy and West Indies which are very small are producing much more sugarcane per hectare than India. While the countries like Brazil, Australia, USA, etc., have recorded sugar recovery percentage of around 14, the sugar recovery in India has remained stagnant at around 10 per cent for the last few years. Although climatic suitability determines the sugar recovery to a great extent, there is a need on the part of sugarcane breeding institutes to take steps towards evolving improved technology for improving sugar recovery. Sugar recovery in India could be improved through undertaking research and evolving high-sucrose sugarcane varieties, replacement of low sucrose sugarcane varieties by high sucrose sugarcane varieties, evolving improved technology in sugar manufacturing terms of inventing modern machinery and using it. In India, the productivity of sugarcane measured in terms of yield per hectare. The productivity of sugarcane in India is still lower, when compared with that in several other countries. In terms of productivity per hectare of sugarcane during 2005, India [61.98 tonnes] stood tenth, the first nine countries being Colombia [92.29 tonnes], Australia [91.06 tonnes], Philippines [81.58 tonnes], Indonesia [72.86 tonnes], Brazil [72.85 tonnes], Mexico [70.61 tonnes], South Africa [69.63 tonnes], United States of America [66.63 tonnes] and China [65.16 tonnes]. Lower productivity of sugarcane in India could be attributed to raising of sugarcane under diverse growing conditions by millions of farmers. This points out to the need for intensifying research, extension and development efforts towards increasing the productivity of sugarcane in India.

The Indian sugar industry is at the crossroads today, where it can leverage opportunities created by global shifts in sugar trade as well as the emergence of sugarcane as a source of renewable energy, through ethanol and cogeneration. While some of these opportunities have been well-researched in the past, there was a need to assess the potential for India and to develop a comprehensive and actionable roadmap that would enable the Indian industry to take its rightful place as a food and energy producer for one of the world's leading economies.

3.6 Future Prospects of the Indian Sugar Industry

The Indian Sugar Industry will have a rosy future, if its potential is fully developed and it is allowed to bloom. The demand for sugar is estimated to increase at a higher rate than increase in sugar production on account of ever-increasing population and change in the food habits of the people. The growth of sugar by food and beverage industries and other non-household users, estimated to account for about 45 per cent of total consumption, could provide additional impetus to long-term market growth unless in the meantime the Government allows the food and beverage industry to import its sugar requirement directly and putting a ceiling on their stock holding. Although *gur* and *khandsari* are still consumed in rural areas, demand for white sugar is expected to continue to increase. India's good fortune in being climatically suitable for cultivating sugarcane needs to be exploited for maximum benefit to the country. The Government and the Industry need to address certain aspects of the business to create this future and enjoy the benefits thereof. The industry is rightly politically sensitive given its impact on a country's economy as also the number of people it impacts upon. In the past, however, the political arithmetic has led to skewed policies of a short sighted and micro-level nature. These policies have actually ended up damaging the very interest of the parties sought to be protected the farmers. A stable long-term policy is needed in which the shackles are removed which constrain this industry from growing in a healthy manner. The need for the Government to adopt a visionary approach to utilise this great industry for maximising value for all stake holders, in the best interest of the country. Indian Sugar industry can be the global leader provided it comes out of vicious cycle of acute shortage and surplus of sugarcane. The country can maintain this positions only if adequate attention is paid to R and D on various facets of the industry. There is a need on the part of sugar research institutes to take steps towards identifying measures to overcome the problem of high cost of conversion of sugarcane into sugar particularly in co-operative and public sector sugar factories. Considering the need for making Indian sugar globally competitive to meet the challenges of liberalisation policy, the WTO and ICUMSA norms, the National Federation of Cooperative Sugar Factories Limited (NFCSF), set up the Research and Development and Training Center at FC-33, Jasola, New Delhi. In India, The National Sugar Institute, Kanpur; Deccan Sugar Institute, Pune; and Institute of Sugar Technology, Tamil Nadu mainly catering the research, advisor, extension and training needs of the industry. A few laboratories of the Council of Scientific and Industrial Research (CSIR) are engaged in research on various issues of interest to Sugar industry. As the future of Indian Sugar Industry will largely depend on how cost-effective and technically advanced, therefore, the Research and Development department should focus on the following thrust area:

- To improve the quality of sugarcane through high sugar content, high yielding, early maturing, its management for insects, pests and diseases and better sugar recovery.
- To improve the efficiency productivity and quality of sugar to make it internationally competitive.
- To reduce inventory and maintenance cost.
- To reduce steam, fuel, power and water consumption.
- Proper utilisation of all by-products of the sugar industry and setting up co-generation and ethanol projects; etc.
- Research programme should be undertaken in area of sugarcane cultivation, enhancing sugarcane productivity, and sugar recovery. Sugarcane prices should be fixed on the basis of sugar recovery. Attention is to be given on manufacturing quality sugar as per international standards at competitive prices.

In the era of globalisation, sugar industry needs more competitive edge which can be given by way of modernisation, enhancing productivity, and manufacturing excellent quality sugar at competitive prices. It needs quality management at every level of activity to enhance its performance. The need of the hour is to liberalise industry from clutches of unprofessional people. New sugar units should be set-up taking into consideration sugarcane availability.

References

Centre for Monitoring Indian Economy (CMIE), (2004) Agriculture, February, CMIE Pvt. Ltd, Mumbai-400 093.

Devaraja, T.S. (2009). *Financial Performance of Agro-based Industries- The Case of Sugar Industry in Karnataka*, Anmol Publication Pvt. Ltd., New Delhi, India.

Directorate of Sugar, Revitalisation of Sugar Industry, Department of Food and Public Distribution, Ministry of Food, Consumer Affairs and Public Distribution, GOI, Krishi Bhavan, New Delhi, 14th July 2006.

Murthy, S.R.S. (2010). National Bank for Agriculture and Rural Development Department of Economic Analysis and Research, Mumbai-3.

National Federation of Co-operative Sugar Factories Ltd., New Delhi, Co-operative Sugar, Vol. 40 (10) June 2009.

Ray Sarbapriya (2012). Reviewing Performance of Indian Sugar Industry: An Economic Analysis Food Science and Quality Management Vol. 3, 2012 ISSN 2224-6088 (Paper) ISSN 2225-0557 (On-line).

Sanyal, N., Bhagria, R.P. and Ray, S.C. (2008), "Indian Sugar Industry", *Yojna*, 52(4), 13-17.

Pandey, A.P. (2007) 'Indian sugar industry: A strong industrial base for rural India' Banaras Hindu University MPRA Paper No. 6065.

S. Pruthi, (1995). History of Sugar Industry in India, Reliance Publishing House, New Delhi, pp. 1-29.

Rai, Prem Shankar (2001). Uttar Pradesh Mein Chini Udyog Ki Punjee Sunrachana Ph.D. thesis of Deptt. of Economics, B.H.U., Varanasi.

Government of India (2004), "Report of the Committee on Revitalisation of Sugar Industry", (Tuteja Committee), Ministry of Food, Consumer Affairs and Public Distribution, Department of Food and Public Distribution, New Delhi.

ISMA (2004), "Sugar Situation, Indian Sugar Mills Association", http://www. indiansugar.com

Singh, S.P. (2006a), "Technical and Scale Efficiencies in the Indian Sugar Mills: An Inter-state Comparison", *The Asian Economic Review,* Vol. 48 (1), pp. 87-100.

Department of Economic Analysis and Research (2010), National Bank for Agriculture and Rural Development, Mumbai.

Directorate of Sugar (2006), Revitalisation of Sugar Industry, Department of Food and Public Distribution, Ministry of Food, Consumer Affairs and Public Distribution, GoI, Krishi Bhavan, New Delhi.

4

Working Environment Factor—An Analysis

4.1 Introduction

Work environment related issues have been prioritised in labour policy debates all throughout the industrialised nations. When pertaining to a place of employment, the work environment involves the physical location as well as the immediate surroundings of the workplace, such as factory site or office building. Typically, it also involves other factors relating to the place of employment, such as the quality of the air, noise level, and additional perks and benefits of employment. In total work environment is the sum of the inter-relationship that exists within the employees and between the employees and the environment in which the employees work. The work environment according to Opperman (2002) is a composite of three major sub-environments viz., the technical environment, the human environment and the organisational environment. Technical environment refers to tools, equipment, technological infrastructure and other physical or technical elements. This environment creates elements that enable employees perform their respective responsibilities and activities. The human environment refers to peers, others with whom employees relates, team and work groups, interactional issues, the leadership and management. Human environment is designed in such a manner that encourages informal interaction in the work place, so that the opportunity to share knowledge and exchange ideas could be enhanced. This is a basis to attain maximum productivity. Organisational environment include, systems, procedures, practices, values and philosophies. Management has control over organisational environment. For instance, measurement system where people are rewarded on quantity, hence workers will have little interest in helping those workers who are trying to improve quality.

The concept of quality of work life (QWL) deals with the issue of how rewarding or satisfying the time spent in the workplace is. As such, QWL may reflect working conditions and contextual issues such as relationships with colleagues and the intrinsic satisfaction of the job. Basically, the work environment factors affect both the individual quality of work life outcomes as well as organisational outcomes. A healthy workplace is most important for the committed employees. Most of the employees prefer to work honestly and sincerely and try to give their best to the organisation (Joanne Profetto McGrath *et. al.,* 2003). However, an unhealthy work environments lead to absenteeism, ineffectiveness in health-care delivery, stress, and discord among colleagues.

Today, Management's new challenge is to create a work environment that attracts, keeps, and motivates its work force. Management should create a work environment where employee enjoys what they do, feel like they have a purpose, have pride in what they do, and can reach their potential. A good and harmonious working environment is one where all workers are treated with dignity and respect, and where no worker is subjected to harassment by conduct that is related to religious belief or political opinion. Brenner (2004) asserted that the ability of employees within an organisation to share knowledge throughout the system depends on the conditions of their work environment. It is also observed that employees tend to be more productive in a well-facilitated work environment. Workers productivity cannot be optimal, if the conditions of work environment are not favourable. Hence, improved work environment will enhance employee productivity. It is well-acknowledged that work systems cannot only affect commitment, competence, cost effectiveness and congruence but also have long-term consequence for workers' well-being, there is some evidence to indicate that work systems designs may have effects on physical health, mental health and longevity of life itself. Conducive work environment ensures the well-being of employees which invariably will enable them exert themselves to their roles with all vigour that may translate to higher productivity (Akinyele, 2007). These days, for an organisation to be successful and achieve its organisational objectives it is essential that its employees are satisfied with their work, since work occupies an important place in many people's lives, such conditions are likely to affect not only their physical but also a high-level of social, psychological and spiritual well-being. An unstrained work environment ensures good health and psychological conditions which enable the employees to perform job and non-work related functions without inhibitions. It is well-established in the literature that employees with a high-level of psychological well-being are better, more committed, and more productive than employees with a low-level of psychological well-being (Wright and Bonett, 2007; Wright and Cropanzano, 2004). Nonetheless, employees are likely to have higher well-being if they are satisfied with their work and organisation and they perceive their Quality of Work Life (QWL) positively, since an employee's experiences in the workplace and his/her QWL influence his/her health and psychological well-being (Chan and Wyatt, 2007; Srivastava, 2007). Therefore, QWL experience became the focus of attention and workplace wellness is crucial in promoting healthier working environments. Unsafe and hazardous working conditions cause problems to both employers and employees. There may be little advantage to the employer in short-term but in medium and long-terms, it adversely affects the productivity. Therefore, adequate investment must be made to ensure safe and healthy working conditions. Thus, it can be said that QWL can develop jobs and working conditions that are excellent for people as well as for the economic health of the organisation (Kanagalakshmi and Devei, 2003).

Therefore, to survive and grow in this competitive business environment the sugar industry of India must ensure a safe and healthy work environment. There are strong indications that a lot need to be done by employers of sugar mills of Uttar Pradesh (both in the co-operative and private sector) to provide a suitable work environment that would meet employees' expectation as well as increase job satisfaction and enhance productivity of the work force. Therefore, the management has to take extra care to protect its employees. Proper seating arrangement, lighting facilities within the factory, water facility, fresh air, good working conditions and health facilities are very important to the employees who engage themselves in sugar production work. Absence of such good conditions may result in fatigue; back pain and rheumatic pain which in turns frustration and increases the stress level. And this frustration may further lead to lower rate of output, inefficiency and increasing rate of absenteeism. As workplace is the second home of employees, thus physical working conditions at work place is an important factor in measuring Quality of Working Life. In the present study, the researcher has made an attempt to examine/investigate the following issues under the Working Environment Factor:

- Comfortable Personal Work Space.
- Lighting Facility Within the Mill.
- Temperature Within the Mill.

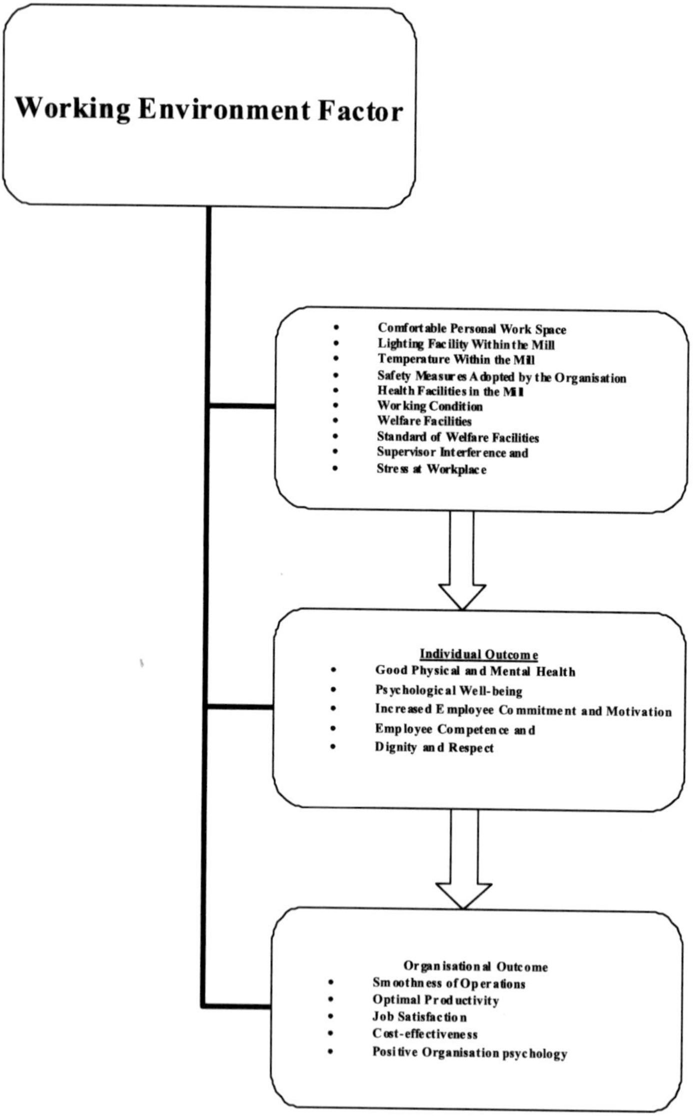

Fig. 4.1. Conceptual Model of Working Environment Factor.

- Safety Measures Adopted by the Organisation,
- Health Facilities in the Mill,
- Working Conditions,
- Welfare Facilities,
- Standard of Welfare Facilities,
- Supervisor Interference, and
- Stress at Workplace.

4.2. Geographical Location-wise Analysis of Working Environment Factor

Table 4.1 reveals the perception of employees regarding working environment factor with geographical location of sugar mills of UP. The geographical location of sugar mills have been divided into three zones namely, Eastern zone, Central zone and Western zone. It can be observed from the table that the proportion of total selected employees, 66.1 per cent have asserted about comfortable work space while 33.9 per cent have denied it. In the case of Eastern UP, 65 per cent employees have asserted in favour of comfortable work space, where as 69.2 per cent employees of Central UP and 64.2 per cent employees of Western UP have responded in favour of comfortable workspace and rest are against it. The Pearson Chi-square test has been applied to test the association between comfortable work space and geographical location of sugar mills. The χ^2 value is (0.769) at two degrees of freedom and descriptive statistics (1.34± .474) between comfortable work space and geographical location indicates that it is not significant at five per cent level of significance (χ^2= 0.769, df=2, P> 0.05, Mean and SD= 1.34± 0.474).

In case of level of temperature and geographical location nearly 77 per cent respondent have replied in favour of bearable level of temperature and rest are against it. In Eastern UP, 79.2 per cent respondents have asserted that level of temperature within the mill is bearable whereas in Central UP (74.2 per cent) and in Western UP (77.5 per cent) respondent are satisfied with this fact and rest are denied it. However, the descriptive statistics (Mean ± SD) and Pearson's Chi-square test shows the two tailed P value is greater than the commonly accepted 0.05 level, hence, no significant differences are found in the perception level of respondent of different zones.

The table also describes the view of respondents regarding workplace stress. It indicates that the proportion of total selected employees approximately 47 per cent respondents are asserted that they feel stress at workplace while 53 per cent respondents denied it. In case of Eastern

Table 4.1: Working Environment Factor Analysis with Geographical Location of Sugar Mills

Sl.No.	Label	Test Applied	Location	Crosstabs			Descriptive	Value of Test			Inference
				Yes	No	Total		Value	d.f	Asymp.Sig	
1.	Do you have a comfortable personal work space?	Pearson Chi-Square	Eastern	78 (65)	42 (35)	120 (100)	1.35±.479	χ^2=.769	2	p>**0.05**	Not Significant
			Central	83 (69.2)	37 (30.8)	120 (100)	1.31±.464				
	(Comfortable Work Space)		Western	77 (64.2)	43 (35.2)	120 (100)	1.36±.482				
			Total	**238 (66.1)**	**122 (33.9)**	**360 (100)**	**1.34±.474**				
2.	The level of temperature within the mill is bearable?	Pearson Chi-Square	Eastern	95 (79.2)	25 (20.8)	120 (100)	1.21±.408	χ^2=.877	2	p>**0.05**	Not Significant
			Central	89 (74.2)	31 25.8)	120 (100)	1.26±.440				
	(Level of Temperature)		Western	93 (77.5)	27 (22.5)	120 (100)	1.23±.419				
			Total	**277 (76.9)**	**83 (23.1)**	**360 (100)**	**1.23±.422**				

(Contd.)

(Contd. Table 4.1)

Sl.No.	*Label*	*Test Applied*	*Location*	*Crosstabs*			*Descriptive*	*Value of Test*			*Inference*
				Yes	*No*	*Total*		*Value*	*d.f*	*Asymp.Sig*	
3.	Do you feel any stress at workplace? **(Workplace Stress)**	**Pearson Chi-Square**	Eastern	62 (51.7)	58 (48.3)	120 (100)	1.48±.502	χ^2=3.309	2	p>**0.05**	Not Significant
			Central	48 (40)	72 (60)	120 (100)	1.60±.492				
			Western	56 (46.7)	64 (53.3)	120 (100)	1.53±.501				
			Total	**166 (46.1)**	**194 (53.9)**	**360 (100)**	**1.54±.499**				

Table 4.2: Working Environment Factor Analysis with Geographical Location of Sugar Mills

S.No.	Test Variable Lists (Label)	Test Applied	Descriptive				Value of Test			Inference
			Location	No.	Mean ±SD	Mean Rank	Value	d.f.	Asymp. Sig	
1.	The lighting facility within the mill is sufficient to work **(Lighting Facility)**	**Kruskal-Wallis (H) Test**	Eastern	120	4.10±.952	196.01				Significant
			Central	120	3.94±1.015	179.18				
			Western	120	3.97±.733	167.31	5.795	2	P<0.05	
			Total	**360**	**4.00±.910**					
2.	The safety measures adopted by the organisation **(Safety Measures)**	**Kruskal-Wallis (H) Test**	Eastern	120	2.47±.987	206.35				
			Central	120	2.22±.812	181.70				
			Western	120	1.98±.855	153.45	17.579	2	p<0.001	Very Highly Significant
			Total	**360**	**2.22±.908**					
3.	The health facilities in the mill are not good **(Health Facility)**	**Kruskal-Wallis (H) Test**	Eastern	120	2.67±1.259	182.98				
			Central	120	2.80±1.357	189.05	2.471	2	P>0.05	Not Significant
			Western	120	2.51±1.335	169.48				
			Total	**360**	**2.66±1.319**					
4.	I am not satisfied with the working condition provided by the organisation **(Working Condition)**	**Kruskal-Wallis (H) Test**	Eastern	120	3.14±1.225	192.45				
			Central	120	3.11±1.228	188.21	7.418	2	P<0.05	Significant
			Western	120	2.73±1.314	160.84				
			Total	**360**	**2.99±1.267**					

(Contd.)

(Contd. Table 4.2)

S.No.	Test Variable Lists (Label)	Test Applied	Descriptive				Value of Test			Inference
			Location	No.	Mean ±SD	Mean Rank	Value	d.f	Asymp. Sig	
5.	The quality of welfare facilities provided by the mill **(Quality of Welfare Facility)**	**Kruskal-Wallis (H) Test**	Eastern	120	2.42±.885	203.83				
			Central	120	2.13±.898	175.68				
			Western	120	2.03±.888	161.99	11.396	2	P<0.05	Significant
			Total	**360**	**2.19±.902**					
6	My supervisor interferes in the given work **(Supervisor interference)**	**Kruskal-Wallis (H) Test**	Eastern	120	1.96±.888	177.09				
			Central	120	2.08±.712	195.07				
			Western	120	1.93±.980	169.34	4.406	2	P>0.05	Not Significant
			Total	**360**	**1.99±.853**					
7.	The welfare facilities provided by the employer **(Type of Welfare Facility)**	**Kruskal-Wallis (H) Test**	Eastern	120	2.12±1.427	198.20				
			Central	120	1.59±.957	177.19				
			Western	120	1.51±.926	166.10	7.734	2	P<0.05	Significant
			Total	**360**	**1.74±1.156**					
8.	**Total Score of Working Environment Factor**	**Kruskal-Wallis (H) Test**	Eastern	120	2.29±.340	206.69				
			Central	120	2.20±.343	189.06				
			Western	120	2.07±.358	145.75	21.955	2	p<0.001	Very Highly Significant
			Total	**360**	**2.19±.357**					

Zone 51.7 per cent respondents feels stress at workplace while in Central Zone (40 per cent) and in Western Zone (53.3 per cent) are in favour of this fact, and rest are disagree with this. The descriptive statistics (1.34± .474) and Chi-Square value (3.309) with corresponding P value is found not-significant at five per cent level of significance. Hence, no significant difference exists in the perception level of the respondents of three different zones.

In the above table (4.2) different variables of working environment factor have been analysed on the basis of the geographical location of UP sugar mills. The geographical location has been divided into three parts, i.e., Eastern Zone, Central Zone and Western Zone. Further, Kruskal-Wallis (H) Test has been applied for the purpose of getting group-wise difference regarding the perception of various variables of relational factor.

The table reveals that out of seven variables only two variables are found to be non-significant, i.e., health facilities and supervisor interference in the given work. However, in four variables, i.e., lighting facility, working condition, quality of welfare facilities and type of welfare facilities the perception of employees from select Zone is found significantly differing at five per cent level of significance ($p<0.05$). On the other hand, very highly significant difference has been observer among employees about the perception of safety measures adopted by the organisation. The P value is found less then (0.001). The employees of Eastern Zone sugar mills have shown highest satisfaction level (206.35) followed by the Central Zone (181.70) and Western Zone (153.45) respectively.

Similarly, the employees of Eastern Zone are more satisfied (196.01) with the lighting facility compare to Central (179.18) and Western Zone (167.31). Statistically, it is also observed that regarding working condition the employees of Eastern Zone shown the highest level of satisfaction (192.45) followed by the Central Zone (188.21) and Western Zone (160.84) respectively. It can also be seen from the above table that regarding type and quality of welfare facilities again the employees of Eastern Zone are more satisfied than the employees of Central and Western Zones respectively.

However, the overall analysis of working environment factor reveals that the average satisfaction level of employees of three zones is differing highly and significantly ($H= 21.955$, d.f. = 2, $p<0.001$). Out of the three zones, Eastern Zone has got highest mean rank (206.69) followed by Central Zone (189.06) and Western Zone (145.75) respectively.

4.3 Nature of Organisation-wise Analysis of Working Environment Factor

The Table 4.3 shows the analysis of working environment factor with nature of sugar mills in UP. Under working environment factor three items, i.e., comfortable work space, level of temperature and work-place stress have been analysed.

Regarding comfortable work space in private sector sugar mills 68.5 per cent employees asserted that they have comfortable work space, followed by 58.9 per cent in co-operative sector sugar mills. On an overall basis majority of respondent (66.1 per cent) have replied that they have comfortable personal workspace and rest of (33.9 per cent) replied that they do not have comfortable personal work space. The Pearson Chi-square test has been applied to test the association between private and co-operative sugar mills with regards to comfortable personal work space. It shows that two tailed P-value is greater than commonly accepted level of 0.05 levels. Thus, it can be concluded that there is no significant difference regarding comfortable personal work space in both the private and co-operative sector sugar mills (χ^2=2.794, df= 1, P> 0.05).

In case of level of temperature, majority of respondent (80.4 per cent) from private sector asserted that level of temperature within the sugar mill is bearable. While in co-operative sector sugar mills 69.3 per cent respondent replied that the level of temperature within the mill is bearable. On an overall basis 76.9 per cent are agreed with this while rest are disagree with this fact. The χ^2 value (7.145) and corresponding P value is found less than 0.05 level. Thus, it found that there is significant difference between private and co-operative sugar mill employees regarding the perception of level of temperature within the mill. However, the evidence may be confirmed by seeing the descriptive statistics also.

In case of work place stress there seems to be almost similar response in both the private and co-operative sector sugar mills. 48.2 per cent employees from co-operative sector feel stress at work place followed by 45.2 per cent in private sector and rests are replied that they do not feel stress at work place. Overall, 53.9 per cent employees asserted that they do not feel any stress at work place. The χ^2 value (0.373) and corresponding P value is more than five per cent level of significance, hence no significant difference have been found in the perception level of private and co-operative sector employees with regards to work place stress. The average mean score obtained by both the private and co-operative sector are almost same.

Table 4.3: Working Environment Factor Analysis with Nature of Organisation (Sugar Mills)

Sl. No.	*Label*	*Test Applied*	*Location*	*Crosstabs*			*Descriptive*	*Value of Test*			*Inference*
				Yes	*No*	*Total*		*Value*	*d.f*	*Asymp. Sig*	
1.	Do you have a comfortable personal work space? **(Comfortable Work Space)**	**Pearson Chi-Square**	Private	185 (68.5)	85 (31.5)	270 (100)	1.31±.465	χ^2=2.794	1	p>**0.05**	Not Significant
			Co-operative	53 (58.9)	37 (41.1)	90 (100)	1.41±.495				
			Total	**238 (66.1)**	**122 (33.9)**	**360 (100)**	**1.34±.474**				
2.	The level of temperature within the mill is bearable? **(Level of Tempreture)**	**Pearson Chi-Square**	Private	217 (80.4)	53 (19.6)	270 (100)	1.20±.398	χ^2=7.145	1	p<0.05	Significant
			Co-operative	60 (69.3)	30 (20.8)	90 (100)	1.33±.474				
			Total	**277 (76.9)**	**83 (23.1)**	**360 (100)**	**1.23±.422**				
3.	Do you feel any stress at workplace? **(work place Stress)**	**Pearson Chi-Square**	Private	122 (45.2)	148 (54.8)	270 (100)	1.55±.499	χ^2=.373	1	p>**0.05**	Not Significant
			Cooperative	44 (48.9)	46 (51.1)	90 (100)	1.51±.503				
			Total	**166 (46.1)**	**194 (53.9)**	**360 (100)**	**1.54±.499**				

Table 4.4: Working Environment Factor Analysis with Nature of Organisation

Sl. No.	Statements	Mill-Wise Statistics				Mann-Whitney U Test	Asymp. Sig (2-tailed)	Inference
		Nature of Mills	No.	Mean Rank	Sum of Rank			
1.	The lighting facility within the mill is sufficient to work **(Lighting Facility)**	Private	270	186.54	50366.5	10518.5	p>0.05	Not Significant
		Coop.	90	162.37	14613.5			
2.	The safety measures adopted by the organisation **(Safety Measures)**	Private	270	194.99	52648	8237	p<0.001	Very Highly Significant
		Coop.	90	137.02	12332			
3.	The health facilities in the mill are not good **(Health Facility)**	Private	270	194.22	52439.5	8445.5	p<0.001	Very Highly Significant
		Coop.	90	139.34	12540.5			
4.	I am not satisfied with the working condition provided by the organisation **(Working Condition)**	Private	270	182.95	49397	11488	p>0.05	Not Significant
		Coop.	90	173.14	15583			

(Contd.)

(Contd. Table 4.4)

Sl. No	Statements	Mill-Wise Statistics				Mann-Whitney U Test	Asymp. Sig (2-tailed)	Inference
		Nature of Mills	No.	Mean Rank	Sum of Rank			
5.	The welfare facilities provided by the employer **(Type of Welfare Facility)**	Private Coop.	270 90	191.41 147.77	51680.5 13299.5	9204.5	p<0.001	Very Highly Significant
6.	The quality of welfare facilities provided **(Quality of Welfare Facility)**	Private Coop.	270 90	195.03 136.90	52659 12321	8226	p<0.001	Very Highly Significant
7.	My supervisor interferes in the given work **(Supervisor Interference)**	Private Coop.	270 90	187.10 160.69	50518 14462	10367	p<0.05	Significant
8.	**Total Score of Working Environment Factor**	Private Coop.	270 90	199.94 122.17	53985 10995	6900	p<0.001	Very Highly Significant

The Table 4.4 describes the analysis of work environment factor with nature of organisation. The table shows the detailed analysis of work environment factor, i.e., lighting facility, safety measures, health facilities, working condition, type of welfare facilities, quality of welfare facilities and supervisor interference in work.

The Mann-Whitney U test result indicates that there is very highly significant difference have been found between the opinion of private and co-operative sugar mills employees regarding safety measures, health facilities, type of welfare facilities and quality of welfare facilities at one per cent level of significance. The average means score obtained by the private and co-operative sector are significantly differing from each other. However, in case of supervisor interference in the given work also shows the significant difference at five per cent level of significance between the opinion of private and co-operative sugar mills.

Statistically it is also found that there is no significant difference among the opinion of private and co-operative sugar mills employees regarding lighting facility and working condition. As a whole, the Mann-Whitney U test results indicate that there is very highly significant difference between the perception of private and public sector sugar mills employees regarding working environment factor at one per cent level of significance ($p<0.001$). It is also observed the average satisfaction score of the respondent, who belongs to private sector (53895) is much higher than the co-operative sector sugar mills employees (10995). Therefore, it can be inferred that private sector sugar mills employees are more satisfied than the co-operative sector employees regarding working environment factor.

4.4 Nature of Employment-wise Analysis of Working Environment Factor

In the Table 4.5 different variables of work environment factor (comfortable work space, level of temperature and workplace stress) has been analysed on the basis of nature of employment in UP sugar mills. Nature of employment has been divided in two categories, i.e., permanent and seasonal employees. Regarding comfortable work space in sugar mills 73.3 per cent permanent employees asserted that they have comfortable work space, followed by 58.9 per cent seasonal employees. On an overall basis majority of respondent (66.1 per cent) have replied that they have comfortable personal workspace and rest of (33.9 per cent) replied that they do not have comfortable personal work space. The Pearson

TableNo. 4.5: Working Environment Factor Analysis with Nature of Employment in Sugar Mills

S.No.	*Label*	*Test Applied*	*Nature of Employment*	*Crosstabs*			*Descriptive*	*Value of Test*			*Inference*
				Yes	*No*	*Total*		*Value*	*d.f*	*Asymp.Sig*	
1.	Do you have a comfortable personal work space? **(Comfortable Work Space)**	**Pearson Chi-Square**	Permanent	132 (73.3)	48 (26.7)	180 (100)	1.27±.443	8.381	1	P<0.05	Significant
			Seasonal	106 (58.9)	74 (41.1)	180 (100)	1.41±.493				
			Total	**238 (66.1)**	**122 (39.9)**	**360 (100)**	**1.34±.474**				
2.	The level of temperature within the mill is bearable? **(Level of Temperature)**	**Pearson Chi-Square**	Permanent	140 (77.8)	40 (22.2)	180 (100)	1.22±.417	0.141	1	P>0.05	Not Significant
			Seasonal	137 (76.1)	43 (23.9)	180 (100)	1.24±.428				
			Total	**277 (76.9)**	**83 (23.1)**	**360 (100)**	**1.23±.422**				
3.	Do you feel any stress at work place? **(Work place Stress)**	**Pearson Chi-Square**	Permanent	65 (36.1)	115 (63.9)	180 (100)	1.64±.482	14.488	1	P<0.001	Very Highly Significant
			Seasonal	101 (56.1)	79 (43.9)	180 (100)	1.44±.498				
			Total	**166 (46.1)**	**194 (53.9)**	**360 (100)**	**1.54±.499**				

Chi-square test has been applied to test the association between private and cooperative sugar mills with regards to comfortable personal work space. P value is found significant at 0.05 levels. Thus, it can be concluded that there is significant difference regarding comfortable personal work space in both the nature of employment (χ^2=8.381, df= 1, P< 0.05).

In case of level of temperature, majority of permanent employees (77.8 per cent) replied that the level of temperature within the sugar mill is bearable followed by (76.1 per cent) seasonal employees. On an overall basis 76.9 per cent are agreed with this while rest are disagree with this fact. The χ^2 value (.141) and corresponding P value is found more than 0.05 level. Thus, it shows that there is no significant difference exists between the permanent and seasonal employees regarding the perception of level of temperature within the mill. However, the evidence may be confirmed by seeing the descriptive statistics also.

In case of workplace stress there seems to be highly significance difference between the opinions of permanent and seasonal employees. 36.1 per cent permanent employees reveal that they feel stress at work place. However, majority of seasonal employees (56.1 per cent) are agreed with this fact. Overall, 53.9 per cent employees asserted that they do not feel any stress at workplace. The χ^2 value (14.488) and corresponding P value is less than one per cent level of significance, hence highly significant difference have been found the perception level of private and co-operative sector employees with regards to workplace stress.

The Table 4.6 reveals the analysis of working environment factor with regards to nature of employment in sugar mills, i.e., permanent and seasonal employees. Analysis has been done with the help of Mann-Whitney U test. It can be observed from the table that out of seven variables, three variables, i.e., health facility, working condition and supervisors interference in give work are found no significant (P<0.05).

Further, the table also shows that regarding lighting facility, safety measures and quality of welfare facilities the opinions of permanent and seasonal employees are differing significantly. In case of lighting facility the mean rank obtained by the permanent employees (M=195.71) shows higher satisfaction compare to seasonal employees (M=165.29). The result of Mann-Whitney U test (13462.5) is found significant at five per cent level of significance.

There is also significance difference found between permanent and seasonal employees regarding the perception of safety measures adopted by the organisation. The mean rank (194.74) obtained by the permanent

Table 4.6: Working Environment Factor Analysis with Nature of Employment in Sugar Mills

Sl. No.	*Test Variable Lists*	*Mill-wise Statistics*					*Mann-Whitney U Test*	*Asymp. Sig (2-tailed)*	*Inference*
		Nature of Mills	*No.*	*Descriptive*	*Mean Rank*	*Sum of Rank*			
1.	The lighting facility within the mill is sufficient to work **(Lighting Facility)**	Permanent	180	4.15±.815	195.71	35227.50	13462.5	P<0.01	Significant
		Seasonal	180	3.86±.975	165.29	29752.50			
2.	The safety measures adopted by the organisation **(Safety Measures)**	Permanent	180	2.38±.901	194.74	35054.00	13636.00	P<0.05	Significant
		Seasonal	180	2.08±.896	166.26	29926.00			
3.	The health facilities in the mill are not good **(Health Facility)**	Permanent	180	2.73±1.311	185.90	33462.00	15228.00	P>0.05	Not significant
		Seasonal	180	2.59±1.328	175.10	31518.00			
4.	I am not satisfied with the working condition provided by the organisation **(Working Condition)**	Permanent	180	3.10±.1.282	188.38	33909.00	14781.00	P>0.05	Not Significant
		Seasonal	180	2.89±1.246	172.62	31071.00			

(Contd.)

(Contd. Table 4.6)

Sl. No.	Test Variable Lists	Mill-wise Statistics					Mann-Whitney U Test	Asymp. Sig (2-tailed)	Inference
		Nature of Mills	No.	Descriptive	Mean Rank	Sum of Rank			
5.	The welfare facilities provided by the employer **(Type of Welfare Facilities)**	Permanent	180	1.31±.859	136.54	24576.50	8286.5	P<0.001	Very Highly Significant
		Seasonal	180	2.17±1.250	224.46	40403.50			
6.	The quality of welfare facilities provided **(Quality of welfare Facilities)**	Permanent	180	2.36±.925	197.60	35568.00	13122.00	P<0.01	Significant
		Seasonal	180	2.03±.852	163.40	29412.00			
7.	My supervisor interferes in the given work **(Supervisors Interference)**	Permanent	180	2.01±.906	181.37	32647.00	16043.00	P>0.05	Not Significant
		Seasonal	180	1.97±.797	179.63	32333.00			
8.	**Total Score of Working Environment Factor**	Permanent	180	2.21±.347	186.69	33605.00			
		Seasonal	180	2.17±.367	174.31	31375.00	15085.00	P>0.05	Not Significant

employees reveals that the safety measure is good enough while mean rank obtained by seasonal employees (165.29) shows that safety measures is satisfactory.

Similarly, the perceptions of employees regarding quality of welfare facilities seem to differ in both the nature of employment at five per cent level of significance. The descriptive result reveals that the employees of permanent nature (M=197.60) are more satisfied than the seasonal employees (163.40) with quality of welfare facilities provided by their organisations.

There is very highly significant difference is found between the perception of permanent and seasonal employees regarding the type of welfare facilities provided by the organisations. The descriptive statistics (1.31±.859) shows that the almost all permanent employees are getting housing, recreational, medical and canteen facility while seasonal employee are getting only recreational, medical and canteen facility (2.17±1.250). Therefore, seasonal employees are not getting the housing facility. The result of Mann-Whitney U test (8286.5) is found significant at one per cent level of significance.

However, regarding the overall working environment factor, no significant difference is found regarding the perception of permanent and seasonal employees.

4.5 Analysis of Work Environment Factor with Select Demographic Variables

The Table 4.7 shows the Perception Score of Work Environment Factor with Select Demographic variables, i.e., experience, income-level, educational level and age. One way Analysis of Variance (One-way ANOVA) is used to compare the means of more than two groups. F-probability of appropriate significance level is considered to determine the significance of the test. Regarding the experience the result of the one-way ANOVA given in Table 1 shows that the calculated value of F (1.661) for four degrees of freedom is found insignificant at 0.05 level ($P>0.05$). Therefore, no significant difference is found to exist in the mean scores of working environment factor between any of the group pairs categorised on the basis of experience. Therefore, the job experience cannot be considered as a discriminating factor of the working environment in the sugar mills.

However, in the case of income level it is seen that the F-value obtained (5.426) is found significant at 0.05 level of significance ($P<0.05$). Therefore, there is significant difference exist regarding the perception of work

Table 4.7: Distribution of Total Perception Score of Work Environment Factor with Select Demographics

Factor	*Descriptive Statistics*			*Test Used*	*Test Value*			*Inference*
Experiences (in Years)	*No.*	*Mean ± SD*	*Range*		*df*	*F*	*Comparison*	
1-5	21	21.90±3.88	13-32	One-Way ANOVA	4	1.661	P>0.05	Not Significant
5-10	60	22.81±3.85	14-32					
10-15	86	21.53±3.83	14-31					
15-20	96	21.46±3.39	13-29					
>20	97	22.10±3.19	14-31					
Total	**360**	**21.90±3.57**	**13-32**	**Decision: In case of experiences H_0 can be accepted**				
Income Level (Rs.)				One-Way ANOVA	2	5.426	P<0.05	Significant
<10,000	139	21.16±3.50	13-20					
10000-20000	177	22.24±3.52	14-32					
>20000	44	22.84±3.62	15-31					
Total	**360**	**21.90±3.57**	**13-32**	**Decision: In case of Income Level H_0 can't be accepted**				
Educational Level								

(Contd.)

(Contd. Table 4.7)

Factor	*Descriptive Statistics*			*Test Used*	*Test Value*			*Inference*
Experiences (in Years)	*No.*	*Mean ± SD*	*Range*		*df*	*F*	*Comparison*	
VI-VIII Standard	14	23.35±3.02	20-31	One-Way ANOVA	5	3.372	P<0.05	Significant
Matriculation	35	20.34±3.19	14-25					
Intermediate	51	22.35±3.79	13-30					
Graduation	156	21.89±3.35	14-31					
Post Graduate	48	22.97±3.84	14-32					
Others	56	21.91±3.69	13-32					
Total	**360**	**21.90±3.57**	**13-32**	**Decision: In case of Educational Level H_0 can't be accepted**				
Age (in Years)								
<30	26	21.69±3.61	13-31					
30-40	88	22.18±4.05	14-32	One-Way ANOVA	3	1.586	P>0.05	Not Significant
40-50	148	22.19±3.57	13-32					
>50	98	21.26±3.03	14-28					
Total	**360**	**21.90±3.57**	**13-32**	**Decision: In case of Age H_0 can be accepted**				

environment factor. The employees of income level more than Rs. 20,000 have shown highest satisfaction (22.84±3.62) regarding working environment factor followed by income group of Rs.10,000-20,000 (22.24±3.52). Thus, income level can be considered as a discriminating variable of work environment factor of QWL.

In case of educational level result of the one-way ANOVA shown in table also reveals that the calculated value of F (3.372) and corresponding P value is found significant at 0.05 level. Therefore, significant difference is found to exist in the mean score of working environment factor among the educational level group. The employees who belongs to secondary education level obtained highest satisfaction score (23.35±3.02) regarding working environment factor followed by Post-graduate level (22.97±3.84) and Intermediate level (22.35±3.79) respectively. The employees who belong to matriculation level have shown lowest level of satisfaction regarding working environment factor (20.34±3.19). Thus, educational level of employees can be considered as a discriminating variable of work environment factor of QWL.

Regarding the age group of employees the result of the one-way ANOVA given in table shows that the calculated value of F-value (1.586) and corresponding P value is found more than 0.05 level at three degrees of freedom. Therefore, no significant difference is found to exist in the mean score of working environment factor between the group pairs categorised on the basis of age. Therefore, the Age of the employees cannot be considered as a discriminating variable of work environment factor of QWL.

Conclusions

An attempt was made in this chapter to study the factors that facilitate the total working environment of sugar industry in Uttar Pradesh. All the factors of work environment are analysed on the basis of geographical location, nature of organisation and nature of employment-wise. Based on the analysis and discussion the following findings are noted:

1. Geographical location-wise analysis reveals that the lighting facility, working condition, type of welfare facilities and quality of welfare facility are found significantly different in three select zones (Eastern, Central and Western zones). However, statistically very highly significant differences have been noticed in the perception of Eastern, Western and Central zones' employees with regards to safety measures and total score of working environment factor. The remaining dimensions are found non-significant.

2. Nature of Organisation-wise analysis reveals that there exists highly significant difference regarding the perception of health facility, safety measures, type of welfare facilities, and quality of welfare facilities between private and co-operative sugar mills employees. Further, significant differences have been observed in the perception of level of temperature. The overall analysis of work environment factor reveals that the opinion of both the sector differs statistically very highly significant. The average satisfactions of private sector employees are more than the co-operative sector employees with regards to work environment factors of quality of work life.

3. Nature of Employment-wise analysis of the study revealed that there exist highly significant difference between the permanent and seasonal employees regarding the perception of work-place stress and type of welfare facilities. While, the perception about lighting facility, safety measures and quality of welfare facilities are differing significantly between the permanent and seasonal employees. There is no significant difference have been found regarding overall score of work environment factor.

4. The demographic analysis of this study also pointed out that level of income and level of education are the key variables that influence the perception of work environment factor in sugar industry.

References

Akinyele, S.T. (2007). A Critical Assessment of Environmental Impact on Workers Productivity in Nigeria. *Res. J. Bus. Manage. 1*(1), 50-61.

Brenner, P. (2004). Workers Physical Surrounding. Impact Bottom Line Accounting: Smarts Pros.com.

Chan, K.W. and Wyatt, T.A. (2007), Quality of Work Life: A Study of Employees in Shanghai, China, *Asia Pacific Business Review, 13*(4), 501-517.

Joanne Profetto-McGrath *et el,* 2003 "A study of critical thinking and research utilisation among nurses", *Western Journal of Nursing Research,* Sage Publications, 25:322.

Kanagalakshmi, L. and Devei, N.B. (2003), "A Study on Perception of Quality of Work Life among Textile Manufacturing Workers in Tirunelveli".

Opperman C.S. (2002). Tropical Business Issues, Partner Price Water House Coopers.

Srivastava, A.K. (2007), Perceived Work Environment and Employees' Health, *Psychological Studies*, 52, (4), 345- 347.

Wright, T.A. and Bonett, D.G. (2007). Job Satisfaction and Psychological Well-being as Non-additive Predictors of Work-place Turnover; *Journal of Management,* 33(2), 141-160.

Wright, T.A. and Cropanzano, R. (2004), The Role of Psychological Well-being in Job Performance: A Fresh Look at an Age-old Quest, *Organisational Dynamics*, 33(4), 338-351.

5

Relational Factor—An Evaluation

5.1 Introduction

The Employee Relation dimension has attracted notice and it gained popularity in the last three decades. The philosophy of Quality of Work Life is based on the belief of worker participation and healthy employer and employees' relationship. Human relation is the art of getting along with the people either as individuals or as a group. Human relations are an integral process through which an individual's attitude and work are integrated with a view to effecting a willing co-operation on his/her part in the achievement of the interests of an organisation as a whole. In the words of Davis, "Human relations in an area of management practice in the integration of people into work situation in a way that motivates them to work together productively, co-operatively and with economic, psychological and social satisfaction". According to V.V. Giri, "Such an association of labour and management at all levels would lead to the promotion of increased productivity for the general benefit of the enterprise, the employer and the community, giving employees better understanding of their role in the working of the industry and in the process of production, satisfaction of the urge of self-expression in employees, thus leading to industrial peace. Better relations and increased co-operation will enable employers to win their confidence and co-operation. Such association of labour with management in a real way at all levels will break the barriers between labour and management and do away with suspicious and mistrust and replace antagonism with co-operation".

Socially, the need for participation arises because modern industry is a social institution with the interests of the capital owner, the employer, the community and the workers equally vested in it. With the increasing strength of the organisation of workmen and with their raising expectations, a stage has now been reached where the workers not only demand improvement in emoluments and status but also want to use the power of their organisation to secure co-partnership. Thus, the concept of workers' participation in management rests on the principle of equality and co-operation between management and workers. Workers will be motivated and their morale will improve if they are involved in the process of decision-making.

In many countries it is statutory for the industrial establishment to constitute joint consultation committee with representative of managers and workers at the plant level. This implies that management must be prepared and willing to allow its employees some say or influence on decisions about conditions or processes which affect their work tasks and environment. It is concerned with maintaining employer-employee relationships that contribute to satisfactory productivity, motivation, and morale. The Industrial Dispute Act 1947 provides to set-up a joint working committee. In the case of an industrial establishment in which 100 or more workmen are employed or have been employed on any day in the preceding twelve months, the Government may by general or special order require the employer to constitute a works committee consisting of representatives of employers and workmen engaged in the establishment.

Therefore, maintaining healthy employee relations in an organisation is a pre-requisite for organisational success. A good employee relation provides fair and consistent treatment to all employees so that they will be committed to the organisation. Effective employee relations require co-operation between managers and employee representative's trade unions. Therefore, the management should develop and implement adequate HR strategies such as cordial relationship, joint decision-making, emotional supervisory support, favourable management attitude, etc., for optimum utilisation of existing human resources in the competitive environment.

In the light of aforesaid discussion it can be concluded that QWL programmes seek to create a culture of work environment in organisations and society at large so as to ensure higher productivity and greater job satisfaction of the employees. In order to improve quality of work life joint efforts of employees and their unions, employers, professional organisations and government are necessary.

Nonetheless, in this chapter, the researcher has made an attempt to evaluate the following issues under the Relational Factor.

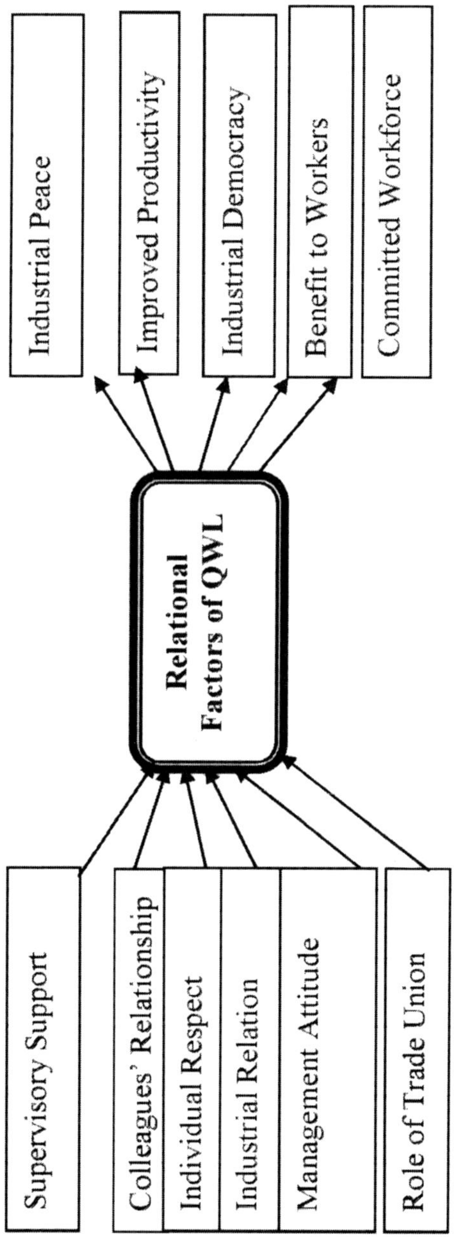

Fig. 5.1: Extractions of Relation Factor and their Positive Outcomes.

- Supervisory Support,
- Relationship with Colleagues and Supervisor,
- Individual Respect,
- Industrial Relation,
- Role of Trade Union, and
- Management Attitude

5.2 Geographical Location-wise Analysis of Relational Factor

In the Table 5.1 different variables of relational factor have been analysed on the basis of the geographical location of UP sugar mills. The geographical location has been divided in to three parts, i.e., Eastern Zone, Central Zone and Western Zone. Kruskal-Wallis (H) Test has been applied for the purpose of getting group-wise difference regarding the perception of various variables of relational factor. The table shows that out of nine variables three variables are found to be non-significant, i.e., supervision quality, industrial relation and management attitude. There are three variables namely, supervisory support, colleagues relationship and supervisory relationship the perception of employees is found significantly difference at five per cent level of significance ($p<0.05$).

However, regarding superiors' relationship; individual respect and role of trade union the difference is found very highly significant at one per cent level of significance. In case of supervisory relationship, the employees of Western Zone sugar mills have shown the highest satisfaction level (202.96) followed by the Eastern Zone (182.23) and Central Zone (156.31) respectively. However, regarding the perception about individual respect, employees of Eastern Zone have shown the highest level of satisfaction (209.56) followed by the Western Zone (171.35) and Central Zone (156.32) respectively. Similarly in the opinion about the role of trade union, employees of Eastern Zone are highly satisfied (210.41).

In the case of trade union role the total mean score (2.81±1.23) shows that employees of Central and Western Zone have less than average satisfaction, i.e., (2.65±1.25) and (2.60±1.25) respectively. But, regarding the overall relational factor, employees of all three groups have highly and significantly different opinions. Out of the three zones, Eastern Zone has got the highest mean rank (202.79) followed by Western (176.77) and Central Zone (161.95). Thus, it can be concluded that regarding relationship factor employees have significantly different opinion in relation to most of the variables. It indicates that in the mills of different zones, the employees' perception towards relational environment is quite different.

Table 5.1: Analysis of Relational Factor with Geographical Location of Sugar Mills

S.No.	Label	Test Applied	Descriptive				Value of Test			Inference
			Location	No.	Mean ±SD	Mean Rank	Value	d.f	Asymp. Sig	
1.	Supervision Quality is not Good. **(Supervision Quality)**	Kruskal-Wallis (H) Test	Eastern	120	3.24±1.32	166.82				
			Central	120	3.53±1.15	185.32				
			Western	120	3.56±1.18	189.37				
			Total	**360**	**3.44±1.21**		**3.829**	**2**	**p>0.05**	Non-significant
2.	Receive Adequate Support from Supervisor. **(Supervisor's Support)**	Kruskal-Wallis (H) Test	Eastern	120	4.09±0.91	199.95				
			Central	120	3.72±1.13	166.80				
			Western	120	3.81±1.09	174.75				
			Total	**360**	**3.88±1.06**		**8.365**	**2**	**p<0.05**	Significant
3.	Relationship with Colleagues is Good. **(Colleagues Relationship)**	Kruskal-Wallis (H) Test	Eastern	120	4.48±0.76	188.34				
			Central	120	4.31±0.75	161.30				
			Western	120	4.52±0.67	191.86				
			Total	**360**	**4.44±0.74**		**7.982**	**2**	**p<0.05**	Significant
4.	Type of Relationship with Supervisor. **(Supervisor's Relationship)**	Kruskal-Wallis (H) Test	Eastern	120	2.54±0.53	186.57				
			Central	120	2.40±0.56	163.22				
			Western	120	2.57±0.55	191.71				
			Total	**360**	**2.50±0.55**		**6.694**	**2**	**p<0.05**	Significant
5.	Relationship with Superiors is Good. **(Superiors Relationship)**	Kruskal-Wallis (H) Test	Eastern	120	4.18±0.83	182.23				
			Central	120	3.93±0.98	156.31				
			Western	120	4.32±0.85	202.96				
			Total	**360**	**4.14±0.90**		**15.212**	**2**	**p<0.001**	Very Highly Significant

(Contd.)

(Contd. Table 5.1)

S. No.	*Label*	*Test Applied*	*Descriptive*				*Value of Test*			*Inference*
			Location	No.	Mean ± S.D.	Mean Rank	Value	d.f	Asymp. Sig.	
6.	Not Treated with Respect in the Organisation. **(Individual Respect)**	Kruskal-Wallis (H) Test	Eastern	120	3.94±1.16	209.56				Very Highly Significant
			Central	120	3.44±1.21	160.59				
			Western	120	3.54±1.27	171.35				
			Total	**360**	**3.64±1.23**		**16.971**	**2**	**p<0.001**	
7.	Union-Management Relationship in Organisation. **(Industrial Relation)**	Kruskal-Wallis (H) Test	Eastern	120	3.08±1.26	192.68				Non-Significant
			Central	120	2.88±1.24	175.43				
			Western	120	2.88±1.01	173.49				
			Total	**360**	**2.95±1.18**		**2.647**	**2**	**p>0.05**	
8.	Trade Union Plays a Major Role to Protect Workers' Interest. **(Role of Trade Union)**	Kruskal-Wallis (H) Test	Eastern	120	3.18±1.10	210.41				Very Highly Significant
			Central	120	2.65±1.25	167.42				
			Western	120	2.60±1.25	163.68				
			Total	**360**	**2.81±1.23**		**15.993**	**2**	**p<0.001**	
9.	Mgt takes Interest to Solve Employees' Work Related Problems. **(Management Attitude)**	Kruskal-Wallis (H) Test	Eastern	120	3.12±0.91	195.87				Non-Significant
			Central	120	2.86±1.09	172.56				
			Western	120	2.92±0.91	173.07				
			Total	**360**	**2.97±0.98**		**4.369**	**2**	**p>0.05**	
10.	Total Score of Relational Factor	Kruskal-Wallis (H) Test	Eastern	120	3.185 ±.501	202.79				Highly Significant

5.3 Nature of Organisation-wise Analysis of Relational Factor

The Table 5.2 depicts the analysis of relational factor with regards to nature of sugar mills. Analysis has been done with the help of Mann-Whitney U test. It can be seen from the table that out of nine variables, six variables, i.e., supervisors support; colleagues relationship; supervisors relationship; superiors' relationship and individual respect are found non-significant at 0.05 level of significance.

Further, it can also be observed from the above table that regarding supervision quality; industrial relation and role of the trade union, the perception of the employees significantly differing ($P<0.05$). In case of supervision quality the descriptive statistics reveals that the employees who belong to co-operative sector sugar mills (197.68) are more satisfied than the employees of private sector sugar mills (174.77). There is also significance difference is found between both the sectors regarding the perception of industrial relation. The mean rank (187.31) obtained by the co-operative sector sugar mills shows higher satisfaction than the private sector sugar mills (160.07) with regards to industrial relation environment. Similarly, the perceptions of employees regarding role of trade unions to protect the worker interest seem to differ in both the private and co-operative sector sugar mills at five per cent level of significance. The descriptive results reveals that the employees of private sector sugar mills (186.57) are more satisfied than the employees who belongs to co-operative sector sugar mills (162.87).

There is highly significant difference is observed regarding the opinion of employees in case of management attitude towards the solution of work related problems in the both sectors of sugar mills. The mean rank of private sector sugar mills (192.05) is significantly higher than the mean score obtained by the co-operative sugar mills (145.84). The result of Mann-Whiteny U test (9030.50) is found significant at one per cent level of significance. Thus, it can be concluded that the management of private sector takes high interest to solve the employees work related problems in comparison to management of co-operative sector sugar mills.

However, regarding the overall relational factor, employees of both the sectors differs significantly. The private sector sugar mills employees have got the highest mean rank (187.78) than the employees of co-operative sugar mills (158.67). The value of Mann-Whiteny U test (10185.00) is found significant at five per cent level of significance. Thus, it can be inferred that regarding relationship factor employees have significantly different opinion in relation to most of thc variables. It indicates that in both the

Table 5.2: Analysis of Relational Factors with Nature of Organisation (Sugar Mills)

Statements	*Mill-wise Statistics*					*Mann-Whitney U Test*	*Asymp.Sig. (2-tailed)*	*Inference*
	Nature of Mill	*No.*	*Mean*	*Mean Rank*	*Sum of Rank*			
Supervision Quality is not Good. **(Supervision Quality)**	Private Cooperative	270 90	3.40±1.18 3.59±1.31	174.77 197.68	47189.00 17791.00	10604.00	$p<0.05$	Significant
Receive Adequate Support from Supervisor. **(Supervisors Support)**	Private Cooperative	270 90	3.94±0.95 3.67±1.31	183.92 170.25	49657.50 15322.50	11227.50	$p>0.05$	Not Significant
Relationship with Colleagues is Good. **(Colleagues Relationship)**	Private Cooperative	270 90	4.42±0.71 4.48±0.81	176.98 191.06	47784.50 17195.50	11199.50	$p>0.05$	Not Significant
Type of Relationship with Supervisor. **(Supervisor Relationship)**	Private Cooperative	270 90	2.53±0.54 2.43±0.56	184.31 169.07	49764.00 15216.00	11121.00	$p>0.05$	Not Significant
Relationship with Superiors is Good. **(Superiors Relationship)**	Private Cooperative	270 90	4.16±0.87 4.10±0.99	180.73 179.81	48797.50 16182.50	12087.50	$p>0.05$	Not Significant
Not Treated with Respect in the Organisation.	Private Cooperative	270 90	3.69±1.11 3.50±1.52	180.10 181.70	48627.00 16353.00	12042.00	$p>0.05$	Not Significant

(Contd.)

(Contd. Table 5.2)

Statements	*Mill-wise Statistics*					*Mann-Whitney U Test*	*Asymp.Sig. (2-tailed)*	*Inference*
	Nature of Mill	*No.*	*Mean*	*Mean Rank*	*Sum of Rank*			
(Individual Respect)								
Union-Management Relationship in Organisation.	Private	270	3.03±1.16	187.31	50573.50	10311.50	$p<0.05$	Significant
	Cooperative	90	2.70±1.20	160.07	14406.00			
(Industrial Relation)								
Trade Union Plays a Major Role to Protect Workers' Interest.	Private	270	2.89±1.21	186.57	50375.00	10510.00	$p<0.05$	Significant
	Cooperative	90	2.58±1.24	162.28	14605.00			
(Role of Trade union)								
Mgt takes Interest to Solve Employees' Work Related Problems.	Private	270	3.09±0.94	192.05	51854.50	9030.50	$p<0.001$	Very Highly Significant
	Cooperative	90	2.62±1.01	145.84	13125.50			
(Management Attitude)								
Total Score of Relational Factor	Private	270	3.46±.535	187.78	50700.00	10185.00	$p<0.05$	Significant
	Cooperative	90	3.29±.627	158.67	14280.00			

mills the perception of employees towards relational environment is quite different.

5.4 Nature of Employment-wise Analysis of Relational Factor

The Table 5.3 reveals the analysis of relational factor with regards to nature of employment sugar mills i.e., permanent and seasonal employees. Analysis has been done with the help of Mann-Whitney U test. It can be observed from the table that out of nine variables, four variables, i.e., supervision quality, Supervisors Support; Colleagues Relationship; and individual respect are found non-significant at 0.05 level of significance.

Further, the table reveals that regarding supervisors relationship perception of the employees significantly differing at five per cent level of significance. The employees of permanent nature asserted that the relationship with their supervisor is harmonious (M=190.46) while in case of seasonal employees the relationship with supervisor is found almost good (M= 170.54). There is also highly significance difference is found between permanent and seasonal employees regarding the perception of superiors' relationship and management attitude to solve the work related problems. The mean rank (193.73) obtained by the permanent employees shows higher satisfaction than the seasonal employees (167.23) with regards to superiors' relationship. Similarly, the perceptions of employees regarding management attitude to solve the work related problems seem to differ in both the nature of employment at five per cent level of significance. The descriptive result reveals that the employees of permanent nature (196.48) are more satisfied than the seasonal employees (164.52) with management attitude.

There is very highly significant difference is found between the perception of permanent and seasonal employees regarding the industrial relation and role of trade union. In case of industrial relation the mean rank obtained by the permanent employees (198.33) is significantly higher than the mean score obtained by the seasonal employees (162.67). The result of Mann-Whitney U test (9030.50) is found significant at one per cent level of significance. Thus, it can be concluded that the permanent employees feels better industrial relation in compare to seasonal employees. Similarly, regarding role of trade union the descriptive result shows that employees of permanent nature are more satisfied (197.74) than the employees who belongs to seasonal nature of employment (163.26). It indicates that trade unions play a major role to protect the interest of permanent employees.

However, regarding the overall relational factor, employees of both the natures differs very highly and significantly. The permanent employees

Table 5.3: Analysis of Relational Factors with Nature of Employment in Sugar Mills

Statements	*Mill-Wise Statistics*					*Mann-Whitney U Test*	*Asymp.Sig. (2-tailed)*	*Inference*
	Nature of Mill	*No.*	*Mean*	*Mean Rank*	*Sum of Rank*			
Supervision Quality is not Good. **(Supervision Quality)**	Permanent	180	3.40±1.28	178.41	32114.00	15824.00	p>0.05	Not-Significant
	Seasonal	180	3.49±1.15	182.59	32866.00			
Receive Adequate Support from Supervisor. **(Supervisors Support)**	Permanent	180	3.94±0.97	185.15	33327.50	15362.50	p>0.05	Not-Significant
	Seasonal	180	3.81±1.11	175.85	31652.50			
Relationship with Colleagues is Good. **(Colleagues Relationship)**	Permanent	180	4.47±0.74	186.44	33559.00	15131.00	p>0.05	Not-Significant
	Seasonal	180	4.40±0.73	174.56	31421.00			
Type of Relationship with Supervisor. **(Supervisor Relationship)**	Permanent	180	2.57±0.52	190.46	34282.00	14408.00	p<0.05	Significant
	Seasonal	180	2.44±0.57	170.54	30698.00			
Relationship with Superiors is Good. **(Superiors Relationship)**	Permanent	180	4.26±0.85	193.73	34871.00	13819.00	p<0.01	Highly Significant
	Seasonal	180	4.03±0.93	167.27	30109.00			
Not Treated with Respect in the Organisation.	Permanent	180	3.78±1.13	189.70	34145.50	14544.50	p>0.05	Not-Significant
	Seasonal	180	3.51±1.31	171.30	30834.50			

(Contd.)

(Contd. Table 5.3)

Statements	*Mill-Wise Statistics*					*Mann-Whitney U Test*	*Asymp.Sig. (2-tailed)*	*Inference*
	Nature of Mill	*No.*	*Mean*	*Mean Rank*	*Sum of Rank*			
(Individual Respect) Union-Management Relationship in Organisation.	Permanent	180	3.15±1.16	198.33	35699.50	12990.50	p<0.001	Very Highly Significant
	Seasonal	180	2.74±1.16	162.67	29280.50			
(Industrial Relation) Trade Union Plays a Major Role to Protect Workers' Interest.	Permanent	180	3.02±1.25	197.74	35594.00	13096.00	p<0.001	Very Highly Significant
	Seasonal	180	2.60±1.17	163.26	29386.00			
(Role of Trade Union) Mgt takes Interest to Solve Employees' Work Related Problems.	Permanent	180	3.13±0.91	196.48	35366.50	13323.50	p<0.01	Highly Significant
	Seasonal	180	2.81±1.02	164.52	29613.50			
(Management Attitude) Total Score of Relational Factor	Permanent	180	3.46±.535	200.54	36097.50	12592.50	p<0.001	Very Highly Significant
	Seasonal	180	3.29±.627	160.46	28882.50			

have got the highest mean rank (200.54) than the seasonal employees (160.46). The value of Mann-Whitney U test (10185.00) is found significant at one per cent level of significance. Thus, it can be concluded that regarding relationship factor employees have significantly different opinion in relation to most of the variables. It indicates that perception of permanent employees is positive towards relational environment.

5.5 Analysis of Relational Factor with Select Demographic Variables

The Table 5.4 reveals the perception score of relational factor with select demographic variables, i.e., experience, income level, educational level and age. One way Analysis of Variance (One-way ANOVA) is used to compare the means of more than two groups. F-probability of appropriate significance level is considered to determine the significance of the test. Regarding the experience the result of the one-way ANOVA given in table shows that the calculated value of F (3.091) for four degrees of freedom is found significant at 0.05 level ($P>0.05$). Therefore, significant difference is exists in the mean scores of relational factor between the different groups of job experience. Therefore, the job experience can be considered as a major variable of the relational factor of quality of work life.

However, in the case of income level it is seen that the F-value obtained (14.801) is found highly significant at 0.01 level of significance ($P<0.01$). Therefore, there is significant difference have been noticed in the perception of relational factor. The employees of income level more than Rs. 20000 have shown highest satisfaction (32.77±4.68) regarding relational factor followed by income group of Rs.10,000-20,000 (31.61±4.91) and below Rs. 10,000 (29.06±4.91). Thus, it can be concluded that income level of employees play is an important key variables that influence the relational factor of quality of work life.

In case of Educational level result of the one-way ANOVA shown in table also reveals that the calculated value of F value (5.33) and corresponding P value is found significant at 0.01 levels. Therefore, significant difference has been observed in the mean score of relational factor among the educational level group. The employees who belongs Post-graduate level obtained the highest satisfaction score (32.47±4.68) regarding relational factor followed by graduate level (31.70±4.84) and Intermediate level (29.76±5.34) respectively. The employees who belong to matriculation level have shown the lowest level of satisfaction regarding relation factor (28.42±5.41). Thus, educational level of employees has significant impact on relational factor of quality of work life.

Table 5.4: Distribution of Total Perception Score of Relational

Factor	*Descriptive Statistics*			*Test Used*	*Test Value*			*Inference*
Experiences	*No.*	*Mean ± SD*	*Range*		*df*	*F*	*Comparison*	
1-5	21	29.52±4.35	19-36	**One-Way ANOVA**	4	3.091	P<0.05	Significant
5-10	60	30.85±5.11	19-39					
10-15	86	30.25±4.86	14-40					
15-20	97	30.04±5.36	18-40					
>20	96	32.21±4.83	18-41					
Total	360	30.77±5.07	14-41	**Decision: In case of experiences H_0 can't be accepted**				
Income Level								
< Rs.10,000	139	29.06±4.91	14-40	**One-Way ANOVA**	2	14.801	P<0.001	Very Highly Significant
Rs.10000-20000	177	31.61±4.91	18-41					
Rs. 20000	44	32.77±4.68	23-40					
Total	360	30.77±5.07	14-41	**Decision: In case of Income Level H_0 can't be accepted**				
Educational Level								
VI-VIII Standard	14	29.21±4.91	19-38	**One-Way ANOVA**	5	5.33	P<0.001	Very Highly Significant
Matriculation	35	28.42±5.41	18-39					
Intermediate	51	29.76±5.34	14-38					
Graduation	156	31.70±4.84	18-41					
Post Graduate	48	32.47±4.68	21-41					
Others	56	29.48±4.61	19-40					
Total	360	30.77±5.07	14-41	**Decision: In case of Educational Level H_0 can't be accepted**				

(Contd.)

(Contd. Table 5.4)

Factor Experiences	*Descriptive Statistics*			*Test Used*	*Test Value*			*Inference*
	No.	*Mean ± SD*	*Range*		*df*	*F*	*Comparison*	
Age								
<30	26	29.65±3.88	19-36					
30-40	88	30.87±5.16	14-40	**One-Way ANOVA**	3	1.780	P>0.05	Not Significant
40-50	148	30.33±5.27	18-41					
>50	98	31.64±4.88	21-40					
Total	360	30.77±5.07	14-41	**Decision: In case of Age H_0 can be accepted Factor with Select Demographic**				

Regarding the age group of employees, the result of the one-way ANOVA given in table shows that the calculated F-value (1.780) and corresponding P value is found more than 0.05 level at three degrees of freedom. Therefore, no significant difference is found in the mean score of relational factor between any of the group pairs categorised on the basis of age. Therefore, the age of the employees cannot be considered as a influencing variable of relational factor of QWL.

Conclusion

The present chapter was undertaken to evaluate the relational factor of quality of work life at three different clusters namely, geographical location-wise, nature of organisation-wise and nature of employment-wise. Based on the analysis and discussion the following findings are noted:

1. There is very highly significant difference is found regarding the perception of superiors' relationship, individual respect and role of trade union among the employees of Eastern, Central and Western Zones. Significant difference has been noticed in case of supervisory support, colleagues' relationship and supervisory relationship. Further, no significant difference is observed in case of supervision quality and industrial relation. The overall analysis of relational factor revealed that the employees of Eastern Zone are more satisfied followed by the Central and Western Zones.

2. There is significant difference have been observed between private and co-operative sector sugar mills with regards to management attitude, supervision quality, industrial relation and role of trade union. Further, no significant difference is found in the perception of six variables namely, supervisors support; Colleagues' relationship; supervisor's relationship; superiors' relationship and individual respect. The overall analysis of relational factor reveals that the opinion of both the sector differs significantly. The average satisfactions of private sector employees are more than the co-operative sector employees with regards to relational factors of quality of work life.

3. The nature of employment-wise analysis revealed that out of nine variables of relational factor, five variables are found significant namely, supervisors' relationship, superiors' relationship, industrial relation, role of trade union and management attitude. However, no significant difference has been noticed in the perception of supervision quality, supervisory support, colleagues' relationship and individual respect between the permanent and seasonal employees. Further, statistically highly and

significant difference has been observed regarding the overall perception of relational factor. Permanent employees are found more satisfied than the seasonal employees with regards to relational factor.

4. There has been found significant relationship of relation factor of quality of work life with job experience, income and education level of employees.

References

Giri, V.V. (1972). *Labour Problems in Indian Industry*, Asia Publishing House, Bombay.

Keith, Davis (1962). *Human Relations in Management*, McGraw Hill Book Co., New York.

6

Job Factor-An Appraisal

6.1 Introduction

Work has occupied an important place in the life of human beings. Work culture plays a significant role in employee job satisfaction and quality of work life. It is an all inclusive scaffold that determines the job activities, organisational philosophy and support, moral, ethics and working life-style of employees (Hofstede, G., 1990). The work culture varies from organisation to organisation due to presence of people with multiple and assorted background, norms and ethics. The work culture in an organisation forms the basis of difference among them. It is the work culture of an organisation that makes a distinction between a good and bad organisation to work for. A good work culture strengthens the employee's loyalty to the organisation and reduces attrition rate whereas if employees are not satisfied or comfortable in a work culture of an organisation, it would result in low productivity. There have been studies that showed that the prevailing work culture is an important rod for measuring divergence (Triandis H.C., 1982). Now-a-day, employees are becoming more and more educated, skilled, affluent and unionised. It is no longer possible to design jobs solely according to the needs of technology completely overlooking the needs of employees. The job which is skill-based, interesting, challenging that provides status and pride, and entails involvement and makes employees feel happy and secure. People moves from job to job due to unhappiness at work, a new direction or career-path or a simple desire to develop themselves and learn multi-skills. Therefore, there is a need for developing more humanised jobs which can satisfy employee's higher needs, employ their higher skill and make them better employees. Hence, the traditional

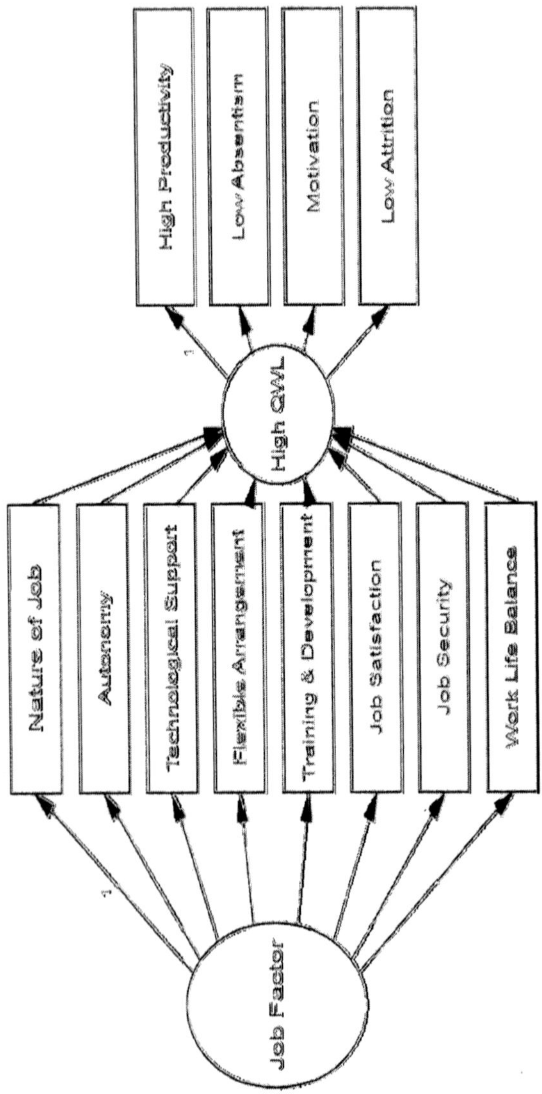

Fig. 6.1: Job Factor and Quality of Work Life: A Conceptual Model.

job design needs to be replaced by enriched job design. It has been completely understood that quality of work is indispensable for an amiable work culture. With such strategies not only the organisational goals aligned to the employee engagement, employee involvement and are accomplished (Bae, J. and Lawler, 2000). The understanding of work culture would facilitate why some organisation have good or bad picture. Therefore, the perceptive observation of different dimension of work culture is important for better performance evaluation (Groeschl, S. 2003). The human resource department has a major role in creating and maintaining the amiable work culture being equipped with the implements like recruitment, good training and development, organisational support, flexible hours, and healthy work life balance strategies. Therefore, this chapter seeks to examine the different variable of job factor or work culture prevailing in the private and co-operative sectors of sugar mills in Uttar Pradesh. The following issues of job factor are covered under the study.

6.2 Geographical Location-wise Analysis of Job Factor

Table 6.1 shows the analysis of job factor with geographical location of sugar mills. The chi-square test has been applied to check the perception of employees regarding select variables, i.e., technological support, work life balance and flexible working arrangement. Statistically, it is observed that there is no significant differences have been found in the opinion of employees regarding technological support and work life balance. However, majority of respondent (57.5 per cent) from Western Zone reported that they do not have opportunity to using new technology in the task. Similarly, in the case of work life balance, employees of all three zones (81.7 per cent) replied that they are able to maintain a healthy work life balance. The chi-square value (1.25) and corresponding P value found more than commonly accepted (0.05) level of significance. Hence, no significant difference is found in the opinion of employee of three different zones.

However, in the case of flexible working hour statistically significant difference has been observed in the perception of employees at five per cent level of significance (χ^2=9.960, d.f= 2, $P<0.05$). Overall analysis shows that about half of the employees (51 per cent) reveals that the organisation do not provide any kind of flexible working arrangement. Majority of respondent (60 per cent) from Western Zone are agreed with this fact.

In the Table 6.2, three variables of job factors have been analysed on the basis of geographical location of sugar mills. Chi-square test has been done to check the association regarding the opinions of different select

Table 6.1: Job Factor Analysis with Geographical Location of Sugar Mills

Sl. No.	Label	Test Applied	Location	Crosstabs			Descriptive	Value of Test			Inference
				Yes	No	Total		Value	d.f	Asymp. Sig	
1.	Is there any opportunity to you for using new technology? **(Technological Support)**	Pearson Chi-Square	Eastern	56 (46.7)	64 (53.3)	120 (100)	1.53±.501	χ^2=.473	2	$p>0.05$	Not Significant
			Central	52 (43.3)	68 (56.7)	120 (100)	1.57±.498				
			Western	51 (42.5)	69 (57.5)	120 (100)	1.58±.496				
			Total	**159 (44.2)**	**122 (55.8)**	**360 (100)**	**1.56±.497**				
2.	Do you able to maintain a healthy balance between work and family life? **(Work Life Balance)**	Pearson Chi-Square	Eastern	98 (81.7)	22 (18.3)	120 (100)	1.18±.389	χ^2=1.25	2	$p>0.05$	Not Significant
			Central	92 (76.7)	28 (23.3)	120 (100)	1.23±.425				
			Western	98 (81.7)	22 (18.3)	120 (100)	1.18±.389				
			Total	**288 (80)**	**72 (20)**	**360 (100)**	**1.23±.422**				
3.	Does the organisation provide you flexible working hour? **(Flexible working hour)**	Pearson Chi-Square	Eastern	72 (60)	48 (40)	120 (100)	1.40±.492	χ^2=9.960	2	$p<0.05$	Significant
			Central	56 (46.7)	64 (53.3)	120 (100)	1.53±.501				
			Western	48 (40)	72 (60)	120 (100)	1.60±.492				
			Total	**176 (48.9)**	**184 (51.1)**	**360 (100)**	**1.51±.501**				

Table 6.2: Job Factor Analysis with Geographical Location of Sugar Mills

Sl. No.	Label	Test Applied	Crosstabs	Location				Value of Test			Inference
				Eastern	Central	Western	Total	Value	d.f	Asymp.Sig	
1.	What are the reasons of your stay at the present job? **(Job Retention)**	Pearson Chi-Square	Salary	86 (71.7)	93 (77.5)	98 (81.7)	277 (71.9)	χ^2=8.843	4	p>0.05	Not Significant
			Challenging Job Benefits	27 (22.5)	17 (14.2)	11 (9.2)	55 (15.3)				
				07 (5.8)	10 (8.3)	11 (9.2)	28 (7.8)				
			Total	**120 (100)**	**120 (100)**	**120 (100)**	**360 (100)**				
			Descriptives	1.34±.587	1.31±.619	1.28±.621	1.31±.608				
2.	Which of the following best describes your usual work schedule? **(Work Schedule)**	Pearson Chi-Square	Day shift	100 (83.3)	99 (82.5)	101 (84.2)	300 (83.3)	χ^2=5.72	6	p>0.05	Not Significant
			Afternoon shift	03 (2.5)	04 (3.3)	07 (5.8)	14 (3.9)				
			Night shift	09 (7.5)	05 (4.2)	05 (4.2)	19 (5.3)				
			Rotating shift	08 (6.7)	12 (10)	07 (5.8)	27 (7.5)				
			Total	**120 (100)**	**120 (100)**	**120 (100)**	**360 (100)**				

(Contd.)

(Contd. Table 6.2)

Sl. No.	Label	Test Applied	Crosstabs	Location				Value of Test			Inference
				Eastern	Central	Western	Total	Value	d.f	Asymp.Sig	
3.	What cause you have the greatest dissatisfaction at work? **(Work-Dissatisfaction)**	Pearson Chi-Square	Descriptives	1.38±.889	1.42±.967	1.32±.889	1.37±.889	χ^2=9.25	6	p>0.05	Not Significant
			Lack of appreciation	64 (53.3)	74 (61.7)	65 (54.2)	203 (56.4)				
			Too much paper work	18 (15)	09 (7.5)	08 (6.7)	35 (9.7)				
			Family issue	03 (2.5)	06 (5.0)	08 (6.7)	17 (4.7)				
			Lack of training and development	35 (29.2)	31 (25.8)	39 (32.5)	105 (29.2)				
			Total	**120 (100)**	**120 (100)**	**120 (100)**	**360 (100)**				
			Descriptives	2.08±1.317	1.95±1.308	2.18±1.376	2.07±1.334				

variables. Statistically, no significant difference has been found in the perception of employees regarding the three variables, i.e., job retention, work schedule and work-satisfaction.

Regarding the opinion of job retention, the overall analysis reveals that almost (72 per cent) respondent replied that salary is most influencing factor to stay at present job followed by the challenging job (15.3 per cent) and benefits (7.8 per cent) respectively. In case of work schedule, almost (83.4 per cent) employees feel that day shift is most appropriate to work in sugar factory. Further, the opinions of employees regarding work dissatisfaction are almost similar. In total (56.4 per cent) employees reported that lack of appreciation is the greatest cause of work-dissatisfaction at workplace. However, about (29.2 per cent) employees feel that lack of training and development is the second most cause of work dissatisfaction. The Chi-square value (9.25) and corresponding P value (P>0.05) reveals that there is no significant difference between the perception of employees of different zones about work-dissatisfaction.

Table 6.3 analysed the opinion of sugar mills employees regarding different variables of job factor, namely, adequate training, employee's interest, additional responsibilities, autonomy, and job security. The analysis has been done on the basis of the geographical location of UP sugar mills. Kruskal-Wallis (H) Test has been applied for the purpose of getting group-wise difference regarding the perception of various variables of job factor. It can be observed from the table that out of five dimensions, three dimensions are found to be non-significant, i.e., (Adequate training, Employee's interest and additional responsibilities).

Statistically, significant difference has been observed between the employees of sugar mills regarding Job autonomy at five per cent level of significance (H=6.323, P<0.05). It reveals that the employees of Eastern Zone showed the highest satisfaction (196.2) followed by the Western (176.45) and Central Zone (168.32).

The table also shows that H value (16.018) is found to be highly significant for the dimension of job security (P<0.001). The highest mean rank (201.58) obtained by the employees of Eastern Zone depicts that they are more satisfied with job security than the employees of Central (188.11) and Western Zone (151.80).

However, regarding the overall job factor, no significant differences have been found among the employees of all three groups (H=2.028, d.f.=2, P>0.05). Therefore, it can be concluded that all the employees of three zones exhibited a similar level of satisfaction regarding job factor of quality of work life.

Table 6.3: Job Factor Analysis with Geographical Location of Sugar Mills

Sl. No.	*Label*	*Test Applied*	*Descriptive*				*Value of Test*			*Inference*
			Location	*No.*	*Mean ±SD*	*Mean Rank*	*Value*	*d.f*	*Asymp. Sig*	
1.	I receive adequate training to do my job well. **(Adequate Training)**	Kruskal-Wallis (H) Test	Eastern	120	3.16±1.414	196.01	4.111	2	P>0.05	Not Significant
			Central	120	3.38±1.354	179.18				
			Western	120	2.94±1.463	167.31				
			Total	360	3.16±1.418	----				
2.	Do you feel your company has your best interest at heart? **(Employee's Interest)**	Kruskal-Wallis (H) Test	Eastern	120	2.25±.625	187.80	3.308	2	P>0.05	Not Significant
			Central	120	2.08±.740	167.53				
			Western	120	2.22±.758	186.17				
			Total	360	2.18±.712	--				
3.	I am ready to take additional responsibility with my job. **(Additional Responsibilities)**	Kruskal-Wallis (H) Test	Eastern	120	3.62±1.109	176.12	.486	2	P>0.05	Not Significant
			Central	120	3.65±1.142	180.78				
			Western	120	3.62±1.284	184.60				
			Total	360	3.63±1.178	—				

(Contd.)

(Contd. Table 6.3)

Sl. No.	*Label*	*Test Applied*	*Descriptive*				*Value of Test*			*Inference*
			Location	*No.*	*Mean ±SD*	*Mean Rank*	*Value*	*d.f*	*Asymp. Sig*	
4.	I have necessary authority to do my job well. **(Autonomy)**	Kruskal-Wallis (H) Test	Eastern	120	3.76±1.045	196.72	6.323	2	P<0.05	Significant
			Central	120	3.40±1.170	168.32				
			Western	120	3.50±1.195	176.45				
			Total	360	2.55±1.145	----				
5.	How satisfied are you with your overall job security? **(Job Security)**	Kruskal-Wallis (H) Test	Eastern	120	2.57±.959	201.58	16.018	2	P<0.001	Very Highly Significant
			Central	120	2.42±.941	188.11				
			Western	120	2.09±1.00	151.80				
			Total	360	2.36±.986	---				
6.	**Total Score of Job Factor**	Kruskal-Wallis (H) Test	Eastern	120	2.20±.301	189.02	2.028	2	P>0.05	Not Significant
			Central	120	2.17±.290	182.26				
			Western	120	2.13±.313	170.22				
			Total	360	2.17±.302	---				

Table 6.4: Job Factor Analysis with Nature of Organisation (Sugar Mills)

Sl. No.	*Label*	*Test Applied*	*Crosstabs*	*Nature of Organisation*			*Value of Test*			*Inference*
				Private	*Co-operative*	*Total*	*Value*	*d.f*	*Asymp.Sig*	
1.	What are the reasons of your stay at the present job? **(Job Retention)**	**Pearson Chi-Square**	Salary	203 (75.2)	74(82.2)	277 (76.9)	χ^2=5.615	2	p>0.05	Not Significant
			Challenging Job	48(17.8)	07(7.8)	55(15.3)				
			Benefits	19(7.0)	09(10.0)	28(7.8)				
			Total	270 (100)	90 (100)	360 (100)				
			Descriptives	**1.32±.599**	**1.28±.636**	**1.31±.608**				
2.	Is there any opportunity to you for using new technology? **(Technological Support)**	**Pearson Chi-Square**	Yes	127(47)	32(35.6)	159(44.2)	χ^2=3.608	1	p<0.05	Significant
			No	143(53)	58(64.4)	201(55.8)				
			Total	270(100)	90(100)	360(100)				
			Descriptives	**1.53±.500**	**1.64±.481**	**1.56±.497**				
3.	Do you able to maintain a healthy balance between work and family life? **(Work-Life Balance)**	**Pearson Chi-Square**	Yes	220(81.5)	68 (75.6)	228 (80)	χ^2=1.481	1	p>0.05	Not Significant
			No	50 (18.5)	22 (24.4)	72 (20)				
			Total	270 (100)	90 (100)	360 (100)				
			Descriptives	**1.19±.389**	**1.24±.432**	**1.20±.401**				

(Contd.)

(Contd. Table 6.4)

Sl. No.	*Label*	*Test Applied*	*Crosstabs*	*Nature of Organisation*			*Value of Test*			*Inference*
				Private	*Co-operative*	*Total*	*Value*	*d.f*	*Asymp.Sig*	
4.	Does the organisation provide you flexible working hour? **(Flexible working hour)**	**Pearson Chi-Square**	Yes	139 (51.5)	37 (41.1)	176 (48.9)				
			No	131 (48.5)	53 (58.9)	184 (51.1)				
			Total	270 (100)	90 (100)	360 (100)	χ^2=2.905	1	p>0.05	Not Significant
			Descriptives	**1.49±.501**	**1.59±.495**	**1.51±.501**				
5.	Which of the following best describes your usual work schedule? **(Work-schedule)**	**Pearson Chi-Square**	Day shift	217 (80.4)	83 (75)	300 (83.3)				
			Afternoon shift	14 (5.2)	00 (00)	14 (3.9)	χ^2=12.774	3	p<0.05	Significant
			Night shift	13 (4.8)	06 (6.7)	19 (5.3)				
			Rotating shift	26 (9.6)	01 (1.1)	27 (7.5)				
			Total	270 (100)	90 (100)	360 (100)				
			Descriptives	**1.44±.961**	**1.17±.585**	**1.25±.889**				
6.	What cause you have the greatest dissatisfaction at work? **(Work-dissatisfaction)**	**Pearson Chi-Square**	Lack of appreciation	149 (55.2)	54 (60)	203 (56.4)				
			Too much paper work	29 (10.7)	06 (6.7)	35 (9.7)	χ^2=1.453	3	p>0.05	Not Significant
			Family issue	13 (4.8)	04 (4.4)	17 (4.7)				
			Lack of training& development	79 (29.3)	26 (28.9)	105 (29.2)				
			Total	270 (100)	90 (100)	360 (100)				
			Descriptives	**2.08±1.331**	**2.02±1.349**	**2.07±1.334**				

6.3 Nature of Organisation-wise Analysis of Job Factor

The Table 6.4 shows the perception level of respondent regarding different dimension of job factor. The analysis has been done on the basis of nature of organisation. Chi-square test is used to indicate the difference between the employees of private and co-operative sugar mills. The table shows that out of six dimensions only two items are there in which P value is found less than five per cent level of significance. Hence, H_0 is found to be rejected in the case of these items. These include item no. 2 (technological support) and item no. 5 (work-schedule).

In the case of technological support, about (55.8 per cent) respondent replied that they have no opportunity to use new technology. Majority of the employees (64.4 per cent) from co-operative sugar mills and (53 per cent) from private sugar mills are agreed with this fact. The value of Chi-square (3.068) with corresponding P value is found significant ($P<0.05$). Thus, the opinion of employees from both the sugar mills is differing significantly at five per cent level of significance.

Regarding the work schedule, overall analysis shows that almost (83 per cent) employees reveal that day shift is the best for working in sugar factory while afternoon shift is the preferred shift (3.9 per cent). The Chi-square value is found significant at five per cent level of significance ($\chi^2=12.774$, $P<0.05$). Hence, significant difference is observed among the perception of the employees of private and co-operative sector regarding the work schedule. On the other hand, no statistically significant differences are found in remaining four variables (job retention, work life balance, flexible working hours and work-dissatisfaction). P value is found more than commonly accepted five per cent level of significance. Majority of employees reveals that present salary is most important reason to stay in the job. Similarly, about 56.4 per cent employees from private and co-operative sector asserted that lack of appreciation is major cause of work dissatisfaction in the sugar industry of Uttar Pradesh.

6.4 Nature of Employment-wise Analysis of Job factor

The table (6.5) reveals the perception of permanent and seasonal employees with regards to different items of job factor. Accordingly analysis has been done with the help of Mann-Whiteny U test. The item includes adequate training, employee's interest, additional responsibilities, and autonomy and job security. It can be seen from the table that out of five variables, only two variables, i.e., adequate training and additional responsibilities are found non-significant at five per cent level of significance.

Table 6.5: Job Factor Analysis with Nature of Employment in Sugar Mills

Sl. No.	*Test Variable Lists*	*Mill-wise Statistics*					*Mann-Whitney U Test*	*Asymp. Sig (2-tailed)*	*Inference*
		Nature of Mills	*No.*	*Descriptive*	*Mean Rank*	*Sum of Rank*			
1.	1. I receive adequate training to do my job well **(Adequate Training)**	Permanent Seasonal	180 180	3.51±1.310 2.81±1.441	185.15 175.85	33327.5 31652.50	15362.5	p>0.05	Not Significant
2.	2. Do you feel your company has your best interest at heart? **(Employee's Interest)**	Permanent Seasonal	180 180	2.32±.751 2.03±.645	200.05 160.95	36009.00 28971.00	12681.00	p<0.001	Very Highly Significant
3.	3. I am ready to take additional responsibility with my job. **(Additional Responsibilities)**	Permanent Seasonal	180 180	3.70±1.172 3.56±1.183	186.84 174.16	33631.00 31349.00	15059.00	p>0.05	Not Significant

(Contd.)

(Contd. Table 6.5)

Sl. No.	*Test Variable Lists*	*Mill-wise Statistics*					*Mann-Whitney U Test*	*Asymp. Sig (2-tailed)*	*Inference*
		Nature of Mills	*No.*	*Descriptive*	*Mean Rank*	*Sum of Rank*			
4.	4. I have necessary authority to do my job well. **(Autonomy)**	Permanent Seasonal	180 180	3.76±.1.021 3.34±1.225	196.79 164.21	35423.00 29557.00	14781.00	p<0.001	Very Highly Significant
5.	5. How satisfied are you with your overall job security? **(Job Security)**	Permanent Seasonal	180 180	2.80±.971 1.92±1.787	225.64 135.36	40615.00 24365.99	8075.00	p<0.001	Very Highly Significant
6.	**6. Total Score of Job Factor**	Permanent Seasonal	180 180	2.21±.304 2.03±.250	211.25 149.75	38025.00 26955.00	10665.00	p<0.001	Very Highly Significant

Further, the table reveals that regarding employee's interest, autonomy and job security the perception of permanent seasonal employees statistically differing very highly and significantly at 0.001 level of significance. The mean rank (200.5) obtained by the permanent employees shows higher satisfaction than the seasonal employees (160.95) with regards to employee's interest. It means the sugar mills employers take extra care of their permanent employees compare to seasonal employees.

Similarly, the perceptions of permanent and seasonal employees regarding autonomy are differing statistically significant. The descriptive result reveals that the employees of permanent nature (196.79) are more satisfied than the seasonal employees (164.21) with the given autonomy. It means the permanent employees have given more autonomy and power than the seasonal employees related to their work.

The table also reveals that in case of job security the mean rank obtained by the permanent employees (225.64) is significantly higher than the mean score obtained by the seasonal employees (135.36). The result of Mann-Whitney U test (8075.00) is found significant at one per cent level of significance. Thus, it can be concluded that the permanent employees feels better job security in compare to seasonal employees.

However, regarding the overall perception of job factor, the employees of both the natures differs very highly and significantly. The permanent employees have got highest mean rank (211.25) than the seasonal employees (149.75). The value of Mann-Whitney U test (10665.00) is found significant at one per cent level of significance. Thus, it can be concluded that regarding the job factor employees have significantly different opinion in relation to most of the variables. It indicates that perception of permanent employees is positive towards job or work culture environment.

6.5 Analysis of Job Factor with Select Demographic Variables

Table 6.6 reveals the Perception Score of job Factor with select demographic variables, i.e., experience, income level, education level and age of the employees. In order to assess the average satisfaction score, mean and standard deviation is used. Further, to find out group-wise difference one-way ANOVA is used. The table reveals that employees with different income level (i.e., below 10,000, 10000-20,000 and above 20,000) differs statistically highly significant with regards to total score of job factor ($F = 10.252$, $P < .001$) at one per cent level of significance. Therefore, it can be inferred that income level is an important variable influencing the job factor of quality of work life. Similarly, employees belonging to different

Table 6.6: Distributions of Total Perception Score of Job Factor with Select Demographics

Factor	*Descriptive Statistics*			*Test Used*	*Test Value*			*Inference*
Experiences	No.	Mean ± SD	Range		**df**	**F**	**Comparison**	
1-5	21	24.66±3.15	17-29	One-Way ANOVA	4	1.683	P>0.05	Not Significant
5-10	60	24.48±3.42	16-23					
10-15	86	23.33±3.39	14-32					
15-20	97	23.61±3.32	16-31					
>20	96	24.15±3.19	17-35					
Total	360	23.90±3.32	14-35	**Decision: In case of experiences H_0 can be accepted**				
Income Level (Rs.)				One-Way ANOVA	2	10.252	P<0.001	Very Highly Significant
<10,000	139	23.23±3.02	16-32					
10000-20000	177	23.95±3.41	14-35					
>20000	44	25.77±3.18	20-32					
Total	360	23.90±3.32	14-35	**Decision: In case of Income Level H_0 can't be accepted**				
Educational Level								

(Contd.)

(Contd. Table 6.6)

Factor	*Descriptive Statistics*			*Test Used*	*Test Value*			*Inference*
VI-VIII Standard	14	23.50±3.65	17-28	One-Way ANOVA	5	2.82	P<0.05	Significant
Matriculation	35	22.80±2.44	18-27					
Intermediate	51	23.03±3.32	14-30					
Graduation	156	24.03±3.43	16-35					
Post Graduate	48	25.06±3.21	17-33					
Others	56	24.08±3.32	18-32					
Total	360	23.90±3.32	14-35	**Decision: In case of Educational Level H_0 can't be accepted**				
Age								
<30	26	29.92±3.11	17-29					
30-40	88	24.06±3.08	17-33	One-Way ANOVA	3	.843	P>0.05	Not Significant
40-50	148	24.09±3.55	14-35					
>50	98	23.44±3.24	17-32					
Total	360	23.90±3.32	14-35	**Decision: In case of Age H_0 can be accepted**				

educational level (secondary, matriculation, intermediate, graduation, post-graduation and other) differs statistically significant with regards to total sore of job factor ($F= 2.82, P<0.05$) at five per cent level of significance. It means that, employees belonging to different education levels have different opinions about the job factor of quality of work life.

However, the sugar mills employees belonging to different age groups, i.e., below 30 years, 30-40 years, 40-50 years and 50 and above years do not differ statistically significant with respect to total score of job factor ($F=0.843, p>0.05$) at five per cent level of significance. It means that, the employees belonging to different age groups have similar opinion with all the variables of job factor. Similarly, it is also noticed that the employees belonging to different years of service experience (1.5 years, 5-10 years, 10-15 years and 20+ years) do not differ statistically significant with respect to total score of job factor scores ($F=5.3014, p<0.05$) at five per cent level of significance. Therefore, it can be concluded that employees belonging to different years of service experience have same perception regarding job factor of quality of work life.

Conclusions

The aim of this chapter was seek to examine the perception of employees of sugar mills in Uttar Pradesh with regards to different dimensions of job factor. The entire analysis has been done on the basis of three different clusters namely, geographical location-wise analysis, nature of organisation-wise analysis and nature of employment-wise analysis. Based on the analysis and discussion the following findings are noted:

1. There is statistically very highly significant difference have been found regarding the perception of job security among the employees of Eastern, Central and Western Zones. The employees of Eastern Zone asserted that they are more satisfied with the job security than the employees of Central and Western Zone respectively. Significant difference has also been noticed in case of flexible working hour and autonomy. Further, no significant difference is observed in case of job retention, work schedule, work dissatisfaction, technological support, work life balance, adequate training, employee's interest, and additional responsibilities. However, regarding the overall job factor, no significant differences have been found among the employees of all three groups. Therefore, it can be concluded that all the employees of three zones exhibited a similar level of satisfaction regarding job factor of quality of work life.

2. There is significant difference have been observed between the opinion private and co-operative sector sugar mills employees with regards to technological support and work schedule at five per cent level of significance and rest of the variables are found not significant.

3. The nature of employment-wise analysis revealed that out of five variables of job factor, three variables are found statistically highly significant namely, employee's intersect, autonomy and job security. However, no significant difference has been noticed in the perception of adequate training and additional responsibilities between the permanent and seasonal employees of Uttar Pradesh Sugar Industry. Further, statistically very highly and significant difference has been observed regarding the overall perception of job factor. Permanent employees are found more satisfied than the seasonal employees with regards to job factor.

4. The demographic analysis revealed that education level and income level of employees have significant relationship with job factor of quality of work life.

References

Bae, J. and Lawler, J.J. (2000). Organisational and HRM Strategies in Korea: Impact of Firms Performance in an Emerging Economy. *Academy of Management Journal,* 43(3); 502-517.

Groeschl, S. (2003). Cultural Implication for the Appraisal Process, Cross Cultural Management, *An International Journal,* 10(1), 67-79.

Hofstede, G. (1990). Managerial Culture and Work-related Values in India. *Organisation Studies*, 11(1). 103-106.

Triandis, H.C. (1982). Review of culture's consequences. *Human Organisation*, 41, 86-90.

7

Financial Factor–An Assessment

7.1 Introduction

One of the most important factors which influence the quality of work Life (QWL) is financial factor. In spite of the importance gained by the other factors now-a-day, compensation plays a greater role in employee's satisfaction. Especially in country like India, where the employee welfare programmes take back seat, compensation is the main source of satisfaction of the employee (Anitha, B., and Rao, Subba, 1998). Therefore, financial support becomes pivotal to make employees feel happy and productive at work. The Study Group of the National Commission on Labour has recommended that "under our conditions, a wage incentive in accordance with an effective utilisation of manpower which is the cheapest, quickest and surest means of increasing productivity. The only practicable and self-sustaining means of improving manpower utilisation is to introduce incentive schemes and stimulate human efforts to provide a positive motivation to greater output".

Compensation is a methodical approach to assigning a monetary value to employees in return for work performed. In earlier times, compensation was limited to money alone in the form of wages and salaries. But with advancement in human civilisation, compensation today has many forms, besides money. Better or higher value of compensation package, helps employees to achieve a better standard of living therefore, employees are motivated to join those organisations which offer better and higher compensation to them. As everyone wants more compensation and therefore, there is a natural competition amongst them and more competent employees are able to get higher paying jobs (Deb, 2009). It is worth mentioning here that the Indian sugar industry employs over five lakhs skilled and unskilled workers mainly from the rural areas (ISMA 2005). And it is also well-known fact that wages and salary is only the key factor for their livelihood. Hence, the adequate and fair wages must be regularly paid to the employees. The fairness of wages is also considered as an important part of Quality of Work Life, but it is difficult to measure (Green, 2006). A fair wage is in general considered as a reflecting a clear connection between the worker's contribution to the performance of the organisation and their pay. The level of fair wages should be change depending upon the cost of living. Beside the compensation package there is one more important issue that comes under financial factor which is called social security. Social security forms an important part of labour welfare providing the "security" which is of great importance to the worker's and their families' well-being. Recently, the concepts of social security measures are gaining importance in Indian industrial scenario. Free of cost hospital facility, group insurance programmes, retirement benefits are some of the important welfare programmes that must provide to the sugar mills employees by their employer.

The concept of social security measure is well reflected in the ILO definition. "It can be taken to mean the protection which society provides for its members, through a series of public measures, against the economic and social distress that otherwise would be caused by the stoppage or substantial reduction of earnings resulting from sickness, maternity, employment injury, unemployment, invalidity, old age and death; the provision of medical care, and the provision of subsidies for families with children". The social security (minimum standards) convention (No.102) adopted by the ILO in 1952 defines the nine branches of social security benefit: They are: Medical care; Sickness benefit; Unemployment benefit; Old age benefit; Employment injury benefit; Family benefit; Maternity benefit and Invalidity benefit. Although the Government enacted different acts in the past, is not found to be very successful for their enforcement at the organisation level. In such a case, it is really difficult to ensure QWL at the organisational level. In other words, we can say that the Government is not monitoring QWL factors as per the rules and regulations and factory owners are disinterested to implement government regulative mechanism. And finally Labour unions are not successful in the process of collective bargaining in order to ensure their members' rights and interests.

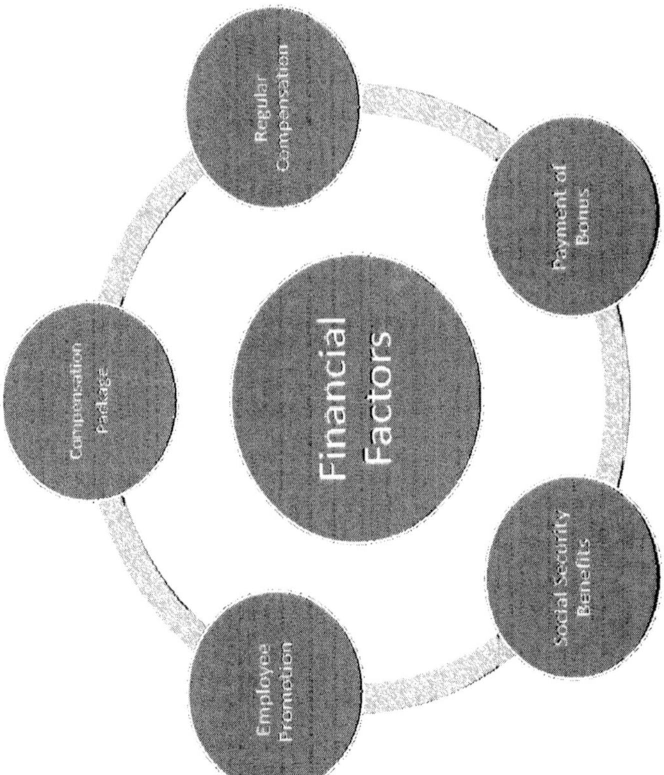

Fig. 7.1: Financial Factors of Quality of Work Life

Therefore, it can be concluded that to ensure the better quality of work life (QWL) every organisation must offer good compensation package and social security benefits to attract and retain the talent pool in the organisation. The management should always remember the fact that if the compensation offered, are not competitive as compared to other organisations, the efficient employees may leave the firm and inefficient workers or those workers who have no other means may continue with the organisation unpleasantly which is not good for the organisation in the long run. However, in the present work the scholar has made an attempt to assess the following issues under the Financial Factor of Quality of Work Life (QWL) in both the co-operative and Private Sugar mills:

- Adequate and Fair Compensation (Pay Package);
- Timely and Regular Compensation;
- Payment of Bonus;
- Social Security Benefit; and
- Employee Promotion.

7.2 Geographical Location-wise Analysis of Financial Factor

The Table 7.1 depicts the analysis of financial factor on the basis of geographical location of the UP sugar mills. The geographical location of Uttar Pradesh sugar industry is spread over three zones, i.e., Eastern Zone, Central Zone and Western Zone. Total four variables have been analysed in the above table with the help of Chi-square (χ^2) test. In case of two variables i.e., timely compensation and adequate bonus, the relationship is found to be very highly significant at two degrees of freedom ($P<0.001$, d.f. 2). Regarding timely compensation the value of Chi-square is found (25.229) at two degrees of freedom and in case of adequate bonus value of Chi-square is (50.164) at two degrees of freedom. The table also reveals that out of three geographical locations maximum employees (77.5 per cent) of Western Zone are satisfied with timely compensation followed by 75 per cent in Central Zone and 50 per cent in Eastern Zone employees respectively. In case of second variable, i.e., adequate bonus, overall 66 per cent employees reveals that they are getting adequate bonus while one third (33.9 per cent) employees asserted that they are not getting adequate bonus.

However, regarding the social security benefits and fair promotion the relationship is found to be not significant even at five per cent level of significance. Around 52 per cent employees revealed that they are getting social security benefit. While, in case of fair promotion majority of

Table 7.1: Analysis of Financial Factor with Geographical Location of Organisation (Sugar Mills)

Sl. No.	*Label*	*Test Applied*	*Location*	*Crosstabs*			*Descriptive*	*Value of Test*			*Inference*
				Yes	*No*	*Total*		*Value*	*d.f*	*Asymp.Sig*	
1.	Do you get timely and regular compensation/ Salary? **(Timely Compensation)**	Pearson Chi-Square	Eastern	60 (50)	60 (50)	120 (100)	1.50±.502	χ^2=25.229	2	p<0.001	Very Highly Significant
			Central	90 (75)	30 (25)	120 (100)	1.25±.435				
			Western	93 (77.5)	27 (22.5)	120 (100)	1.22±.419				
			Total	**243 (67.5)**	**117 (32.5)**	**360 (100)**	**1.32±.469**				
2.	Do you get adequate bonus beside your salary? **(Adequate Bonus)**	Pearson Chi-Square	Eastern	102 (85)	18 (15)	120 (100)	1.15±.359	χ^2=50.164	2	p<0.001	Very Highly Significant
			Central	51 (42.5)	69 (57.5)	120 (100)	1.58±.496				
			Western	85 (70.8)	35 (29.2)	120 (100)	1.29±.456				
			Total	**238 (66.1)**	**122 (33.9)**	**360 (100)**	**1.34±.474**				

(Contd.)

(Contd. Table 7.1)

Sl. No.	Label	Test Applied	Location	Crosstabs			Descriptive	Value of Test			Inference
				Yes	No	Total		Value	d.f	Asymp.Sig	
3.	Does the organisation provide you the social security benefits?	Pearson Chi-Square	Eastern	63 (62.5)	57 (47.5)	120 (100)	1.48±.501				
			Central	57 (47.5)	63 (52.5)	120 (100)	1.52±.501		2	$p>0.05$	Not Significant
	(Social Security Benefits)		Western	66 (55)	54 (45)	120 (100)	1.45±.500	$\chi^2=1.402$			
			Total	**186 (51.7)**	**174 (48.3)**	**360 (100)**	**1.48±.500**				
4.	Are the employee promotion decision handled fairly?		Eastern	41 (34.2)	79 (65.8)	120 (100)	1.66±.476				
	(Fair Promotion)		Central	52 (43.3)	68 (56.7)	120 (100)	1.57±.498	$\chi^2=3.912$	2	$p>0.05$	Not Significant
			Western	38 (31.7)	82 (68.3)	120 (100)	1.68±.467				
			Total	**131 (36.4)**	**229 (63.6)**	**120 (100)**	**1.64±.482**				

Table 7.2: Financial Factor Analysis with Geographical Location of Sugar Mills

Sl. No.	*Label*	*Test Applied*	*Descriptive*				*Value of Test*			*Inference*
			Location	*No.*	*Mean ±SD*	*Mean Rank*	*Value*	*d.f*	*Asymp. Sig*	
1.	Are you satisfied with your pay package? **(Remuneration)**	Kruskal-Wallis (H) Test	Eastern	120	3.19±1.162	190.16	2.761	2	P>0.05	Not Significant
			Central	120	3.22±1.271	182.05				
			Western	120	2.62±1.271	169.29				
			Total	**360**	**3.01±1.263**	----				
2.	Promotion is strictly linked to performance and seniority. **(Promotion Based on Performance and Seniority)**	Kruskal-Wallis (H) Test	Eastern	120	1.284±1.420	182.48	1.625	2	P>0.05	Not Significant
			Central	120	2.91±1.372	187.58				
			Western	120	2.70±1.464	171.44				
			Total	**360**	**2.82±1.418**	--				
3.	Total Score of Financial Factor	Kruskal-Wallis (H) Test	Eastern	120	1.82±.310	188.46	7.967	2	P<0.05	Significant
			Central	120	1.88±.291	193.90				
			Western	120	1.72±.322	159.14				
			Total	**360**	**1.79±.310**	—				

respondent (63.6 per cent) employees feel that promotion decision are not handled fairly in the organisation.

The Table 7.2 shows the analysis of financial factor on the basis of geographical location of the UP sugar mills. It reveals that regarding both the variables, i.e., remuneration and promotion based on performance and seniority, the relationship is not found to be significant at five per cent level of significance (H= 2.761, d f=2, P>0.05). However, the overall analysis indicates that there exists significant difference at five per cent level of significance. Further, the mean rank shows that employees of Central Zone are more satisfied with the financial factor (193.90) followed by Eastern Zone (188.46) and Western Zone (159.1) respectively.

7.3 Nature of Organisation-wise Analysis of Financial Factor

Table 7.3 exhibits the analysis of financial factor with nature of sugar mills in UP. Under financial factor four variables i.e., timely compensation, adequate bonus, social security benefit and fair promotion have been analysed. Chi-square test has been applied to check the association regarding the employee's perception about select variables. There is highly significant difference is found in the opinion of employees regarding timely compensation, social security benefit and fair promotion in the both private and co-operative sectors sugar mills.

Regarding timely compensation about 77.8 per cent employees of private sector sugar mill responded that they are getting timely and regular compensation while in co-operative sector only 36.7 per cent employee are agree with this and remaining 63.7 per cent employees are denied with this fact. On an overall basis about (67.5 per cent) respondent have replied that they are getting timely compensation. The Pearson Chi-square test has been applied to test the association between private and co-operative sugar mills with regards to timely compensation. The χ^2 value (52.004) is found highly significant at one per cent level of significance (P<0.001). Hence, there is highly significant difference is found in the opinion of employees about timely compensation.

In case of social security benefit, majority of respondent, 58.5 per cent from private sector reveals that they are getting social security benefit from their organisation. On the contrary, in co-operative sector sugar mills only 41.5 per cent employees are getting the social security benefits and rest are not. The χ^2 value (20.304) and corresponding P value is found less than 0.01 level. Thus, it has been found that there is significant difference exist in the practice of social security benefit between private and co-operative sugar mills.

Table 7.3: Financial Factor Analysis with Nature of Organisation (Sugar Mills)

Sl. No.	*Label*	*Test Applied*	*Crosstabs*	*Nature of Organisation*			*Value of Test*			*Inference*
				Private	*Cooperative*	*Total*	*Value*	*d.f*	*Asymp. Sig*	
1.	Do you get timely nd regular compensation/ Salary? **(Timely Compensation)**	Pearson Chi-Square	Yes	210 (77.8)	33 (36.7)	243 (67.5)	χ^2=52.004	2	P<0.001	Very Highly Significant
			No	60 (57)	57 (63.3)	117 (32.5)				
			Total	**270 (100)**	**90 (100)**	**360 (100)**				
			Descriptive	**2.43±1.246**	**1.37±.800**	**2.16±1.277**				
2.	Do you get adequate bonus beside your salary? **(Adequate Bonus)**	Pearson Chi-Square	Yes	187 (69.3)	51 (56.7)	238 (44.2)	χ^2=4.778	1	P<0.05	Significant
			No	83 (30.7)	39 (43.3)	122 (33.9)				
			Total	**270 (100)**	**90 (100)**	**360 (100)**				
			Descriptive	**1.31±.462**	**1.43±.498**	**1.34±.474**				

(Contd.)

(Contd. Table 7.3)

Sl. No.	Label	Test Applied	Crosstabs	Nature of Organisation			Value of Test			Inference
				Private	Cooperative	Total	Value	d.f	Asymp. Sig	
3.	Does the organisation provide you the social security benefits? **(Social Security Benefits)**	Pearson Chi-Square	Yes	158 (58.5)	28 (38.1)	186 (52.7)	χ^2=20.304	1	P<0.001	Very Highly Significant
			No	112 (41.5)	62 (68.9)	174 (48.3)				
			Total	**270 (100)**	**70 (100)**	**360 (100)**				
			Descriptive	**1.41±.494**	**1.69±.466**	**1.48±.500**				
4.	Are the employee promotion decision handled fairly? **(Fair Promotion)**	Pearson Chi-Square	Yes	121 (44.8)	10 (11.1)	131 (36.4)	χ^2=33.125	1	P<0.001	Very Highly Significant
			No	149 (55.2)	80 (88.9)	229 (63.6)				
			Total	**170 (100)**	**90 (100)**	**360 (100)**				
			Descriptive	**1.55±.498**	**1.89±.316**	**1.64±.482**				

Table 7.4: Financial Factor Analysis with Nature of Organisation (Sugar Mills)

Test Variable Lists	*Mill-wise Statistics*					*Mann-Whitney U Test*	*Asymp. Sig (2-tailed)*	*Inference*
	Nature of Mills	*No.*	*Descriptive*	*Mean Rank*	*Sum of Ranks*			
1. Are you satisfied with your pay package? **(Remuneration)**	Private	270	2.43±1.296	204.32	55167.00	5718.00	P<0.001	Very Highly Significant
	Co-operative	90	1.37±.800	109.03	9813.00			
2. Promotion is strictly linked to performance and seniority. **(Performance and Seniority-based Promotion)**	Private	270	3.10±1.353	200.05	54343.00	6642.00	P<0.001	Very Highly Significant
	Cooperative	90	1.97±1.267	119.30	10737.00			
3. Total Score of Financial Factor	Private	270	1.83±.319	196.03	52828.00	7957.00	P<0.001	Very Highly Significant
	Co-operative	90	1.66±.239	133.91	12052.00			

Further, regarding the fair promotion the opinion of employees are found to be very highly and significantly differing in private and co-operative sugar mill. Majority of the respondent (88.9 per cent) replied that employee's promotion decisions are not handled fairly. About 55.2 per cent employees from private sector sugar mills are agreed with this fact. The χ^2 value (33.125) and corresponding P value is found highly significant at one per cent level of significance, hence there is highly significant difference exist between the perception level of private and co-operative sector employees. The average mean score obtained by both the sector are almost same. However, about the practice of adequate bonus significant difference have been observed in both the private and co-operative sector ($P<0.05$)

The Table 7.4 analyses the two variables of financial factor, i.e., remuneration and promotion, based on performance and seniority on the basis of nature of organisation. In both the cases, the relationship is found to be very highly significant ($P<0.001$). Mean rank shows that private sector employees are more satisfied (204.32) with remuneration — compare to co-operative sector employees (109.03). In case of second variables, same perception has been found and private sector employees feel better regarding their promotion opportunity (200.5) than co-operative sector employees (119.30). Finally, in the last part of the table indicate the perception of employees regarding financial factors which again shows that the private sector employees have higher satisfaction (196.03) rather than co-operative sector employees (133.91). P value is found to be less than (0.001) level of significance. Therefore, highly significant difference is found regarding the practice of financial factor in both the nature of organisations.

7.4 Nature of Employment-wise Analysis of Financial Factor

The Table 7.5 shows the analysis of financial factor with regards to nature of employment in sugar mills, i.e., permanent and seasonal employees. Analysis has been done with the help of Chi-square test. The statistical analysis reveals that there is highly significant difference is exist in the opinion social security benefits between permanent and seasonal employees (χ^2=17.798, d.f.=1 and $P<0.001$). About 62.8 per cent permanent employees asserted that they are getting social security benefits. On the contrary, only 40.6 per cent seasonal employees are getting the same benefit and rest are not. On an overall analysis, the table shows that about (52.7 per cent) are getting the social security benefits and rest denied with this fact.

Table 7.5: Financial Factor Analysis with Nature of Employment

Sl. No.	*Label*	*Test Applied*	*Crosstabs*	*Nature of Organisation*			*Value of Test*			*Inference*
				Permanent	*Seasonal*	*Total*	*Value*	*d.f*	*Asymp.Sig*	
1.	Do you get timely and regular compensation/ Salary? **(Timely Compensation)**	Pearson Chi-Square	Yes	130 (72.2)	113 (62.8)	243 (67.5)	χ^2=3.659	1	P<0.05	Significant
			No	50 (27.0)	67 (37.2)	117 (32.5)				
			Total	**180 (100)**	**180 (100)**	**360 (100)**				
			Descriptive	**1.28±.449**	**1.37±.485**	**1.32±.469**				
2.	Do you get adequate bonus beside your salary? **(Adequate Bonus)**	Pearson Chi-Square	Yes	124 (68.9)	114 (31.1)	238 (66.1)	χ^2=1.240	1	P>0.05	Not Significant
			No	56 (63.3)	66 (36.7)	122 (33.9)				
			Total	**180 (180)**	**180 (180)**	**360 (360)**				
			Descriptive	**1.34±.464**	**1.32±.483**	**1.34±.474**				

(Contd.)

(Contd. Table 7.5)

Sl. No.	Label	Test Applied	Crosstabs	Nature of Organisation			Value of Test			Inference
				Permanent	Seasonal	Total	Value	d.f	Asymp.Sig	
3.	Does the organisation provide you the social security benefits? **(Social Security Benefits)**	Pearson Chi-Square	Yes	113 (62.8)	73 (40.6)	186. (51.7)	χ^2=17.798	1	P<0.001	Very Highly Significant
			No	67 (37.2)	107 (59.4)	174 (48.3)				
			Total	**270 (100)**	**90 (100)**	**360 (100)**				
			Descriptive	**1.37±.485**	**1.59±.492**	**1.48±.500**				
4.	Are the employee promotion decision handled fairly? **(Fair Promotion)**	Pearson Chi-Square	Yes	76 (42.2)	55 (30.6)	131 (36.4)	χ^2=5.292	1	P<0.05	Significant
			No	104 (57.8)	125 (69.4)	229 (63.6)				
			Total	**180 (100)**	**90 (100)**	**360 (100)**				
			Descriptive	**1.58±.495**	**1.69±.462**	**1.64±.482**				

Table 7.6: Financial Factor Analysis with Nature of Employment (Sugar Mills)

Test Variable Lists	*Mill-wise Statistics*					*Mann-Whitney U Test*	*Asymp.Sig (2-tailed)*	*Inference*
	Nature of Mills	*No.*	*Descriptive*	*Mean Rank*	*Sum of Ranks*			
1. Are you satisfied with your pay package? **(Remuneration)**	Permanent	180	2.59±1.397	209.90	37782.00	10908.00	P<0.001	Very Highly Significant
	Seasonal	180	1.73±.972	151.10	27198.00			
2. Promotion is strictly linked to performance and seniority. **(Promotion-based on performance and seniority)**	Permanent	180	3.01±1.449	194.36	34985.00	13704.500	P<0.05	Significant
	Seasonal	180	2.62±1.363	166.64	29994.5			
3. **Total Score of Financial Factor**	Permanent	180	1.83±.319	201.73	36311.50	12378.50	P<0.001	Very Highly Significant
	Seasonal	180	1.66±.239	159.27	28688.50			

There is also significant difference has been observed regarding the perception of timely compensation and fair promotion. In case of timely compensation (72.2 per cent) permanent employees reveals that they are getting timely and regular compensation while (62.8 per cent) seasonal employees are agree with this fact. However, in total about 67.5 per cent employees are getting timely compensation and rests are not. The value of χ^2 (3.569) is found significant at five per cent level of significance ($P<0.005$). Similarly, the perceptions of employees regarding fair promotion seems to differ in both the nature of employment at five per cent level of significance. Overall (63.6 per cent) employees are said that promotion policy is not handled fairly. About (69.4 per cent) seasonal employees area greed this fact followed by (57.8 per cent) permanent employees.

However, regarding the adequate bonus no significant difference is found between the perception of permanent and seasonal employees. About 68.9 per cent permanent employees revealed that they are getting adequate bonus. On the contrary, majority of seasonal employees (63.3 per cent) responded that they are not getting adequate bonus.

The Table 7.6 reveals the analysis of financial factor with regards to nature of employment sugar mills, i.e., permanent and seasonal employees. Analysis has been done with the help of Mann-Whitney U test. The analysis of above table depicts that in case of remuneration, the perception of employees is to be found very highly and significantly differing. The descriptive statistics reveals that the permanent employees are neither satisfy nor dissatisfied (2.59± 1.397) with the remuneration or pay package they are getting. On the contrary, seasonal employees are almost dissatisfied with their compensation package. The result of Mann-Whitney U test (10908.00) is found significant at (0.001) level of significance. Further, regarding the promotion policy of sugar mills, the permanent employees are more satisfied (194.36) than the seasonal employees (166.64). The value of Mann-Whitney U test (13704.500) is found significant at five per cent level of significance. However, overall analysis again shows that the permanent employees are more satisfied with the financial factor (201.73) than the seasonal employees (159.27). The difference is found to be very highly significant ($P<0.001$).

7.5 Analysis of Financial Factor with Select Demographic Variables

The Table 7.7 depicts the Perception Score of Financial Factor with Select Demographic variables, i.e., experience, income level, educational level and age. One way Analysis of Variance is used to compare the means

Table 7.7: Distributions of Total Perception Score of Financial Factor with Select Demographics

Factor	*Descriptive Statistics*			*Test Used*	*Test Value*			*Inference*
	N	Mean ± SD	Range		**df**	**F**	**Comparison**	
Experiences								
1-5	21	11.09±1.57	7-14					
5-10	60	11.36±1.87	7-15					
10-15	86	10.37±1.73	7-14	One-Way ANOVA	4	2.831	$P<0.05$	Significant
15-20	97	10.64±1.82	8-15					
>20	96	10.78±1.92	7-18					
Total	**360**	**10.76±1.86**	**7-18**		**Decision: In case of experiences H_0 can't be accepted**			
Income Level								
<10,000	139	10.31±1.64	7-16	One-way ANOVA	2	17.838	$P<0.001$	Very Highly Significant
10000-20000	177	10.76±1.86	7-18					
>20000	44	12.15±1.87	8-15					
Total	**360**	**10.76±1.86**	**7-18**		**Decision: In case of Income Level H_0 can't be accepted**			
Educational Level								
VI-VIII Standard	14	10.57±1.34	9-14					
Matriculation	35	10.28±1.46	8-14	One-Way ANOVA	5	3.421	$P<0.05$	Significant
Intermediate	51	10.45±1.91	7-15					
Graduation	156	11.65±1.72	7-18					
Post-graduate	48	10.68±2.07	7-15					
Others	56	10.91±1.77	7-15					
Total	**360**	**10.76±1.86**	**7-18**		**Decision: In case of Educational Level H_0 can't be accepted**			

(Contd.)

(Contd. Table 7.7)

Factor	*Descriptive Statistics*			*Test Used*	*Test Value*			*Inference*
Age								
<30	26	11.00±1.71	8-15	One-way ANOVA	3	1.783	P>0.05	Not Significant
30-40	88	10.79±1.97	7-15					
40-50	148	10.93±1.83	7-18					
>50	98	10.40±1.81	7-15					
Total	**360**	**10.76±1.86**	**7-18**	**Decision: In case of Age H_0 can be accepted**				

of more than two groups. F-probability of appropriate significance level is considered to determine the significance of the test. Regarding the experience, the result of the one-way ANOVA given in above table shows that the calculated value of F (2.831) for four degrees of freedom is found significant at 0.05 level ($P<0.05$). Therefore, significant difference is found to exist in the mean scores of financial factor between the group pairs categorised on the basis of experience. Therefore, the job experience may be considered as an influencing variable of QWL in the sugar mills.

However, in the case of income level, the F-value (5.426) is found very highly significant at 0.001 level of significance ($P<0.001$). Therefore, there is significant difference exist regarding the perception of financial factor. The employees of income level more than Rs. 20000 have shown the highest satisfaction (12.15 ± 1.87) regarding financial factor followed by income group of Rs. 10,000-20,000 (10.76 ± 1.86). Thus, it can be inferred that higher income level leads to better quality of work life.

In case of Educational level, result of the one-way ANOVA shown in table also reveals that the calculated value of F value (3.421) and corresponding P value is found significant at 0.05 levels. Therefore, significant difference is found to exist in the mean score of financial factor among the educational level group. The employees who belongs to graduation level obtained the highest satisfaction score (11.65 ± 1.72) regarding financial factor followed by others (10.91 ± 1.77) and Post-graduate level (10.68 ± 2.07) respective. Thus, educational level of employees can be considered as an impotent variable that affects the financial factor of quality of work life.

Regarding the age group of employees the result of the one-way ANOVA given in table shows that the calculated value of F-value (1.783) and corresponding P value is found more than 0.05 levels at three degrees of freedom. Therefore, no significant difference is found to exist in the mean score of financial factor between the group pairs categorised on the basis of age. Therefore, it may be concluded that the Age group of employees does not have any impact of financial factor of quality of work life.

Conclusions

In this chapter, an endeavour has been made to analyse the six variables of financial factor which affect the quality of working life in sugar industry. The analysis has been done on the basis of three major criteria, i.e., (i) geographical location-wise analysis; (ii) nature of organisation-wise analysis; and nature of employment-wise analysis. The above analysis of factors affecting quality of work life reveals that:

1. There is highly significant difference have been observed in the practice of two variables namely, timely compensation and adequate bonus among Eastern, Central and Western Zone of sugar mills. Further, no significant difference was observed in the case of remuneration, social security benefits and fair promotion. However, overall score of financial factor is also differing significantly, Zone-wise. The employees of Central Zone are more satisfied with the financial factor followed by Eastern Zone and Western Zone respectively.

2. There is very highly significant difference have been found regarding the perception of remuneration, timely compensation, performance and seniority-based promotion, social security benefits and fair promotion between private and co-operative sugar mills employees. The private sector employees have shown higher satisfaction with financial factor than the co-operative sector employees.

3. The nature of employment-wise analysis divulge that here is significant difference is exist in the perception of permanent and seasonal employees regarding the issues of remuneration, timely compensation, promotion based on performance and seniority, social security benefit, fair promotion. The overall score of financial factor are also differing significantly. The statistical analysis shows that permanent employees are more satisfied with the financial factor than the seasonal employees.

4. The Table 7.7 of this chapter shows that there is significant impact of income level, job experience and education level on the financial factor of quality of work life.

References

Anitha, B., and Rao, Subba (1998). *Quality of Work Life in Commercial Banks*, Discovery Publishing House, New Delhi, 17.

Green, F. (2006). Demanding Work. The paradox of Job Quality in the Affluent Economy Princeton, NJ: Princeton University Press.

International Labour Office (1984) "Introduction to Social Security", Geneva,p.3.

8

Factors of QWL–An Effectiveness and Impact Analysis

8.1 Introduction

Analysis and interpretation are central steps in the research process. The aim of the analysis is to organise, classify and summarise the collected data so that they can be better comprehended and interpreted to give answers to the questions that triggered the research interpretation is the search for the broader meaning of research findings. Analysis is not fulfilled without interpretation; and interpretation cannot proceed without analysis. So, both are interdependent.

This chapter deals with the overall impact, analysis of quality of work life (QWL). It has been divided into two sections. In the first phase, the main effects of work environment variables, relational variables, job variables and financial variables are studied separately by using standard (simultaneous) Regression Analysis. In the second phase, overall thirty six variables from four factors namely, working environment, relational, job and financial related factors have been considered as independent variables and its impact on five variables namely, employees productivity, workers participation in management, job satisfaction, motivation and organisational loyalty are analysed using binary logistic regression, and the ordinal regression model.

8.2 First Phase of Impact Factor Analysis

Regression models are created to understand the impact of work environment variables, relational variables, job variables and financial variables on overall QWL. Standard (simultaneous) Regression method is used to examine the relationship between dependent variable and independent variables.

Fig. 8.1. Extraction of Quality of Work Life Variables.

Table 8.1: Model Summary: 1-Working Environment with Total Score of QWL

Model	*R*	*Adjusted R Square*	*Std. Error of the estimate*	*Significance F Change*	*F*	*Sig.*	*Durbin Watson*
1	.842[a]	.700	5.688	.000	84.900	0.000	1.876

(a) Predictors: (Constant), Workplace stress, Supervisor interference, Type of welfare facilities, Health facilities, Level of temperature, safety measures, Comfortable work space, Working conditions, Lighting facilities, and Quality of welfare facilities.

(b) Dependent Variable: Total score of QWL

To find out the impact of work environment factor on total score of QWL or to test the hypothesis 1; standard (simultaneous) regression

Table 8.2: Coefficient of Model-1

Model-I	*Unstandardised Coefficient*		*Standardised Coefficient*	*t*	*Sig.*	*Collinearity Statistics*	
	β	*Std. Error*	*Beta*			*Tolerance*	*VIF*
Constant	47.667	2.769	–	17.212	.000	–	–
Comfortable Work Space	.590	.737	.027	.801	.424	.738	1.355
Lighting Facilities	2.757	.401	.241	6.577	.000	.678	1.475
Level of Temperature	-.514	.801	-.021	-.641	.522	.789	1.268
Safety Measures	3.139	.402	.274	7.799	.000	.676	1.480
Health Facilities	1.146	.266	.146	4.309	.000	.732	1.367
Working Condition	1.730	.276	.211	6.257	.000	.735	1.360
Type of welfare Facilities	.582	.274	.065	2.125	.034	.899	1.113
Quality of Welfare facilities	3.479	.421	.302	8.268	.000	.625	1.600
Supervisor Interference	.411	.359	.034	1.144	.254	.962	1.039
Workplace stress	2.483	.654	.119	3.797	.000	.846	1.182

analysis method is used. The Table 8.1 has shown the result of model summary. The correlation coefficient is (+842). The adjusted R^2 of the model is 700 which imply that the predictor variables explain 70 per cent of the variance in the quality of work life (QWL), and the result is found to be statistically significant at the level of 0.001. Further, in the Table 8.2 all the variables of work environment are shown with their respective regression co-efficient (Beta) and computed '*t*' statistics along with their respective significance level. The result of regression analysis reveals that out of ten variables, six variables, lighting facilities, safety measures, health facilities, working condition, quality of welfare facilities and workplace stress are statistically found to be significant at one per cent level of significance. The six variables have positive and significant relationship with QWL in which lighting facilities explain (24 per cent), safety measures (27.4 per cent), health facilities (14.6 per cent), working condition (21 per cent), quality of welfare facilities (30.2 per cent) and workplace stress (11.9 per cent) respectively of total variance. On the other hand, comfortable work space, type of welfare facilities and supervisor interference has no significant relationship with QWL. The finding also reveals that the variable such as level of temperature is exhibit the negative relationship with quality of work life. Therefore, it is inferred that working environment factor significantly influence QWL in a positive way and QWL is radically dependent on these six variables simultaneously.

Table 8.3: Model Summary: 2 – Relational Factor with Total Score of QWL

Model	*R*	*Adjusted R Square*	*Std. Error of the estimate*	*Significance F Change*	*F*	*Sig.*	*Durbin Watson*
1	.845[a]	.707	5.628	.000	97.127	0.000	1.557

(a) Predictors: (Constant), Management Attitude, Colleague's Relationship Quality of Supervision, Individual Respect, Superior's Relationship, Industrial Relations, Supervisory Support, Supervisory Relationship, Role of Trade Union.

(b) Dependent Variable: Total score of QWL.

To test the relationship between the variables of relational factor on total score of QWL Standard (Simultaneous) Regression Analysis has been used. The above Table 8.3 has shown the result of model summary. The correlation of coefficient is (+.845). The adjusted R-square of the model is .707 which demonstrates that the predictor variables explain 70.7

Table 8.4: Coefficient of Model-2

Model-2	*Unstandardised Coefficient*		*Standardised Coefficient*	*t*	*Sig.*	*Collinearity Statistics*	
	β	*Std. Error*	*Beta*			*Tolerance*	*VIF*
Constant	39.111	2.226	--	17.572	.000	–	--
Quality of Supervision	.980	.259	.114	3.789	.000	.896	1.116
Supervisory Support	2.217	.320	.226	6.918	.000	.769	1.301
Colleagues' Relationship	.759	.449	.054	1.691	.092	.808	1.238
Supervisory Relationship	.794	.643	.042	1.234	.218	.709	1.410
Superior's Relationship	1.839	.367	.159	5.011	.000	.810	1.235
Individual Respect	1.242	.266	.147	4.675	.000	.827	1.209
Industrial Relations	1.220	.296	.138	4.113	.000	.724	1.382
Role of Trade Union	2.139	.289	.253	7.406	.000	.702	1.424
Management Attitude	3.083	.366	.290	8430	.000	.691	1.447

per cent of the variance in the quality of work life (QWL), and the result is found to be statistically significant at the level of 0.001. Further, in the co-efficient Table 8.4 all the variables of relational factor are shown with their respective regression co-efficient (Beta) and computed *'t'* statistics along with their respective significance level. The result of regression analysis shows that out of nine variables, seven variables are found to be very positively and significantly related with quality of work life. These are: quality of supervision, supervisory support, superiors' relationship, individual respect, industrial relations, role of trade union and management attitude. These seven variables are statistically significant at the level of 0.001. Quality of supervision has positive and significant impact on QWL which explain 11.4 per cent of the total variance. Similarly, supervisory support has positive impact with quality of work life that explained about 22.6 per cent of the total variance. In the same way, superiors' relationship (15.9 per cent), Individual respect (14.7 per cent), industrial relation (13.8 per cent), role of trade union (25.3 per cent) and management attitude (29 per cent) respectively explained of the total variance. On the contrary, colleagues' relationship and supervisor's relationship have no significant relationship with QWL. Therefore, it is inferred that relational factor significantly influence QWL in a positive way and QWL is fundamentally dependent on these seven variables simultaneously.

Table 8.5: Model Summary: 3 - Job Factor with Total Score of QWL

Model	*R*	*Adjusted R Square*	*Std. Error of the estimate*	*Significance F Change*	*F*	*Sig.*	*Durbin Watson*
3	.825[a]	.670	5.972	0.000	67.202	0.000	1.848

(a) Predictors: (Constant), Work dissatisfaction, Work Life Balance, Work schedule, Job retention, Additional responsibility, Flexi-hours, Employees interest, Technological support, Autonomy, Adequate training and Job security.

(b) Dependent Variable: Total score of QWL

From Table 8.6 it is observed that the variables of job factor account for about 67 per cent of the total variance in the quality of work life ($R^2 = .670, F = 67.202, p < 0.001$). The model is statistically found to be significant at 0.001 levels. Further, in the co-efficient Table 8.6 all the variables of job

Table 8.6: Coefficient of Model-3

Model-3	*Unstandardised Coefficient*		*Standardised Coefficient*	*t*	*Sig.*	*Collinearity Statistics*	
	β	*Std. Error*	*Beta*			*Tolerance*	*VIF*
Constant	45.143	3.138	–	14.386	.000	–	–
Job retention	2.344	.547	.137	4.283	.000	.897	1.114
Technological Support	-.477	.717	-.023	-.665	.507	.782	1.279
Adequate training	2.014	.275	.275	7.332	.000	.655	1.526
Employees Interest	3.989	.503	.273	7.930	.000	.775	1.290
Additional responsibility	1.336	.288	.151	4.645	.000	.866	1.154
Autonomy	2.234	.315	.246	7.093	.000	.763	1.310
Work Life Balance	-.817	.867	-.031	-.943	-.346	.824	1.213
Flexi-Hours	.756	.701	.036	1.078	.282	.807	1.239
Work Schedule	1.010	.374	.086	2.700	.007	.898	1.113
Job Security	2.882	.397	.273	7.259	.000	.648	1.542
Work Dissatisfaction	1.774	.253	.228	7.011	.000	.872	1.146

factor are shown with their respective regression co-efficient (Beta) and computed *'t'* statistics along with their respective significance level. The result of regression analysis shows that seven variables of job factor have positive and significant effect on QWL. These are; job rotation (ß = .137, p< 0.001), adequate training (ß = .275, p< 0.001), employees interest (ß = .273, p< 0.001) additional responsibility (ß= .151, p< 0.001), work schedule (ß = .086, p< 0.05), job security (ß = .273, p< 0.001) and work dissatisfaction (ß = .228, p< 0.001). The finding also reveals that the variables such as technological support and work life balance exhibit the negative relationship with quality of work life.

Table 8.7: Model Summary: 4 - Financial Factor with Total Score of QWL

Model	*R*	*Adjusted R Square*	*Std. Error of the estimate*	*Significance F Change*	*F*	*Sig.*	*Durbin Watson*
4	.694	.473	7.547	.000	54.656	.000	1.897

(a) Predictors: (Constant), Performance-based promotion, Adequate bonus, Regular compensation, Social security benefits, Remuneration, and Fair promotion.

(b) Dependent Variable: Total score of QWL

Table 8.8: Coefficient of Model-4

Model-3	*Unstandardised Coefficient*		*Standardised Coefficient*	*t*	*Sig.*	*Collinearity Statistics*	
	β	*Std. Error*	*Beta*			*Tolerance*	*VIF*
Constant	72.780	3.315	--	21.957	.000	--	--
Remuneration	3.393	.375	.417	9.056	.000	.693	1.442
Regular Compensation	.447	.951	.020	.470	.639	.798	1.253
Adequate Bonus	-.513	.868	-.023	-.591	.555	.938	1.066
Social Security Benefits	-.490	.952	-.024	-.515	.607	.699	1.430
Fair Promotion	-.016	1.156	.000	-.014	.989	.512	1.953
Performance based Promotion	2.864	.391	.391	7.327	.000	.517	1.936

From the regression analysis (Table 8.8), the adjusted R square value is found to be to be .473 meaning thereby, financial factor count about 42.5 per cent of the variability in the quality of work life of employees. The result is statistically found to be significant at one per cent level of significance. Further, the co-efficient table reports that out of six variables only two variables have significant and positive relationship with quality of work life. Remuneration (pay-package) has positive and significant impact on QWL which explain 41.7 per cent of the total variance (ß = .417, p< 0.001). Similarly, performance has positive impact with quality of work life that explained about 39.1 per cent of the total variance (ß = .417, p< 0.001). On the contrary, four variables such as regular compensation, adequate bonus, social security benefit and fair promotion have no significant impact on quality of work life.

8.3 Second Phase of Impact Factor Analysis

In this segment, overall thirty six variables from four factors namely, working environment, relational, job and financial related factors have been considered as independent variables and its impact on five variables namely, employees productivity, workers participation in management, job satisfaction, motivation and organisational loyalty are analysed using binary logistic regression, and the ordinal regression model.

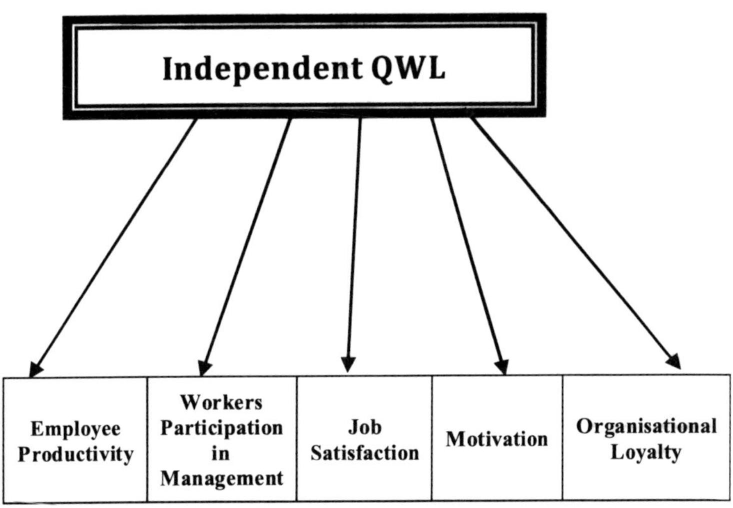

Fig. 8.2. Dependent QWL Variables.

8.3.1 Impact of Multiple Independent QWL Variables on Employees Productivity (Binary Logistic Regression Analysis)

Current American Psychological Association research findings show that people want contentment, love and happiness derived from meaningful work. They want nourishing personal relationships, a healthy mind and body, a spiritual core and a reason for living (Tam Marilyn, 2013). QWL stimulates the employee job satisfaction (Ruzevicius, 2007), and is essential for improving organisational and operational productivity (Sink and Tuttle, 1989).

To understand influence of independent QWL variables on employees' productivity logistic regression analysis have been used. The data of the study strongly support the logistic regression analysis:

- Logistic regression does not assume a linear relationship between the dependent and independent variables.
- The dependent variable must be a dichotomy (2 categories).
- The independent variables need not be interval, nor normally distributed, nor linearly related, nor of equal variance within each group.
- The categories (groups) must be mutually exclusive and exhaustive; a case can only be in one group and every case must be a member of one of the groups.
- Larger samples are needed than for linear regression because maximum likelihood coefficients are large sample estimates. A minimum of 50 cases per predictor is recommended.

Logistic regression is useful for situations when is to predict the presence or absence of a characteristic or outcome based on values of a set of predictor variables. It is similar to a linear regression model but is suited to models where the dependent variable is dichotomous. Logistic regression coefficients can be used to estimate odds ratios for each of the independent variables in the model. Logistic regression is applicable to a broader range of research situations than discriminant analysis.

The first Table 8.9 (Omnibus Tests of Models Coefficients) gives general tests of how well the models performs. The Chi-square of 202.679

Table 8.9: Omnibus Tests of Model Coefficients

Step 1	*Chi-square*	*d.f*	*Sig.*
Step	202.679	36	.000
Block	202.679	36	.000
Model	202.679	36	.000

on 36 d.f, significant beyond .001. This is a test of the null hypothesis that adding the QWL variables to the model has not significantly increased an ability to predict the decisions made by our subjects.

Table 8.10: Model Summary

Step	*-2 Log likelihood*	*Cox & Snell R Square*	*Nagelkerke R Square*
1	279.352[a]	.431	.583

Statistical Significance: Although there is no close analogous statistic in logistic regression to the coefficient of determination $\mathbf{R^2}$ the Model Summary (Table 8.10) provides some approximations. ***Cox and Snell's R-Square*** attempts to imitate multiple R-Square based on 'likelihood', but its maximum can be (and usually is) less than 1.0, making it difficult to interpret. Here, it is indicating that 43 per cent of the variation in the DV is explained by the logistic model. The *Nagelkerke* modification that does range from 0 to 1 is a more reliable measure of the relationship. *Nagelkerke's* R^2 will normally be higher than the *Cox and Snell* measure. *Nagelkerke's* R^2 is part of SPSS output in the 'Model Summary' table; 2 and is the most-reported of the *R*-squared estimates. In this case it is .583, indicating a moderately strong relationship of 58.3 per cent between the predictors and the prediction.

Another statistical test that is used is the *Hosmer and Lemeshow goodness of fit,* which test how well the model fit. Lack of significance on this test is a good thing-in this case (Table 8.11), with a significance value of .108, the test is completely insignificant, meaning that there is no significant difference between the model predictions and observed values.

Table 8.11: Hosmer and Lemeshow Test

Step	*Chi-square*	*df*	*Sig.*
1	13.099	8	.108

In classification Table 8.12, which summarise the results of prediction about employees' productivity-based on thirty-six (36) QWL issues in targetted sugar mills in UP. It can be observed that the model correctly predicts 85.8 per cent of employees' positive opinion (yes) towards enhancing productivity and 75.9 per cent in negative response (No). Overall the model predicts 81.9 per cent of the cases correctly.

Table 8.12: Classification Table[a]

Step 1	*Observed*		*Predicted*		
			Whether available facilities help you to enhance the productivity?		*Percentage correct*
			Yes	*No*	
	Whether available facilities help you to enhance the productivity?	Yes	188	31	85.8
		No	34	107	75.9
	Overall Percentage				81.9
(a) The cut value is .500					

The variables in the equation table (Table: 8.13) has several important elements. The Wald statistic and associated probabilities provide an index of the significance of each predictor in the equation. The Wald statistic has a Chi-square distribution. The simplest way to assess Wald is to take the significance values and if less than .05 reject the null hypothesis as the variable does make a significant contribution. In this case, it can be noted that level of temperature, working conditions, and qualities of welfare facilities, workplace stress, supervisory relationship, regular compensation, adequate bonus, fair compensation and performance-based promotion contributed significantly to the prediction.

8.3.2 Impact of Multiple Independent QWL Variables on Workers Participation in Management (Binary Logistic Regression Analysis)

Participation refers to the mental and emotional involvement of a person in a group situation which encourages him to contribute goals and share in the responsibility of achieving them (Keith Davis, 1975). To understand whether existing practices of QWL really induce workers to participate voluntarily in decision-making process. In similar to last model thirty six QWL issues impact on workers participation in management have been examined by using Binary logistic regression analysis. In our case, model Chi-square (Table 8.14) has 36 degrees of freedom, a value of 222.747 and a probability of $p < 0.000$. Thus, the indication is that the model has a good fit, with the model containing only the constant indicating that the predictors do have a significant effect and create essentially a different model.

For regression models with a categorical dependent variable, it is not possible to compute a single R^2 statistic that has all of the characteristics

Table 8.13: Variables in the Equation

Variables	*Step 1[a]*	*β*	*S.E.*	*Wald*	*df*	*Sig.*	*Exp(β)*
Comfortable Workspace	WEF1	.285	.366	.605	1	.437	1.329
Lighting Facilities	WEF2	.001	.218	.000	1	.995	1.001
Level of Temperature	WEF3	.896	.422	4.507	1	.034	2.451
Safety Measures	WEF4	.296	.225	1.729	1	.189	1.344
Health Facilities	WEF5	-.281	.155	3.293	1	.070	.755
Working Condition	WEF6	.594	.169	12.293	1	.000	1.810
Type of Welfare Facilities	WEF7	-.181	.146	1.537	1	.215	.835
Qualities of Welfare facilities	WEF8	-.493	.250	3.896	1	.048	.611
Supervisor Interference	WEF9	-.040	.209	.036	1	.849	.961
Workplace Stress	WEF10	-.864	.339	6.504	1	.011	.421
Supervision Quality	RF1	-.246	.150	2.668	1	.102	.782
Supervisory Support	RF2	-.129	.185	.483	1	.487	.879
Colleagues Relationship	RF3	.056	.252	.050	1	.823	1.058
Supervisory Relationship	RF4	.904	.365	6.134	1	.013	2.469
Superior's Relationship	RF5	.011	.206	.003	1	.958	1.011
Individual respect	RF6	-.286	.153	3.497	1	.061	.751
Industrial relations	RF7	-.254	.156	2.639	1	.104	.776
Role of trade union	RF8	.129	.172	.564	1	.452	1.138

(Contd.)

(Contd. Table 8.13)

Variables	*Step 1*[a]	β	*S.E.*	*Wald*	*df*	*Sig.*	*Exp(β)*
Management Attitude	RF9	.141	.208	.457	1	.499	1.151
Job retention	JF1	-.433	.304	2.034	1	.154	.648
Technological Support	JF2	-.092	.366	.063	1	.802	.912
Adequate Training	JF3	.271	.149	3.289	1	.070	1.311
Employees Interest	JF4	-.028	.267	.011	1	.915	.972
Additional responsibility	JF5	.041	.150	.077	1	.782	1.042
Autonomy	JF6	-.296	.168	3.118	1	.077	.744
Work life Balance	JF7	-.014	.453	.001	1	.975	.986
Flexi Hours	JF8	-.124	.376	.109	1	.742	.883
Work schedule	JF9	-.284	.199	2.043	1	.153	.753
Job Security	JF10	-.074	.213	.121	1	.728	.929
Work Dissatisfaction	JF11	.118	.133	.790	1	.374	1.125
Remuneration	FF1	-.266	.187	2.034	1	.154	.766
Regular Compensation	FF2	1.101	.356	9.554	1	.002	3.007
Adequate Bonus	FF3	.759	.383	3.917	1	.048	2.136
Social Security benefits	FF4	.332	.368	.813	1	.367	1.393
Fair Promotion	FF5	.994	.467	4.536	1	.033	2.703
Performance based Promotion	FF6	-.561	.154	13.283	1	.000	.571
	Constant	-2.574	2.54	1.026	1	.311	.076

Table 8.14: Omnibus Tests of Model Coefficients

Step 1	*Chi-square*	*df*	*Sig.*
Step	222.747	36	.000
Block	222.747	36	.000
Model	222.747	36	.000

of R^2 in the linear regression model, so these approximations are computed instead. The following methods (Table 8.15) are used to estimate the coefficient of determination. What constitutes a "good" R^2 value varies between different areas of application. While these statistics can be suggestive on their own, they are most useful when comparing competing models for the same data. The model with the largest R^2 statistic is "best" according to this measure. *Nagelkerke's R^2* will normally be higher than the *Cox and Snell* measure. *Nagelkerke's R^2* is the most-reported of the R-squared estimates. In this case it is 0.617 (Table 8.15), indicating a moderate relationship of 61.7 per cent between the predictors and the prediction.

Table 8.15: Model Summary

Step	*-2 Log likelihood*	*Cox & Snell R Square*	*Nagelkerke R Square*
1	273.471[a]	.461	.617

a. Estimation terminated at iteration number 6 because parameter estimates changed by less than .001.

The high p-value (.108) on the Hosmer and Lemeshow Test (Table 8.16) suggests that it is extremely likely that there is no significant difference between the model predictions and observed values, indicating a good model.

Table 8.16: Hosmer and Lemeshow Test

Step	*Chi-square*	*df*	*Sig.*
1	13.118	8	.108

Rather than using a goodness-of-fit statistic, the table (8.17) shows the proportion of cases to classify correctly. The table shows how many of the cases where the observed values of the dependent variable were 1 or 0 respectively have been correctly predicted. In the Classification table (Table 8.17), the columns are the two predicted values of the dependent, while the rows are the two observed (actual) values of the dependent. In a

Table 8.17: Classification Table[a]

Step 1	*Observed*		*Predicted*		
			Does the management provide opportunities to workers in decision-making process?		*Percentage Correct*
			Yes	*No*	
	Does the management provide opportunites to workers in decision-making process?	Yes	132	32	80.5
		No	29	167	85.2
	Overall Percentage				83.1
(a) The cut value is .500					

perfect model, all cases will be on the diagonal and the overall per cent correct will be 100 per cent. In this study, 80.5 per cent were correctly classified for *the yes* group and 85.2 per cent for *the no* group. Overall 83.1 per cent were correctly classified.

The last table gives Beta coefficients for the independent variables along with their significance. The Wald criterion (Table 8.18) demonstrated that seven variables namely, supervisory support, industrial relations,

Table 8.18: Variables in the Equation

Variable	*Step 1[a]*	*β*	*S.E.*	*Wald*	*df*	*Sig.*	*Exp (β)*
Comfortable Workspace	WEF1	-.259	.369	.492	1	.483	.772
Lighting Facilities	WEF2	-.238	.245	.947	1	.331	.788
Level of Temperature	WEF3	.498	.455	1.197	1	.274	1.645
Safety Measures	WEF4	-.095	.234	.165	1	.685	.909
Health Facilities	WEF5	-.250	.156	2.588	1	.108	.778
Working Condition	WEF6	.089	.158	.319	1	.572	1.093
Type of Welfare Facilities	WEF7	.166	.162	1.047	1	.306	1.180
Qualities of Welfare facilities	WEF8	-.191	.254	.561	1	.454	.826

(Contd.)

(Contd. Table 8.18)

Variable	*Step 1*[a]	*β*	*S.E.*	*Wald*	*df*	*Sig.*	*Exp (β)*
Supervisor Interference	WEF9	-.004	.214	.000	1	.985	.996
Workplace Stress	WEF10	.294	.349	.707	1	.400	1.341
Supervision Quality	RF1	-.096	.152	.399	1	.527	.909
Supervisory Support	RF2	-.748	.246	9.284	1	.002	.473
Colleagues Relationship	RF3	-.368	.257	2.056	1	.152	.692
Supervisory Relationship	RF4	.268	.362	.550	1	.458	1.307
Superior's Relationship	RF5	.349	.199	3.080	1	.079	1.418
Individual respect	RF6	.139	.165	.708	1	.400	1.149
Industrial relations	RF7	-.493	.169	8.515	1	.004	.611
Role of trade union	RF8	.222	.174	1.626	1	.202	1.249
Management Attitude	RF9	-.429	.211	4.142	1	.042	.651
Job retention	JF1	-.068	.299	.052	1	.819	.934
Technological Support	JF2	1.074	.356	9.098	1	.003	2.928
Adequate Training	JF3	-.081	.156	.271	1	.603	.922
Employees Interest	JF4	.084	.285	.086	1	.769	1.087
Additional responsibility	JF5	.257	.169	2.298	1	.130	1.293
Autonomy	JF6	-.529	.196	7.309	1	.007	.589
Work life Balance	JF7	-.184	.504	.133	1	.716	.832
Flexi Hours	JF8	.096	.351	.075	1	.784	1.101
Work schedule	JF9	-.129	.212	.367	1	.545	.879
Job Security	JF10	-.293	.210	1.943	1	.163	.746
Work Dissatisfaction	JF11	-.131	.134	.961	1	.327	.877
Remuneration	FF1	.020	.169	.015	1	.904	1.021
Regular Compensation	FF2	.638	.379	2.830	1	.093	1.892
Adequate Bonus	FF3	.094	.383	.060	1	.806	1.099
Social Security benefits	FF4	.246	.393	.391	1	.532	1.278
Fair Promotion	FF5	.950	.420	5.109	1	.024	2.586
Performance-based Promotion	FF6	-.340	.155	4.772	1	.029	.712
	Constant	4.392	2.571	2.917	1	.088	80.777

management attitude, technological support, autonomy, fair promotion and performance-based promotion made a significant contribution to prediction.

8.3.3 Impact of Multiple Independent QWL Variables on Job Satisfaction (The Ordinal Regression Model)

Job satisfaction can be understood by explaining people want to come to work. Locke (1976) defined job satisfaction as "a positive emotional state resulting from the appraisal of one's job or job experiences". Though various researchers identified it in different ways and conclude that it's a combination of physiological, psychological and environmental circumstances, the result of this combination is a person's job satisfaction. Job satisfaction in recent year has become associated with quality of work life movement (http://ezinearticles.com). Many researchers have studied the relationship between organisational support and work-life quality of workers and have found it to have a positive impact on job satisfaction (Rhoades and Eisenberger, 2002; Dixon and Sagas, 2007). For measuring the influence of thirty six (36) select QWL initiatives on job satisfaction the ordinal regression analysis have been performed. Before application of regression analysis using PLUM (**Polytomous Universal Model)** the assumption of the model has been kept into consideration.

Prior to conducting ordinal regression the details of thirty-six independent variables have been examined with their marginal percentage (Table 8.18). The case processing summary also highlights opinions of target respondents in select variables. The predictive value of the model i.e., model fitting information gives the – 2 likelihood (-2ll, Table 8.19) values for the base line and the final model, and SPSS performs a Chi-square test the difference between the -2LL for the two models. The significant Chi-square statistic ($p<.001$) indicates that the final model gives a significant improvement over the baseline intercept only model. This tells that the model gives better predictions than the guessed based on the marginal probabilities for the outcome categories.

The next table in the output is the Goodness-of-Fit (Table 8.21). This table contains Pearson's Chi-square statistic for the model and another Chi-square statistic based on the deviance. These statistics are intended to test whether the observed data are inconsistent with the fitted model. If they are not-that is, if the significance values are large-then it would be concluded that the data and the model predictions are similar and that you have a good model. In this case p value is very large and it can be concluded that absolutely significant and the assumption of good fit is to be accepted.

Another useful statistics for measuring goodness of fit is pseudo R^2 statistics which for ordinal regression models is not possible to compute the same R^2 statistic as in linear regression so three approximations are

Table 8.19: Case Processing Summary

Variable	*Scale*	*No.*	*Marginal Percentage*	*Variable*	*Level*	*No.*	*Marginal Percentage*
Job satisfaction (Dependent Variable)	Highly dissatisfied	41	11.4	Working condition	Strongly agree	41	11.4
	Dissatisfied	131	36.4		Agree	133	36.9
	Unknown	03	8		Unknown	06	1.7
	Satisfied	154	42.8		Disagree	147	40.8
	Highly satisfied	31	8.6		Strongly disagree	33	9.2
Comfortable Workspace	Yes	238	66.1	Type of welfare facilities	Housing/recreation/Medical/ Canteen	220	61.1
	No	122	33.9		Housing/recreation/Medical/	76	21.1
Lighting Facilities	Strongly disagree	09	2.5		Canteen	19	5.3
	Disagree	30	8.3		Medical	27	7.8
	Unknown	04	1.1		None	17	4.7
	Agree	225	62.5	Quality of welfare facilities	Poor	82	22.8
	Strongly agree	92	25.6		Satisfactory	162	95
Level of Temperature	Yes	227	76.9		Good	80	22.2
	No	83	23.1		Excellent	36	10

(Contd.)

(Contd. Table 8.19)

Variable	*Scale*	*No.*	*Marginal Percentage*	*Variable*	*Level*	*No.*	*Marginal Percentage*
Safety Measures	Poor	78	21.7	Supervisor interference	Never	113	31.4
	Satisfactory	164	45.6		Sometimes	159	44.2
	Good	79	21.9		Often	68	18.9
	Excellent	39	10.8		Always	20	5.6
Health facilities	Strongly agree	73	20.3	Workplace stress	Yes	116	46.1
	Agree	145	40.3		No	194	53.9
	Unknown	5	1.4	Supervision Quality	Strongly agree	4	1.1
	Disagree	106	29.4		Agree	8	2.2
	Strongly disagree	31	8.6		Unknown	5	1.4
					Disagree	153	42.5
					Strongly disagree	190	52.8
Supervisory Support	Strongly disagree	19	5.3	Industrial relations	Can't say	54	15
Colleagues Relationship	Disagree	34	9.4		Poor	71	19.7
	Unknown	10	2.8	Supervision Quality	Satisfactory	101	28.1
	Agree	207	57.5		Good	108	30.0
	Strongly agree	90	25.0	Role of trade union	Very good	26	7.2
	Strongly disagree	4	1.1		Strongly disagree	68	18.9
					Disagree	89	24.7
	Disagree	8	2.2				

(Contd.)

(Contd. Table 8.19)

Variable	*Scale*	*No.*	*Marginal Percentage*	*Variable*	*Level*	*No.*	*Marginal Percentage*
	Unknown	5	1.4		Unknown	64	17.8
Supervisory	Agree	153	42.5		Agree	121	33.6
Relationship	Strongly agree	190	52.8	Supervision	Strongly agree	18	6
	Conflicting	9	2.5	Quality	Agree	8	2.2
	Normal	161	44.7	Management	Unknown	5	1.4
	Harmonious	190	52.8	attitude	Disagree	153	42.5
					Never	39	10.8
					Rarely	60	16.3
Superior's	Strongly	8	2.2		Sometimes	134	37.2
Relationship	disagree						
Individual	Disagree	23	6.4	Supervision	Always	127	35.3
respect	Unknown	6	1.7	Quality	Salary	177	76.9
	Agree	195	54.2	Job retention	Challenging job	55	15.3
	Strongly agree	128	35.6	Technological	Benefits	28	7.8
	Strongly agree	32	8.9	support	Yes	159	44.2

(Contd.)

(Contd. Table 8.19)

Variable	*Scale*	*No.*	*Marginal Percentage*	*Variable*	*Level*	*No.*	*Marginal Percentage*
	Agree	50	13.9		No	201	55.8
Supervisory Support	Unknown	17	4.7	Adequate training	Strongly disagree	59	16.4
	Disagree	177	49.2	Supervision Quality	Disagree	94	26.1
	Strongly disagree	84	23.3		Unknown	4	1.1
	Strongly disagree	31	8.6	Industrial relations	Agree	137	58.1
	Strongly disagree	19	5.3		Strongly agree	66	18.31
					Can't say	54	15
	Disagree	34	9.4		Poor	71	19.7
Colleagues Relationship	Unknown	10	2.8		Satisfactory	101	28.1
	Agree	207	57.5	Supervision Quality	Good	108	30.0
	Strongly agree	90	25.0		Very good	26	7.2
	Strongly disagree	4	1.1	Role of trade union	Strongly disagree	68	18.9
		8	2.2				
	Disagree	5	1.4				
	Unknown						

(Contd.)

(Contd. Table 8.19)

Variable	*Scale*	*No.*	*Marginal Percentage*	*Variable*	*Level*	*No.*	*Marginal Percentage*
Employees Interest	Never	64	17.8	Work dissatisfaction	Lack of appreciation	203	56.4
Additional responsibility	Sometimes	166	46.1	Supervision Quality	Too much paper work	35	9.7
	Most of the time	130	36.1		Family issue	17	4.7
	Strongly disagree	24	6.7	Role of trade union	Lack of R & D	105	29.2
	Disagree	64	17.8	Remuneration	Highly disagree	141	39.2
	Unknown	04	1.1		Disagree	127	35.3
Autonomy	Agree	197	54.7		Unknown	03	.8
	Strongly agree	71	19.7	Supervision Quality	Agree	10	19.4
	Strongly disagree	30	8.3		Highly agree	19	5.3
	Disagree	56	15.6	Role of trade union	Yes	243	67.5
				Regular compensation			

(Contd.)

(Contd. Table 8.19)

Variable	*Scale*	*No.*	*Marginal Percentage*	*Variable*	*Level*	*No.*	*Marginal Percentage*
	Unknown	04	1.1		No	117	32.5
Work life balance	Agree	225	62.5	Adequate bonus	Yes	238	66.1
	Strongly agree	45	12.5	Supervision	No	122	33.9
	Yes	288	80	Quality	Yes	186	51.7
	No	72	20	Role of trade union	No	174	48.3
				Social security benefits			
Flexi-hours	Yes	176	48.9	Fair promotion	Yes	131	36.4
Work Schedule	No	184	51.1		No	229	63.6
	Day shift	300	83.3	Performance-based promotion	Strongly disagree	91	25.3
	Afternoon shift	14	3.9		Disagree	87	24.2
	Night shift	19	5.3		Unknown	19	5.3
	Rotating shift	27	7.5		Agree	123	34.2
Job security	Highly dissatisfied	76	21.1		Strongly Agree	40	11.1
Employees Interest	Dissatisfied	135	37.5				
	Satisfied	92	25.6	Work dissatisfaction			
	Highly satisfied	57	15.8				
	Never	64	17.8		Lack of appreciation	203	56.4

Table 8.20: Model Fitting Information

Model	*-2 Log Likelihood*	*Chi-square*	*df*	*Sig.*
Intercept Only	885.300			
Final	551.774	333.526	101	.000

Link function: *Logit.*

Table 8.21: Goodness-of-Fit

	Chi-square	*df*	*Sig.*
Pearson	2746.302	1327	.000
Deviance	551.774	1327	1.000

Link function: *Logit.*

computed instead (Table 8.22). What constitutes a "good" R^2 value depends upon the nature of the outcome and the explanatory variables. Here, the pseudo R^2 values (e.g., **Nagelkerke = 60.4 per cent; Cox and Snell = 66.1 per cent and McFadden = 37.7 per cent**) indicates that thirty six variables of QWL practices explains a relatively higher proportion of the variation in job satisfaction.

Table 8.22: Pseudo R-Square Statistics

Cox and Snell	.604
Nagelkerke	.661
McFadden	.377

Link function: *Logit.*

Table 8.23: Test of Parallel Lines[b]

Model	*-2 Log Likelihood*	*Chi-Square*	*df*	*Sig.*
Null Hypothesis	551.774			
General	.000[a]	551.774	303	.000

The null hypothesis states that the location parameters (slope coefficients) are the same across response categories.

(a) The log-likelihood value is practically zero. There may be a complete separation in the data. The maximum likelihood estimates do not exist.

(b) Link function: Logit

The result of the test of parallelism is in Table 8.23. The row labelled null hypothesis contains –2-log-likelihood for the constrained model, the model that assumes the lines are parallel. The row labelled General is for the model with separate lines or planes. It can be observed that the general model results in a sizeable improvement in fit from the null hypothesis model. The entry labelled Chi-square is the difference between the two –2- log-likelihood values. If the lines or planes are parallel, the observed significance level for the change should be large, since the general model doesn't improve the fit very much. The parallel model is adequate.

8.3.4 Impact of Multiple Independent QWL Variables on Motivation (The Ordinal Regression Model)

It is well-known that employee intrinsic motivation has an impact on organisational performance and Herzberg *et. al.* (1959) had shown that motivated employees tend to performs better. Company needs to find out the factors that influence employees' motivation and to ensure their quality of work life (Gilgeous, 1998), to understand whether existing practices of QWL motivating the employees to what extent. It is observed from the Table 8.24 that majority of employees (52.25 per cent) feels it motivates them normally, whereas 15 per cent asserted extremely.

Table 8.24: Effects of QWL Facilities on Motivation

	Scale	*Frequency*	*Per cent*	*Valid Per cent*	*Cumulative Per cent*
Valid	Slowly	118	32.8	32.8	32.8
	Normally	188	52.2	52.2	85.0
	Extremely	54	15.0	15.0	100.0
	Total	360	100.0	100.0	

From Table 8.25 it can be observed that the difference between the two log-likelihoods—the Chi square—has an observed significance level of less than 0.05. This means that we can reject the null hypothesis that the model without predictors is as good as the model with the predictors.

The next table in the output is the *Goodness-of-Fit table* (Table 8.26). This table contains Pearson's Chi-square statistic for the model (as well as another Chi-square statistic based on the deviance). These statistics are intended to test whether the observed data are consistent with the fitted

Table 8.25: Model Fitting Information

Model	*-2 Log Likelihood*	*Chi-square*	*df*	*Sig.*
Intercept Only	712.401			
Final	444.519	267.882	101	.000

Link function: Logit.

model. In this case p value is very large, so that it can be concluded that the data and the model predictions are similar and have a good model.

Table 8.26: Goodness-of-Fit

Model	*Chi-square*	*df*	*Sig.*
Pearson	1104.836	613	.000
Deviance	444.519	613	1.000

Link function: Logit.

Table 8.27: Pseudo R-Square

Cox and Snell	.525
Nagelkerke	.609
McFadden	.376

Link function: Logit.

Table 8.28: Test of Parallel Lines

Model	*-2 Log Likelihood*	*Chi-Square*	*df*	*Sig.*
Null Hypothesis	444.519			
General	338.068[a]	106.451[b]	101	.336

(a) The null hypothesis states that the location parameters (slope coefficients) are the same across response categories.

(b) The Chi-square statistic is computed based on the log-likelihood value of the last iteration of the general model. Validity of the test is uncertain.

(c) Link function: Logit.

The Table 8.27 of the analysis shows, the pseudo R^2 values (e.g., **Nagelkerke = 60.9 per cent; Cox and Snell = 52.5 per cent and McFadden = 37.6 per cent**) indicates that thirty-six variables of QWL practices explains a relatively higher proportion of the variation in motivation. The test of parallel lines (Table 8.28) is used to assess whether the assumption that the parameters are the same for all categories is reasonable. This test compares the estimated model with one set of coefficients for all categories to a model with a separate set of coefficients for each category. It can be seen that the general model (with separate parameters for each category) gives a significant improvement in the model fit.

8.3.5 Impact of Multiple Independent QWL Variables on Organisational Loyalty (The Ordinal Regression Model)

In present modern world, human resource has become a competitive privilege in organisations. Unsuitable staff can result in failure of business. Normal staff can keep the business and reach the head to head point, while fine staff ever can lead to summit of even moderate businesses (Deal, 2003). In order to become successful in future, the organisations must thus not only employ the best staff, but also must make them loyal to the organisation to keep them (Barnet, 2003). To speak concisely, loyalty in an organisation has direct effect on occupational efficiency and causes less translocation of staff, more efficient use of resources, and higher efficiency (Burgi, 2001). An attempt has been made to understand the influences of QWL indicators on organisational loyalty. It is visible (Table 8.29) that 62.2 per cent of employees believe that available practices are very important to be loyal to the organisation whereas only 3.1 per cent asserts that important.

Table 8.29: Employees Perception towards Organisational Loyalty

	Scale	*Frequency*	*Per cent*	*Valid Per cent*	*Cumulative Per cent*
Valid	Not Important	11	3.1	3.1	3.1
	Important	55	15.3	15.3	18.3
	Highly Important	70	19.4	19.4	37.8
	Very Important	224	62.2	62.2	100.0
	Total	**360**	**100.0**	**100.0**	

Table 8.30: Model Fitting Information

Model	*-2 Log Likelihood*	*Chi-square*	*df*	*Sig.*
Intercept Only	725.228			
Final	552.134	173.094	101	.000

Link function: *Logit.*

The model fitting information gives the (Table 8.30) likelihood difference between base line and the final model. The significant Chi-square statistic (p<.001) indicates that the final model gives a significant improvement over the baseline intercept-only model. It clarifies that the model gives better predictions than the guessed-based on the marginal probabilities for the outcome categories.

Table 8.31: Goodness-of-Fit

	Chi-square	*df*	*Sig.*
Pearson	924.760	970	.848
Deviance	552.134	970	1.000

The Goodness-of-Fit (Table 8.31) contains Pearson's Chi-square statistic for the model and another Chi-square statistic based on the deviance. It is intended to test whether the observed data are inconsistent with the fitted model. If the significance values are large then it can be concluded that the data and the model predictions are similar and that have a good model. In this case, *p* value is very large and it can be concluded that absolutely significant and the assumption of good fit is to be accepted.

Table 8.32: Pseudo R-Square

Cox and Snell	.382
Nagelkerke	.440
McFadden	.239

Link function: Logit.

The null hypothesis states that the location parameters (slope coefficients) are the same across response categories.

(a) The log-likelihood value cannot be further increased after maximum number of step-halving.

(b) The Chi-square statistic is computed based on the log-likelihood value of the last iteration of the general model. Validity of the test is uncertain.

(c) Link function: Logit.

For measuring goodness of fit of the model, pseudo R^2 statistics have been used (Table 8.32). The pseudo R^2 values (e.g., **Nagelkerke = 44 per cent; Cox and Snell= 38.2 per cent and McFadden=23.9 per cent**) shows that thirty six variables of QWL practices explains a relatively moderate proportion of the variation in organisational loyalty. The result of the test of parallelism is in Table 8.33. It can be observed that the general model results in a sizeable improvement in fit from the null hypothesis model.

Table 8.33: Test of Parallel Lines[c]

Model	*-2 Log Likelihood*	*Chi-square*	*df*	*Sig.*
Null Hypothesis	552.134			
General	394.251[a]	157.883[b]	202	.990

Conclusions

The first phase impact factor analysis reveals that out of the thirty- six (36) variables of working environment factor, relational factor, job factor and financial factor, twenty-three (23) variables such as, (1) lighting facilities, (2) safety measures, (3) health facilities, (4) working condition, (5) quality of welfare facilities, (6) workplace stress, (7) quality of supervision, (8) supervisory support, (9) superiors' relationship, (10) individual respect, (11) industrial relations, (12) role of trade union, (12) management attitude, (13) job rotation, (14) adequate training, (15) employees interest, (16) additional responsibility, (17) work schedule, (18) job security, (19) work dissatisfaction, (20) additional responsibilities, (21) remuneration (Pay-package), and (22) Performance-based promotion were found positively significant (.000) and rest of variables were found not significant.

Logistic regression has many analogies to linear regression: logit coefficients correspond to *b* coefficients in the logistic regression equation, the standardised logit coefficients correspond to *beta* weights, and the Wald statistic, a pseudo R^2 statistic, is available to summarise the strength of the relationship. The success of the logistic regression can be assessed by looking at the classification table, showing correct and incorrect classifications of the dependent. Also, goodness-of-fit tests such as model Chi-square are available as indicators of model appropriateness, as is the Wald statistic to test the significance of individual independent variables. The EXP (β) value indicates the increase in odds from a one unit increase in the selected variable.

A logistic regression analysis was conducted to predict employees' productivity and workers participation in management with three hundred and sixty respondents (360) using thirty-six variables of QWL issues as predictors. A test of the full model against a constant only model was statistically significant, indicating that the predictors as a set reliably distinguished between positive and negative response towards QWL improves productivity (Chi-square = 202.679, $p < .001$ with df = 36). Nagelkerke's R^2 of .583 indicated a moderately strong relationship between prediction and grouping. Prediction success overall was 81.9 per cent (85.8 per cent for accept and 75.9 per cent for accept). The Wald criterion demonstrated that nine variables made a significant contribution to prediction.

In the second case, the prediction of workers participation in management, the model was found statistically significant (Chi-square = 222.747, $p < .000$ with df = 36. Nagelkerke's R^2 of .617 shows sound relationship between prediction and grouping. Further the Wald criterion projected that six variables made a major contribution in prediction.

The third case QWL activities and its influence on job satisfaction. The difference (Chi-square statistics) is = 333.526 which is significant at á=0.05, $p < 0.001$. The conclusion is that there is association between the dependent and independent variable(s) in complimentary Log-log link function. The goodness of fit statistics concludes that the observed data were consistent with the estimated values in the fitted model since the p was insignificant, $p = 1.00 > 0.05$. The Pseudo R-Square Statistics i.e., Nagelkerke full model predicts the outcome as its likelihood of R-squared = .661. Several factors namely, lighting facilities, safety measures, adequate support, colleagues relationship, technological support, adequate bonus and adequate bonus found statistically significant and therefore these are influence job satisfaction in sugar mills of UP. Further the significance $p = 1.000 > 0.05$ indicated that there was no significant difference for the corresponding slope coefficients across the response categories, suggesting that the model assumption of parallel lines was not violated in the model with the Complementary Log-log link.

The third cases constructing ordinal regression model using motivation as dependent variables. The presence of a relationship was found between the dependent variable and combination of independent variables, since the statistical significance ($p<.001$) of the final model. The Pearson test for Goodness of Fit is used to measure the degree of the relationship between the linear related variables. In this case also the observed data were found consistent with the estimated values in the fitted model since the p was insignificant, $p = 1.00 > 0.05$. The Nagelkerke (The Pseudo R-Square Statistics) predicts outcome as its likelihood $R^2 = .609$. Further, Wald statistics found influential variables influencing employees' motivation namely, lighting facilities, working condition, supervisory interference, superiors' relationship, role of trade union, job retention, flexible working hour, fair promotion and performance-based promotion.

Finally, influence of QWL initiatives have been examined on organisational loyalty using ordinal regression model. In model fitting summary, statistical significance ($p<.001$) have been observed between independent and dependent variables. Pearson is widely used in statistics to measure the degree of the relationship between the linear related variables. Deviance is a likelihood-ratio test used under full maximum likelihood. The observed data were found consistent with the estimated values in the fitted model since the p was insignificant, $p = 1.00 > 0.05$. The Pseudo R-Square Statistics (Nagelkerke's $R^{2)}$) of .440 indicated a moderate relationship between prediction and grouping. The Wald test of significance (parameter estimates) identifies eight variables which sound statistically significance includes lighting facilities, supervision quality, adequate support, supervisory relationship, respect, additional responsibility, work schedule and regular compensation. Further the assumption of parallel lines have not been violated since significance value of $p = .990 > .05$.

References

Barnet, S. (2003). Employee loyalty, (http://www.seattlepi.com).

Deal, J. (2003). How to creat employee loyalty, (http://www.deal consulting.com).

Dixon, M. and Sagas, M. 2007. The relationship between organisational support, work family conflict, and the job-life satisfaction of university coaches. *Research Quarterly for Exercise and Sport,* 78, 236-247.

Gilgeous, V., (1998), "Manufacturing managers: their quality of working life", *Integrated Manufacturing System,* Vol. 9, No. 3, pp.173-181.

Herzberg, F., Mausner, B., and Snyderman, B. (1959), "The Motivation to Work" (2nd Ed.) New York: John Wiley.

Locke, E. (1976), "The Nature and Causes of Job Satisfaction, in Handbook of Industrial and Organisational Psychology Edited by M.D. Dunnette (Chicago: Rand McNally, 1976), pp. 901-969.

Rhoades, L. and Eisenberger, R. (2002). Perceived Organisational Support: A Review of the Literature, *Journal of Applied Psychology*, Volume 87(4) 698-714.

Ruzevicius, J. (2007) Working Life Quality and Its Measurement, *Forum Ware International,* 2.

Davis Keith (1975). Human Relations at Work, Tata McGraw Hill. p. 288.

Tam Marilyn (2013). A Happy Worker Is a Productive Worker, retrieved from http:// www. huffingtonpost.com/marilyn-tam/how-to-be-happy-at-work_b_3648000.html.

Sink, D.S. and Tuttle, T.C. (1989) *Planning and Measurement in Your Organisation of the Future*, IE Press: Norcross, GA.

9

Summary of Findings, Conclusions and Suggestions

9.1 Introduction

India is known as the original home of sugar and sugarcane. In global sugar economy, the Indian sugar industry has achieved a number of milestones. India is the second largest producer of sugarcane next to Brazil. The Indian sugar industry comprises about 20 per cent of sugar mills and 15 per cent of sugar production of the world. The industry is a key driver of rural development, supporting over about 55 million sugarcane farmers, their dependents and a large mass of agricultural labourers involved in sugarcane cultivation, harvesting, machine manufacturing, etc., of almost 527 sugar mills and ancillary activities, and constituting 7.5 per cent of the rural population. It is worth mentioning that the industry employs over five lakh skilled and unskilled workers mainly from the rural areas. Uttar Pradesh is the largest sugarcane-producing state in the country and a major chunk of the sugar mills in the state are in the private and co-operative sector-based. They play an important role in the production of sugar and generation of employment. The primary aim of Uttar Pradesh sugar industry is to promote the welfare of the members by uplifting the economically manufacturing poor, development of locality and benefitting the people at large. But the development of this sector seriously affected, due to the existence of various problems. Consequent to this a number of units in this sector are becoming sick and unviable and are increasing day by day. Many organisations lag behind due to insufficient human resource department. Very few have fully fledged human resource/personnel department and many have only labour welfare officers, limiting such sections role to welfare activities and maintain the time office. Some of the challenges for poor performance are obsolete technology, poor financial performance, poor working condition, discriminatory government policies, high political influence, frequent changes in management, limited modernisation and diversification and unprofessional management.

An organisation performs best when all the HR practices are managed well. In companies with effective Human Resource management, employees tend to be more satisfied, and the companies tend to be more innovative, have greater productivity and develop a more favourable reputation in the community. For achieving the objectives of the industrial estates proper man power management and suitable quality of work life programmes are essential. Quality of work life covers all aspects of worker's life with special reference to his interaction with his work and his working environment. Quality of work life is the degree by which members of a work organisation are able to satisfy their personal needs through their experience in the organisation. Its focus is on the problem of creating a human work environment where employees work cooperatively and contribute to organisational objectives. Quality of work life is reflected by job involvement, job satisfaction and productivity. The healthy quality of work life is essential in sugar industry to find and keep the best possible fit between their social system and technical system.

Therefore, in the present research work an endeavour is made to highlight dimensions and status of quality of working life (QWL) in sugar industry. The study has greater managerial implication as it would help to re-orient the attitude of management towards employees and thereby increase the morale of the employees. This may lead to sincere involvement of workers in their work and thereby increase productivity. Moreover, any change in this field would affect each and every individual, because prosperity in the industrial sector is directly connected with the society and nation as a whole.

Objectives of the Study

The study has been designed with the following objectives:

Main Objective: The main objective of the study is **to assess the effectiveness of the various dimensions (working environment factor, relational factor, job factor and financial factor) of Quality of Working Life of Employees in Sugar Industry of Uttar Pradesh.**

Sub Objectives: The sub objectives of the study are as follows:

1. To assess the existing QWL practices of employees with regard to various zones (Eastern, Central, and Western) of UP sugar mills;
2. To investigate whether there is any significant difference between private and co-operative sugar mill employees perception regarding QWL issues;
3. To compare perceived level of QWL between permanent and seasonal employees of sugar mills in UP;
4. To explore the influence of demographic variables (experience, income, education level and age) on QWL dimensions; and
5. To investigate the impact of QWL on job satisfaction, workers participation in management, organisational loyalty, employee productivity, and motivation.

9.2 The Design and Methodology of the Study

The present study is an empirical one, based on both primary and secondary data. The study was conducted in entire Uttar Pradesh consisting three zones namely, Western, Central and Eastern Zones. The study was conducted in two phases.

In the first phase, all available secondary data were collected from the published sources like annual reports of Indian Sugar Mills Association (ISMA) New Delhi, Reports of Sugar Year Books, and Handbooks on Sugar Statistics, Department of Economics and Statistics, Economic Survey and Reports of individual sugar mills. The secondary data related to quality of work life was gathered from different books of Quality of Work Life and human resource management, articles, research papers, publication and other documents, newsletters and websites, etc.

In the second phase, primary data was collected by a field survey. A structured questionnaire was used for this purpose. Initially 50 employees were selected for pilot study according to convenience of the researcher and the questionnaire has been finalised after making necessary corrections. The population of the study consists of all the employees/workers of the private and co-operative sugar mills of Uttar Pradesh. In the first stage, the state of Uttar Pradesh has been divided into three zones: Eastern, Central and Western Zones. Accordingly 12 sugar mills (4 mills from each zone) have selected for the survey, of which nine were private sugar mills and three were co-operative sugar mills. The stratified random sampling method was, then, adopted for the selection of respondent for the study. In total the sample consists of 360 respondents. The ratio of sample between private and co-operative was 3:1, i.e., 270 respondents were from private sector and 70 were co-operative sector sugar mills.

The data so collected were analysed with the help of computers, keeping in view of the objectives of the study. Appropriate statistical tools such as Descriptive statistics, Correlation statistics, Chi-square, one way ANOVA, Kruskal-wallis test, Man-Whitney (U) test and Regression analysis (binary logistic regression, linear regression and ordinal regression) have been used.

In the preceding chapters an attempt has been made to study the practicing Quality of Work Life in the sugar mills of Uttar Pradesh. This is the last chapter of report and purely devoted to summaries the findings of those chapters, draw conclusions and make recommendations on the basis of the finding of the study. Therefore, this chapter is divided into three sections. **Section A** provides a summary of the entire study and its findings. **Section B** deals with conclusions drawn from the study and **Section C** contains the recommendations or suggestions in the area of Quality of Working Life for fostering a healthy work environment in the industry.

SECTION-A

9.3 Summary of Chapters

(I) The **first chapter** deals with the conceptual framework of 'Quality of Work Life'. It makes a brief review of the meaning, concepts and indicators of QWL. Evolution of QWL, dimensions of QWL, techniques for improving QWL and gained from improved quality of work life are studied in this chapter.

(II) In **the second chapter**, a brief review of existing literature in the field of Quality of Work Life is presented. It also contains objective of the study, hypotheses for the study, identified variables, significance of the study, research design, sampling design, brief profile of selected sugar mills, analysis of demographic variables, limitations of the study and the chapter layout, etc.

(III) Th**e third chapter** deals with an overview of sugar industry in India. It covers evolution, growth and development of Sugar Industry in India vis-à-vis, Uttar Pradesh. It also focussed global sugar industry scenario.

(IV) In **fourth chapter** shows an analysis of Working Environment Factor of Quality of Work Life.

(V) The **fifth chapter** deals with the evaluation of Relational Factor of Quality of Work Life.

(VI) In **Chapter six** gives analytical measures of Job Factor of Quality of Work Life.

(VII) The **Chapter seven** covers the analysis of Financial Factor of Quality of Work Life.

(VIII) The **Chapter eight** deals with factors of Quality of Work Life and their effectiveness and impact analysis.

(IX) The **ninth and the last chapter** presents a summary of the findings in the foregoing chapters, conclusions and suggestions based on the findings of the study.

9.4 Findings of the Study

The followings are the Major Findings of the Study:

- It has been proved in the present research that high quality of work life ensures employees' higher loyalty, better participation, low absenteeism, reduced turnover, and improved organisational image and enhanced overall performance of the employees and organisation.
- The sugar industry in India plays a vital role towards socio-economic and inclusive development in the rural areas by mobilising rural resources and generating higher income and employment opportunities. About 7.5 per cent of the rural population, covering about 45 million sugarcane farmers, their dependents and a large number of agricultural labourers are involved in sugarcane cultivation, harvesting and ancillary activities. About half a million skilled and semi-skilled workers, mostly from the rural areas are also engaged in the sugar industry.
- With respect to the position of twenty four important sugar production countries in the world, India is the second largest producer of sugarcane next to Brazil (accounting 15 per cent of the world's sugar production). However, regarding the largest sugar consumers, India is the topmost rank in the top ten countries in the international, followed by EU-27, China, Brazil, and USA and finally Egypt, Arab Republic.
- Sugar firms in India are operating under three types of ownership structures viz., public, private and co-operative sectors. Recently, in the country there are 651 licensed sugar factories with an average installed capacity of 18 million tonnes have been spread among large sugarcane growing states like Uttar Pradesh, Maharashtra, Karnataka, Gujarat, Tamil Nadu, and Andhra Pradesh. The co-operative sector dominates with the 320 co-operative sugar firms. It is apparent from the data that 49 per cent of sugar firms are installed under the co-operative sector as compared to the 40.55 per cent under private ownership and 9.50 per cent under public ownership.

• Uttar Pradesh is the foremost state in production of sugar and sugarcane in the country. The state tops the list of sugarcane producing states, whereas, it ranks second in sugar production. Sugar industry of the state has a symbiotic relationship with the rural masses and serves as a nerve centre for the rural development. There are 128 operational sugar mills running in the State at the end of crushing season 2010-11. The entire sugar industry consist of Public, Private and Co-operative sector mills that spread over three zones, i.e., Eastern, Central and Western Uttar Pradesh. Almost 50 per cent of sugar mills are in private sector and rest of the mills are in other sectors.

• The average recovery of sugar at the all India level was 10.48 per cent in 2000-01 and 10.17 per cent in 2010-11 whereas the average recovery of sugar in Uttar Pradesh was 9.73 per cent and 9.7 per cent. The recovery percentage has decreased in Uttar Pradesh due to use obsolete technology, poor financial performance and poor working condition.

Personal Profile of Employees

• In the present study the total sample includes 50 per cent permanent employees (180) and 50 per cent seasonal employees (180). Further, it is discernible that the largest majority of the samples respondents, i.e., 75 per cent are belong to private sector and rest of the (25 per cent) from co-operative sector.

• All the respondents of the sample were male employees. The reason for the larger number of male employees is that sugar industry is essentially a labour-intensive industry, which requires more physical work. Hence, the number of women employed is almost negligible.

• The predominant age group of the respondents in the private and co-operative sugar mills was 41-50 years (41 per cent), followed by the age group of 50 and above years (27.2 per cent). The employees belonging to younger age group were far fewer in the sugar mills of Uttar Pradesh. The major reason for this is the absence of direct recruitment for officers, supervisors and workmen in the sugar mills.

• A large number of employees (99 per cent) are married, as only 7.2 per cent of the respondents are below 30 years. Most of the respondents are above 40 years of age and their job settlement leads to marriage.

• Out of 360 respondent majority of employees (42 per cent) were belongs to technical cadre followed by clerical and accounting cadre (40 per cent).

• It has been found that 49 per cent of employees in the UP sugar mills are drawing Rs. 10,000 to 20,000 as their monthly salary. More than one third employees (38.6 per cent) are getting below Rs. 10,000 as monthly salary. The lowest percentage (12.2 per cent) of the respondents is earning a monthly income above Rs. 20,000. Their income is found to be just sufficient to bread and butter, which happens to be the minimum comfort today.

- It is found out that 43.3 per cent of the employees in the UP sugar mills have educational qualification up to Graduation followed by intermediate (14 per cent) and post graduates (13 per cent). The reason is that most of the employees in the sugar mills are technical workmen, who need sound technical knowledge of plant and machinery. Only nine per cent employees belong to high school level.
- The 52 per cent of employees have more than five dependents. Only a very small number of respondents (38 per cent) have four or less than four dependants. Therefore, the number of the respondents having dependants more than five.
- The 68 per cent of the sample employees are belongs to rural area and rest are (32 per cent) residing in urban areas. It shows that most of the rural people are primarily dependent on sugar mills of Uttar Pradesh.

Statistical Findings

Finding Based on Working Environment Factor (10 Variables):

- Geographical location-wise analysis of working environment factor reveals that the lighting facility, working condition, type of welfare facilities and quality of welfare facility are found significantly different in three select zones (Eastern, Central and Western Zones) at five per cent level of significance. However, statistically very highly significant differences have been noticed in the perception of Eastern, Western and Central Zone's employees with regards to safety measures and total score of working environment factor ($P < .001$). The remaining dimensions are found non-significant.
- There is statistically highly significant difference have been observed regarding the perception of health facility, safety measures, type of welfare facilities, and quality of welfare facilities between private and co-operative sugar mills employees. Further, significant differences have been observed in the perception of level of temperature. The overall analysis of work environment factor reveals that the opinion of both the sector differs statistically very highly significant. The average satisfactions of private sector employees are more than the co-operative sector employees with regards to work environment factors of quality of work life.

• Nature of employment-wise analysis of the study revealed that there exists highly significant difference between the permanent and seasonal employees regarding the perception of work-place stress and type of welfare facilities at one per cent level of significance. While, the perception about lighting facility, safety measures and quality of welfare facilities are statistically differing significantly ($P<0.05$) between the permanent and seasonal employees. There is no significant difference have been found regarding overall score of work environment factor.

• The demographic analysis of this study also pointed out that level of income and level of education are the key variables that influence the perception of work environment factor in sugar industry. Further, job experience and age group of employees are significantly not associated with working environment factor of quality of work life.

Finding Based on Relational Factor (Nine Variables)

• Statistically, there was found very highly significant difference regarding the perception of superiors' relationship, individual respect and role of trade union among the employees of Eastern, Central and Western Zone at one per cent level of significance ($P<0.001$). Significant difference has been noticed in case of supervisory support, colleagues' relationship and supervisory relationship at five per cent level of significance. Further, no significant difference is observed in case of supervision quality and industrial relation. The overall mean score of relational factor revealed that the employees of Eastern Zone (202.79) are more satisfied followed by the Western Zone (176.77) and Central Zone (161.95) respectively.

• There is statistically, significant difference were investigated between private and co-operative sector sugar mills employees with regards to management attitude, supervision quality, industrial relation and role of trade union. Further, no significant difference is found in the perception of six variables namely, supervisors support; Colleagues' relationship; supervisor's relationship; superiors' relationship and individual respect. The overall analysis of relational factor reveals that the opinion of both the sector differs significantly at five per cent level of significance ($P<0.05$). The average satisfaction of private sector employees is more than the co-operative sector employees with regards to relational factors of quality of work life. Therefore, it can be concluded that employers of private sugar mills giving more importance to their employees to maintaining harmonious relationship.

• The nature of employment-wise analysis revealed that out of nine variables of relational factor, five variables are found statistically significant namely, supervisors' relationship, superiors' relationship, industrial relation, role of trade union and management attitude. However, no significant difference has been noticed in the perception of supervision quality, supervisory support, colleagues' relationship and individual respect between the permanent and seasonal employees. Further, statistically highly and significant difference has been observed regarding the overall perception of relational factor. Permanent employees are found more satisfied than the seasonal employees with regards to relational factor.

- There has been found significant relationship of relation factor of quality of work life with job experience, income and education level of employees. However, no significant difference in scores was noticed among the age groups of employees.

Findings Based on Job Factor (Eleven Variables)

- There was found very highly significant difference regarding the perception of job security among the employees of Eastern, Central and Western Zone. The employees of Eastern Zone asserted that they are more satisfied with the job security than the employees of Central and Western Zone respectively. Significant difference has also been noticed in case of flexible working hour and autonomy. Further, no significant difference is observed in case of job retention, work schedule, work dissatisfaction, technological support, work life balance, adequate training, employee's interest, and additional responsibilities. However, regarding the perception of overall job factor, no significant differences have been found among the employees of all three groups. Therefore, it can be concluded that all the employees of three zones exhibited a similar level of satisfaction regarding job factor of quality of work life.
- Statistically, significant difference have been observed between the opinion private and co-operative sugar mills employees with regards to technological support and work schedule at five per cent level of significance. On the other hand, no significant differences was found in remaining four variables, i.e., job retention, work life balance, flexible working hours and work dissatisfaction.
- The nature of employment-wise analysis revealed that out of five variables of job factor, three variables are found statistically highly significant namely, employee's intersect, autonomy and job security at five per cent level of significance. However, no significant difference has been noticed in the perception of adequate training and additional responsibilities between the permanent and seasonal employees of Uttar

Pradesh Sugar Industry. Further, statistically very highly and significant difference has been observed regarding the overall perception of job factor. The researcher found that most of the permanent employees are found slightly more satisfied than the seasonal employees with regards to job factor of QWL.

- The demographic analysis revealed that education level and income level of employees have significant relationship with job factor of quality of work life. However, age and experience of employees was not found significantly related to job factor of quality of work life.

Findings based on Financial Factor (Six Variables)

- The study established that there is highly significant difference have been observed in the practice of two variables namely, timely compensation and adequate bonus among Eastern, Central and Western Zone of sugar mills ($P<.01$). Further, no significant difference was observed in the case of remuneration, social security benefits and fair promotion. However, overall score of financial factor is also differing significantly, Zone-wise. The mean score obtained by the three zones revealed that employees of Central Zone are slightly more satisfied with the financial factor followed by Eastern Zone and Western Zone respectively.
- There is very highly significant difference have been found regarding the perception of remuneration, timely compensation, performance and seniority-based promotion, social security benefits and fair promotion between private and co-operative sugar mills employees. The private sector employees have shown higher satisfaction with financial factor than the cooperative sector employees.
- The nature of employment-wise analysis divulge that significant difference is exist in the perception of permanent and seasonal employees regarding the issues of remuneration, timely compensation, promotion based on performance and seniority, social security benefit, fair promotion. The overall score of financial factor are also differing significantly. The statistical analysis shows that permanent employees are more satisfied with the financial factor than the seasonal employees.
- The last Table 7.7 of this chapter emerged that there is significant impact of income level, job experience and education level on the financial factor of quality of work life. But age of employees has no significant impact on financial factor of QWL.

Findings based on Impact Factor Analysis (Five Variables)

- To understand the influences of thirty-six independent on employees' productivity a logistic regression analysis was conducted with sample size of three hundred sixty respondents. **Nagelkerke's R^2 of .583** indicated a moderately strong relationship between prediction and grouping. Prediction success overall was 81.9 per cent (85.8 per cent for accept and 75.9 per cent for accept). The Wald criterion demonstrated that nine variables made a significant contribution to prediction.

- In the second case, the prediction of workers participation in management, the model was found statistically significant (Chi-square = 222.747, p <.000 with df=36. **Nagelkerke's R^2 of .617** shows sound relationship between prediction and grouping. Further the Wald criterion projected that six variables made a major contribution in prediction.
- The third case, i.e., influence of QWL initiatives on job satisfaction. The difference (Chi-square statistics) is = 333.526 which is significant at á=0.05, p< 0.001. The conclusion 's that there is association between the dependent and independent variable(s) in complimentary Log-log link function. The goodness of fit statistics concludes that the observed data were consistent with the estimated values in the fitted model since the *p* was insignificant, p = 1.00 > 0.05. **The Pseudo R-Square Statistics i.e., Nagelkerke** full model predicts the outcome as its likelihood of R-squared = .661. Several factors namely lighting facilities, safety measures, adequate support, colleagues relationship, technological support, adequate bonus and adequate bonus found statistically significant and therefore these are influence job satisfaction in sugar mills of UP.
- The ordinal regression model (PLUM) using motivation as dependent variables. The presence of a relationship was found between the dependent variable and combination **of independent variables. The Nagelkerke** (The Pseudo R-Square Statistics) predicts outcome as its likelihood **R^2= .609**. Further, Wald statistics found influential variables influencing employees' motivation namely, lighting facilities, working condition, supervisory interference, superiors' relationship, role of trade union, job retention, flexible working hour, fair promotion and performance-based promotion.
- Lastly, influences QWL initiatives have been examined taking organisational loyalty as dependent variables using ordinal regression model. In model fitting summary, **statistical significance (p<.001)** have been observed the between independent and dependent variables. The observed data were found consistent with the estimated values in the fitted model since the *p* was insignificant, *p* = 1.00 > 0.05. The Pseudo R-Square Statistics **(Nagelkerke's $R^{2)}$ of .440** indicated a moderate relationship between prediction and grouping. The Wald test of

significance (parameter estimates) identifies eight variables which sound statistically significance includes lighting facilities, supervision quality, adequate support, supervisory relationship, respect, additional responsibility, work schedule and regular compensation. Further the assumption of parallel lines have not been violated since significance value of $p = .990 > .05$.

SECTION- B

9.5 Conclusion of the Study

After a comprehensive analysis and discussion of the various aspects of the quality of work life in the sugar industry of Uttar Pradesh, it can be concluded that regarding the working environment factor the perception score of sugar mills employees were not found homogeneous. In some cases it was significantly differing geographical location-wise, nature of organisation-wise and nature of employment-wise. Whereas, in some cases similar practice have been observed. The study reveals that the perception of employees regarding lighting facility, safety measures, working condition, type of welfare facilities and quality of welfare facility are found significantly different in three select zones. Although the employees are moderately satisfied with the above dimensions but the employees of Western and Central Zones are slightly less satisfied. The remaining variables such as comfortable work space, level of temperature, work-place stress, health facilities and supervisor interference are not found significant.

The nature of sugar mills analysis reported that the average satisfactions of private sector employees are more than the co-operative sector employees with regards to work environment factors of quality of work life. Therefore, it can be concluded that in the private sector sugar mills the working environment factor is more favourable than the co-operative sector. Although, the statistical result revered that there is no significant difference have been observed in the opinion of permanent and seasonal employees. But in some cases like as comfortable work-space, work-place stress, safety measures, and type of welfare facilities, the seasonal employees asserted less satisfaction compare to permanent employees. The analysis also reveals that the income level and education level are the key variables that influence the perception of work environment factor in sugar industry.

The total perception score with regard to relational factor in different region varying widely. In central region projects poor mean perception score regarding supervisory/ individual/colleagues support, etc. The nature organisation-wise distribution shows poor performance in case of co-operative employees. It is quite evident from the study that relationship of seasonal employees with superiors, colleagues and others found very poor. The role of trade union for seasonal employees found very meaningless. Further, it is also cleared that experiences, income and education level influences job factor irrespective of location, nature of employment and organisation.

In job factor analysis with location-wise found uniform practice regarding job retention, adequate training, autonomy, work life balance and work schedule except job security which shows poor satisfaction score in western region. The same picture also depicts in private and co-operative sugar mills showing moderate evidence with regard to job factor issues. In several cases namely, employees' interest, authority, and job security seasonal employees' position is worst in comparison to permanent employees. In fact, overall job condition of seasonal employees QWL shows very poor. Further, income level of employees also not matched with job and found wide disparity among permanent/seasonal and private/co-operative employees.

There has been wide variance of employees' opinion with regard to financial issues in location, nature of employment and organisation-wise. In geographical location i.e., Eastern, Central and Western region it is visualised that majority cases of financial issues projects moderate satisfaction score despite of statistical difference. The nature-wise, i.e., in private and co-operative sugar mills empirical evidence shows few cases namely, regular compensation, fair compensation found statistical difference and co-operative sugar mills show poor performance and rest of the cases observed moderate score. In nature of employment-wise empirical result shows negative score towards fair compensation, and regular compensation in both the case, but regarding remuneration, seasonal workers reports extreme negative opinions. It is quite evident that income, education and income level creates significant variation in financial factor.

In the first phase of impact factor analysis the standard (simultaneous) regression method is used to identify the potential predictor of quality of work life.This analysis reveals that out of the thirty six (36) variables, twenty three (23) variables were found positively significant (.000) and rest of variables were found not significant.

Finally, it can be concluded that QWL initiatives in UP sugar mills have significant influences on employees' productivity, workers participation in management, job satisfaction and motivation. It is to be noted that only few selective initiatives are found as causing variables as far as its effectiveness is concerned. It also observed that various explanatory variables do not create much influence on organisational loyalty.

SECTION- C

9.6 Suggestions

From the foregoing analysis and findings, it is brought to limelight that most of the private and co-operative sugar mills in the Uttar Pradesh had numerous problems and have been incurring financial losses due to many internal and external factors. The management of human resources is the most difficult job in the mills. In order to strengthen the quality of working life as well as human resource functions of the sugar mills, the following suggestions are made:

(I) In Uttar Pradesh, sugar industry plays a dominant role in the rural development of the state. The sugar industrial units under the study are the oldest industries which have seen the ups and downs since their inception due to the fluctuations of the sugar policy of the central and state governments. Hence, there is need for conducting government sponsored studies in the area of sugar policy in the changing economic environment.

(II) Modernisation and rehabilitation of sugar mills are the main problems being faced by the sugar industry of Uttar Pradesh, because most of these sugar units were set-up in early fifties and sixties. These mills have outlived their normal economic life and are contributing less efficiency and high cost of production. Thus, there is a need of considerable changes in sugar industry. Therefore, the management of sugar mills is suggested to gradually replace old and outdated machinery and plants.

(III) Working conditions refer to mental, physical and social well-being of the workers in the industry. Improvement in productivity lies in better working conditions, reduced absenteeism, minimised industrial unrest and improved employee morale. Therefore, it is suggested that every co-operative sugar mills should ensure total Occupational Safety and Health Administration.

(IV) Although workers in the sugar mills are provided some welfare facilities by their employers like housing facilities, medical facilities, recreational facilities and canteen facilities. But it is observed that the standards of welfare facilities are not satisfactory. Therefore, to ensure the high quality of work life the employer should pay a greater attention in the improvement of standard of welfare facilities.

(V) Although quality of relationship with superiors, colleagues and supervisor's are satisfactory in the case of permanent employees but its massive improvement in seasonal workers are required. Further, it is also need of the hour to strengthen the role of trade union of seasonal workers.

(VI) It is widely opined by the employees that the lack of appreciation and training and development are the main reasons for work dissatisfaction. In the private and co-operative sugar mills of Uttar Pradesh, training programmes are much delayed and negligible. Some sugar mills do not have any formal training programme either for workmen or for administrative staff. Therefore, it is suggested that the organisation should classify the various categories of jobs and assess the developmental needs in order to provide need-based training to the employees to increase their efficiency. In fact overall job condition of seasonal workers needs to be revisited.

(VII) Remuneration, Regular and Adequate and fair pay is a pre-requisite for employee satisfaction and commitment. In this regard, it is felt by a majority of employees in co-operative sector and seasonal workers the present pay levels in the industry are inadequate and they are not getting timely payment. Therefore, it is suggested that continuous monitoring of the compensation, remuneration and the incentive system should be introduced taking into consideration organisational requirements and employee motivation dimensions. The pay structure of permanent and seasonal is found imbalanced. To tune up the human resource environment and commitment in the industry such discretions in the pay fixation should be non-partisan and the fixation should be based upon the skills, experience, qualifications and training. The salary structure should be such as to help to retain qualified and competent people.

(VIII) Since the pay structure of industrial workers have been decided by wage board, the study suggests that inequalities in remuneration can be resolved by statutory binding of wage board recommendations.

(IX) The study established that the promotional policy in the sugar units is vague. Most of the employees revealed that promotion policy is not handled fairly. Therefore, management of sugar units must be ready to give promotion opportunities to the employees after a fixed period of time. Qualified employees should be properly motivated by giving higher grade promotion and increment.

(X) Out of several initiatives (36 issues) of enhancing QWL in sugar mills only 23 variables found effective contribution in effective QWL score. Now, it is important for policy-makers, mill owners to introspect the non-effective QWL issues. So that expenditure in QWL initiatives be viable and can be implemented in strategic way.

(XI) All of practicing QWL are not influencing uniformly on employees productivity, motivation, workers participation in management, organisational loyalty and job satisfaction. It is suggested that mill owners has to apply the specific combination of QWL measures for organisational effectiveness.

9.7 Scope for Further Research

- This research was restricted to the geographic location of Uttar Pradesh only. Therefore, future researches can be extended to other regions in India which will help in gaining further insights into the phenomenon.
- The present research explores the key dimensions of the quality of work life in the sugar industry. A total of 36 parameters of five dimensions were used to measure employees' satisfaction regarding QWL. Although an attempt has been made to extensively identify the attributes of the employees QWL, yet there is possibility of missing the key dimensions influencing the quality of work life (QWL).
- A study may also be conducted on larger sample and analysing the findings using parametric tests for better accuracy and efficiency. Different methods of investigations like case-study participatory action research or bench-marking study may further help in augmenting the depth of knowledge in this area.
- Some other untouched area need to be addressed, i.e., impact of each component of QWL on sugar productivity and firm performance.

Annexure-A

Quality of Working Life Questionnaire for Survey

Dear Respondents

Myself, Dr. S.C. Das, Associate Professor, Faculty of Commerce, Banaras Hindu University, Varanasi, have undertaken a University Grants Commission (UGC), MAJOR RESEARCH PROJECT on **"Quality of Working Life of Employees in Sugar Industry of Uttar Pradesh: An Empirical Investigation".** For exploration of results regarding the study, the researcher needs concrete answer of the questions/statements mentioned below. It's my promise that the information given by you will be kept confidential and use for research purpose only.

Please extend your kind support in fillings up of this questionnaire by putting Mark (√) where applicable.

(A) PERSONAL INFORMATION OF EMPLOYEES

1. Geographical Location of the Organisation:

   (a) Eastern ☐ (b) Central ☐ (c) Western ☐

2. Nature of organisation:

   (a) Private ☐ (b) Co-operatives ☐

3. Nature of employment:

   (a) Permanent ☐ (b) Seasonal ☐

4. Contractual period of service (only for seasonal employees):
   (a) None ☐ (b) 1-4 ☐ (c) 1-5 ☐

5. Position in the organisation:
   (a) Clerical ☐ (b) Accounting ☐ (c) Administration ☐

   (d) Managerial ☐ (e) Sales and Marketing ☐

   (f) Technical ☐ (g) If other please specify [.............]

6. Experience in the present job: ....

7. Income (gross salary) per month:.................

8. Educational Qualification (tick (√) whatever is applicable)
   Below Matriculation **(V – VIII)** Matriculation **(10th Pass)**
   Intermediate **(12th Pass)** Graduation Post - graduation
   Others (Technical Diploma if any)

9. Age (in Years) - (a) Below 30 ☐ (b) 30-40 ☐

   (c) 41-50 ☐ (d) 50 and above ☐

10. Gender: - (a) Male ☐ (b) Female ☐

11. Marital Status: - (a) Married ☐ (b) Unmarried ☐

12. No. of family members:
    (a) Up to 4 ☐ (b) 5-6 ☐
    (c) 1- 7 ☐

13. Area which you are belong to:
    (a) Rural Area ☐ (b) Urban Area ☐

(B) **WORKING ENVIRONMENT FACTOR**

14. **Comfortable workspace:** Do you have a comfortable personal work space?

    (a) Yes ☐ (b) No ☐

15. **Lighting facilities:** The lighting facility within the mill is sufficient to work.

    (a) Strongly Agree ☐ (b) Agree ☐ (c) Unknown ☐

    (d) Disagree ☐ (e) Strongly Disagree ☐

16. **Level of temperature:** The level of temperature within the mill is bearable?

    (a) Yes ☐ (b) No ☐

17. **Safety measures:** The safety measures adopted by the organisation is

    (a) Excellent ☐ (b) Good ☐

    (c) Satisfactory ☐ (d) Poor ☐

18. **Health facilities**: The health facilities in the mill are not good.

    (a) Strongly Agree ☐ (b) Agree ☐

    (c) Unknown ☐ (d) Disagree ☐

    (e) Strongly Disagree

19. **Working condition:** I am not satisfied with the working condition provided by the organisation.

    (a) Strongly Agree ☐ (b) Agree ☐

    (c) Unknown ☐ (d) Disagree ☐

    (e) Strongly Disagree ☐

20. **Type of welfare facilities:** The welfare facilities provided by the employer are (Tick (√) whatever is applicable)

    (a) Housing/ Recreational / Medical/Canteen ☐

    (b) Recreational/Medical/Canteen ☐

    (c) Medical/ Canteen ☐ (d) Medical ☐

    (e) None ☐

21. **Qualities of welfare facilities:** The welfare facilities provided are

    (a) Excellent ☐ (b) Good ☐ (c) Poor ☐

    (d) Poor ☐

22. **Supervisor' interference:** My supervisor interferes in the given work.
    (a) Always ☐ (b) Often ☐
    (c) Sometime ☐ (d) Never ☐
23. **Workplace stress:** Do you feel any stress at workplace?
    (a) Yes ☐ (b) No ☐

(C) RELATIONAL FACTOR

24. **Supervision quality:** The Quality of supervision is not good.
    (a) Strongly Agree ☐ (b) Agree ☐
    (c) Unknown ☐ (d) Disagree ☐
    (e) Strongly Disagree ☐
25. **Supervisory support:** I receive adequate support from my supervisor.
    (a) Strongly Agree ☐ (b) Agree ☐
    (c) Unknown ☐ (d) Disagree ☐
    (e) Strongly Disagree ☐
26. **Colleagues relationship:** The relationship with our colleagues is good.
    (a) Strongly Agree ☐ (b) Agree ☐
    (c) Unknown ☐ (d) Disagree ☐
    (e) Strongly Disagree ☐
27. **Supervisory relationship:** Which type of relationship you have with your supervisor?
    (a) Harmonious ☐ (b) Normal ☐
    (c) Conflicting ☐
28. **Superior's relationship:** The relationship with our superiors is good.
    (a) Strongly Agree ☐ (b) Agree ☐ (c) Unknown ☐
    (d) Disagree ☐ (e) Strongly Disagree ☐
29. **Individual respect:** I am not treated with respect in the organisation.
    (a) Strongly Agree ☐ (b) Agree ☐ (c) Unknown ☐
    (d) Disagree ☐ (e) Strongly Disagree ☐
30. **Industrial relations:** How are union-management relations in your organisation?
    (a) Very Good ☐ (b) Good ☐ (c) Satisfactory ☐
    (d) Poor ☐ (e) can't say ☐

31. **Role of trade union:** Trade union plays a major role to protect the workers interest.
    (a) Strongly Agree ☐ (b) Agree ☐
    (c) Unknown ☐ (d) Disagree ☐ (e) Strongly Disagree ☐
32. **Management attitude:** The management takes interest to solve employee's work related problems
    (a) Always ☐ (b) Sometime ☐
    (c) Rarely ☐ (d) Never ☐

(D) JOB FACTOR

33. **Job retention:** What are the reasons of your stay at the present job? (Tick (√) any one)
    (a) Salary ☐ (b) Challenging job (c) Benefits
34. **Technological support:** Is there any opportunity to you for using new technology?
    (a) Yes ☐ (b) No ☐
35. **Adequate training:** I receive adequate training to do my job well.
    (a) Strongly Agree ☐ (b) Agree ☐ (c) Unknown ☐
    (d) Disagree ☐ (e) Strongly Disagree ☐
36. **Employees' interest:** Do you feel your company has your best interest at heart?
    (a) Most of the time ☐ (b) Sometime ☐
    (c) Never ☐
37. **Additional responsibility:** I am ready to take additional responsibility with my job.
    (a) Strongly Agree ☐ (b) Agree ☐ (c) Unknown ☐
    (d) Disagree ☐ (e) Strongly Disagree ☐
38. **Autonomy:** I have necessary authority to do my job well.
    (a) Strongly Agree ☐ (b) Agree ☐ (c) Unknown ☐
    (d) Disagree ☐ (e) Strongly Disagree ☐
39. **Work-life balance:** Do you able to maintain a healthy balance between work and family life?
    (a) Yes ☐ (b) No ☐

40. **Flexi-hours:** Does the organisation provide you flexible working hour?
    (a) Yes ☐ (b) No ☐
41. **Work schedule:** Which of the following best describes your usual work schedule?
    (a) Day sift ☐ (b) Afternoon shift ☐
    (c) Night shift ☐ (d) Rotating shift ☐
42. **Job security:** How satisfied are you with your overall job security?
    (a) Highly satisfied ☐ (b) Satisfied ☐
    (c) Dissatisfied ☐ (d) Highly dissatisfied ☐
43. **Work dissatisfaction:** What causes you have the greatest dissatisfaction at work? (Tick (√) any one).
    (a) Lack of appreciation ☐ (b) Too much paper work ☐
    (c) Family issue ☐ (d) Lack of T & D ☐

(E) FINANCIAL FACTOR

44. **Remuneration**: Are you satisfied with your pay package?
    (a) Highly satisfied ☐ (b) Satisfied ☐ (c) Unknown ☐
    (d) Dissatisfied ☐ (e) Highly dissatisfied ☐
45. **Regular compensation:** Do you get timely and regular compensation/ Salary?
    (a) Yes ☐ (b) No ☐
46. **Adequate bonus:** Do you get adequate bonus beside your salary?
    (a) Yes ☐ (b) No ☐
47. **Social security benefits:** Does the organisation provide you the social security benefits?
    (a) Yes ☐ (b) No ☐
48. **Fair promotion:** Are the employee promotion decision handled fairly?
    (a) Yes ☐ (b) No ☐
49. **Performance-based promotion:** Promotion is strictly linked to performance and seniority.
    (a) Strongly Agree ☐ (b) Agree ☐ (c) Unknown ☐
    (d) Disagree ☐ (e) Strongly Disagree

(F) IMPACT FACTOR

50. **Job satisfaction:** Taking all things into consideration, how satisfied are you with your service here?

    (a) Highly satisfied ☐ (b) Satisfied ☐ (c) Unknown ☐

    (d) Dissatisfied ☐ (e) Highly dissatisfied ☐

51. **Team spirit:** How satisfied you are with your team spirit?

    (a) Highly satisfied ☐ (b) Satisfied ☐

    (c) Unknown ☐ (d) Dissatisfied ☐

    (e) Highly dissatisfied ☐

52. **Workers participation in management:** Does the management provide opportunities to workers in decision-making process?

    (a) Yes ☐ (b) No ☐

53. **Organisational loyalty:** How important is organisation loyalty to you?

    (a) Very important ☐ (b) Highly important ☐

    (c) Important ☐ (d) Not important

54. **Communication:** Whether the organisation clearly communicates its goals and strategies to employees?

    (a) Yes ☐ (b) No ☐

55. **Skill utilisation:** I am fully able to use my skill in the present position.

    (a) Strongly Agree ☐ (b) Agree ☐ (c) Unknown ☐

    (d) Disagree ☐ (e) Strongly Disagree ☐

56. **Confident:** I am confident of my abilities to succeed of my work.

    (a) Strongly Agree ☐ (b) Agree ☐ (c) Unknown ☐

    (d) Disagree ☐ (e) Strongly Disagree ☐

57. **Sense of failure:** I often feel a sense of failure in my work.

    (a) Strongly Agree ☐ (b) Agree ☐

    (c) Unknown ☐ (d) Disagree ☐ (e) Strongly Disagree ☐

58. **Productivity:** Whether available facilities help you to enhance the productivity?

    (a) Yes ☐ (b) No ☐

59. **Motivation:** While performing your job, work related facilities effectively motivates the employees

    (a) Extremely ☐ (b) Normally ☐ (c) Slowly ☐

60. **Supervisory style:** Whether the supervision style of your supervisor affects your productivity positively?

    (a) Yes ☐ (b) No ☐

Annexure-B

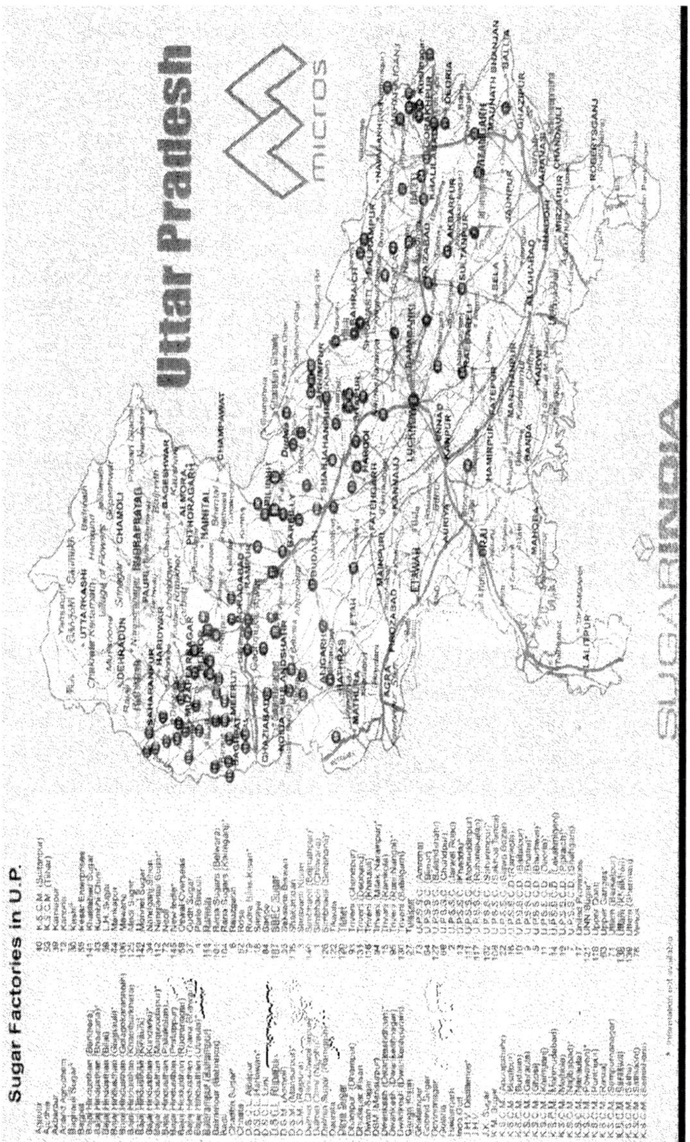

Bibliography

BOOKS:

Anitha, B., and Rao, Subba (1998). *Quality of Work Life in Commercial Banks*, Discovery Publishing House, New Delhi, 17.

Bowditch, James L. and Buono Anthony F. (1982). *Quality of Work Life Assessment:A Survey-Based Approach.* Boston, Massachusetts: Auburn House Publishing Company.

Davis Keith (1975). *Human relations at Work,* Tata McGraw Hill Publication.

Dessler, Gary (2004). *Human Resource Management*, Prentice-Hall of India (P) Ltd., New Delhi.

Devaraja, T.S., (2009). *Finanacial Performance of Agro-based Industries- The Case of Sugar Industry in Karnataka*, Anmol Publication Pvt. Ltd. New Delhi, India.

Gandhi, M.P. (2010). *Problems of Sugar Industry in India-Scope and Prospect of Re-organisation in Post-War Period,* Gandhi and Co. Publisher, Bombay (India).

Giri, V.V. (1972). *Labour Problems in Indian Industry*, Asia Publishing House, Bombay.

Green, F. (2006). *Demanding Work: The Paradox of Job Quality in the Affluent Economy,* Princeton, NJ: Princeton University Press.

Herzberg, F., Mausner, B., and Snyderman, B. (1959), "The Motivation to Work" (2nd Ed.) New York: John Wiley.

Jain, Sangeeta (1991). *Quality of Work Life*, Deep and Deep Publication.

Janson, R. (1981) "*Work Redesign: A Result-oriented Strategy That Works*," in J.H. Donnelly, J.L. Gibson, and J.M. Ivanceich (eds.) Fundamentals of Management Plano, Tex: Business Publication.

Jayamma V., Naik Krishna, C.N. (2006). *Quality of Work Life.* Sonali Publication, New Delhi, India.

K. Chittaranjan (1994). *Sugar Industry Management,* Deep and Deep Publication, New Delhi.

Katzell, R.A., Yankelovich D., Fein M., Ornate, D.A. and Nash A. (1975). *Work productivity and job satisfaction.* The psychological corporation: New York.

Keith Davic, (1981). *'Human Behaviour at Work'*, Tata McGraw Hill Publishing Co. Ltd., New Delhi.

Keith, Davis (1962). *Human Relations in Management*, McGraw Hill Book Co., New York.

Klatt, Murdick and Schuster, (1985). Human Resource Management, Chartex E. Merrill Publishing Company, Ohio.

Kuhlmann, M. (2002), *Group Work and Democracy, in Docherty*, Forslin, J., Shani, R. (eds). Creating Sustainable Work System: Emerging Perspectives and Practice, London: Routledge.

Likert Rensis, (1967). *The Human Organisation, Its Management and Value,* McGraw-Hill Book Company, New York.

Littler, C., Salaman, G. (1984). *Class at Work: The Design, Allocation and Control of Jobs*, London: Bastford.

Luthans, Fred (1981), *Organisational Behaviour*, McGraw-Hill International Book Company.

Mathur, R.N. (1989). *Quality of Working Life of Women Construction Workers.* New Delhi, India: Commonwealth Publishers.

McGregor, D. (1960). 'The Human Side of the Enterprse,' McGraw Hill, New York.

Nikam, G.A. ((2006). Indian Sugar Industry - A Comparative Study, Shree Publishers and Distributors, New Delhi.

Rossi Anna Maria, Perrewe Pamela L. and Sauter Steven L. (2006). *Stress and Quality of Working Life - Current Perspective in Occupational Health.* Greenwich, Connecticut: Information Age Publishing.

Senge, P. (1990), *The Fifth Discipline: The Art and Practice of Learning Organisation*, New York: Double-day.

Sharma, A. and Khandelkar, A. (2010*). Strategic Human Resource Management: An Indian Perspective.* New Delhi, India: Response Books.

Singh, Mangal (1994). *Efficient Management of Sugar Factories.* Somaiya Publication Pvt. Ltd. Bombay (India).

S. Pruthi, (1995). *History of Sugar Industry in India,* Reliance Publishing House, New Delhi, pp. 1-29.

Sugar India Year Book (2011). Pulse of Indian Sugar Industry, Anekant Prakashan, Jaysingpur, Kolhapur (MS).

Thompson, P. (1983*), The Nature of Work, London:* MacMillan.

Trehan, Ruchi. (2008). *Work Environment and Quality of Life.* New Delhi, India: Regal Publication.

Tyagi, R.C. (1995). *Problem and Prospects of Sugar Industry in India: Alternative Strategies for Development.* Mittal Publication, New Delhi (India).

Walker, K.F. (1975) '*Worker's Attitude- A Key to the Quality of Life'*, L.E. Davis and Cherns, A. The Quality of Working Life. The Free Press.

Walton, R.E., (1977). '*Criteria for quality of working life*' in Davis L., *et al.,* The Free Press London, 91-112.

Yusuf Anawar S.M. (1995). *Quality of Working Life: As a Function of Socio-technical System*. New Delhi, India: Mittal Publication.

Ph.D. THESIS

G. Jagadeesh Chandran (2007). Quality of Work Life in the Industrial Estates of Kerala, Mahatma Gandhi University Kottayam.

Rai, Prem Shankar (2001). Uttar Pradesh Mein Chini Udyog Ki Punjee Sunrachana Ph.D. thesis of Deptt. of Economics, BHU, Varanasi.

Rao, Rukmini V. (1986). A Study of Quality of Work Life, Self-concept, Aspiration and Family Life of Working Women, Ph.D. Thesis Submitted to University of Delhi, Delhi.

Sathees Kumar, L. (2009). *A study of human resource management practices in private sugar mills in Tamil Nadu,* Post Graduate and Research Department of Commerce Nehru Memorial College (Autonomous) Tiruchirappalli, Tamil Nadu.

Singh, B.K. (2001). Industrial Relation Practices in Sugar Industry in UP: Sectoral Differences, Banaras Hindu University, UP, India.

Subbaiah, B (2013). *Human resource management in sugar industry: a study with special reference to Sugar Mills in Krishna and West Godavari Districts of Andhra Pradesh,* Department of Commerce and Management Studies, Andhra University Visakhapatnam.

Tomar, A.S. (1993). Problems of Sugar Industries in India with Special Reference to Units Located in Eastern UP, Banaras Hindu University, UP.

RESEARCH PAPERS AND ARTICLES

Akinyele, S.T. (2007). A Critical Assessment of Environmental Impact on Workers Productivity in Nigeria. *Res. J. Bus. Manage. 1*(1), 50-61.

Arthi, J. and Chitramani, P., (2011). Impact of Quality of Work Life on Organisational Commitment among ITES Employees in Coimbatore. *The*

International Journal of Social Sciences and Management, 1 (5), 154-168.

Baba, V.V. and Jamal, M. (1991). Reutilisation of job context and job content as related employees Quality of working life: a study of psychiatric nurses, *Journal of Organisational Behaviour, 12,*. 379-386.

Bae, J. and Lawler, J.J. (2000). Organisational and HRM Strategies in Korea: Impact of Firms Performance in an Emerging Economy. *Academy of Management Journal,* 43(3); 502-517.

Beer, M., and Huse, E.F. (1972). System approach to organisation development, *Applied Behavioural Science, 8*, 79-109.

Biswas, S.K. (1993), Quality of Work Life, What Is It? *The Indian Journal of Labour Economics,* 36 (4), 759-64.

Boisvert, M.P. (1977). The quality of working life: An analysis. *Human Relation, 30 (II),* 155-160.

Carlson, C. (1978). General Motor's Quality of work life efforts, 55(4): 11-23.

Carr, J. Z., Schmidt, A. M., Ford, J., and DeShon, R.P. (2003). Climate perceptions matter: A meta-analytic path analysis relating molar climate, cognitive and affective states, and individual level work outcome, *Journal of Applied Psychology, 88*, 605–619.

Centre for Monitoring Indian Economy (CMIE), (2004) Agriculture, February, CMIE Pvt. Ltd, Mumbai-400093.

Chan, K.W. and Wyatt, T.A. (2007), Quality of Work Life: A Study of Employees in Shanghai, China, *Asia Pacific Business Review, 13*(4), 501-517.

Chander, Subash and Singh, Prampal (1993). Quality of work-life in a university: An Empirical Investigation, *Management and Labour Studies,* 18 (2), 97-107.

Cherns, A.B. (1973). 'Better Working Lives; A Social Scientists View', *Journal of Occupational Psychology, 47*, 23-28.

______.(1975). 'Perspective on the Quality of Working Life, *Journal of Occupational Psychology, 48*, 153-167.

______ (1979). "Using the Social Sciences," London: Routledge and Kegan Paul.

Che Rose, R; Beh L.S, Uli, J, and Idris K. (2006). An analysis of Quality of Work Life (QWL) and career-related Variables, *American Journal of Applied Science*, 3 (12), 2151-2159.

Cooper, M.S., B.S. Morgan, P.M. Foley, and L.B. Kaplan, (1979). "Changing Employee Values: Deepening Discontent?" *Harvard Business Review* 57:1, pp. 117-25.

Cunningham, J.B. and T. Eberle, (1990). A guide to job enrichment and redesign. *Personnel,* 67, 56-61.

Davis, L.E. and A.B. Cherns *et al.*, (1975). The Quality of Working Life. Volume One: Problems, Prospects and the State of the Art. New York: *The Free Press.*

Davis, L.E. (1957). Job design research, *Journal of Industrial Engineering.*

______(1972a). The coming crisis for production management. In L.E. Davis and J.C. Taylor (eds.), Design of Jobs, Harmondsworth: Penguin.

______ (1972b). Readying the unready: Post-industrial jobs. In L.E. Davis and J.C. Taylor (eds.), Design of Jobs, Harmondsworth: Penguin.

______ (1972c). The design of jobs. In L.E. Davis and J.C. Taylor (eds.), Design of Jobs, Harmondsworth: Penguin.

______(1972d). Job satisfaction research: The post-industrial view. In L.E. Davis and J.C. Taylor (eds.), Design of Jobs, Harmondsworth: Penguin.

______(1975). Work revamping can help workers and efficiency. LMRS *Newsletter*. National League of Cities, Washington, D.C., *6* (12), 3.

Davis, L.E. (1976). Developments in job design. In P.B. Warr (ed.) Personal goals and work design. London: Wiley.

______(1977). Evolving alternative organisation design: Their socio-technical bases. *Human Relations*, 39 (3), 261-273.

Dayal and Sharma (1975). The Meaning of Work to Bank Employees, Jamshedpur, XLRI (*Mimeographed.)*

Deal, J. (2003). How to creat employee loyalty, (Http://www.deal consulting.com).

Delamotte, Y. and Takezawa, S. (1974). 'QWL in International Perspective', International Labour Organisation, Geneva.

Delamotte, Y. and Walker, K. F., (1974). Humanisation of Work and the Quality of Working Life —Trends and Issues, *International Institute for Labour Studies Bulletin,* 11, 3-14.

D'souza, and Keith C. (1984). QWL: An Evolutionary Perspective, *Abhigyan,* Vol. Autumn, 1-15.

De, Nitish. R. (1982) Inter-linkage between Quality of work life and Quality of life, *Productivity,* 22(4), 89-91.

De, N.R. (1984). 'Towards an appreciation of quality of life and quality of work life'. *Economic and Political Weekly,* 19 (20-21): M46-M57.

De, N.R. (1976). 'Some Dimensions of Quality of Working Life', paper presented at the National Seminar on Quality of Working Life, Bombay, pp. 22-27.

_______(1977). 'Diflusion of Work System Redesign on Participative Design in a Large Complex Engineering Factory, (mimeo), National Labour Institute, New Delhi.

_______(1980). 'Redesign of work system and Quality of Work Life', Joshi, N.C and Kesary, V.G. (eds) Reading in Managements. Allahabad: A. H. Wheeler.

De, N.R. (1984). "Towards an appreciation of Quality of Life and Quality of Work Life." *Economic and Political Weekly. 19* (20-21): M46-M57.

Department of Economic Analysis and Research (2010). National Bank for Agriculture and Rural Development, Mumbai.

Directorate of Sugar, Revitalisation of Sugar Industry, Department of Food and Public Distribution, Ministry of Food, Consumer Affairs and Public Distribution, GOI, Krishi Bhavan, New Delhi, 14 July 2006.

Directorate of Sugar (2006), Revitalisation of Sugar Industry, Department of Food and Public Distribution, Ministry of Food, Consumer Affairs and Public Distribution, GOI, Krishi Bhavan, New Delhi.

Dixon, M. and Sagas, M. 2007. The relationship between organisational support, work-family conflict, and the job-life satisfaction of university coaches. Research Quarterly for Exercise and Sport, 78, 236-247.

E.F. Huse, Organisation Development and Change (Minneapolis: West, 1980), p. 508.

Emery, E.F. and Thorsurd, E (1969). "Form and the Content in Industrial Democracy" Tavistock, London.

EPOC (1997). New Forms of Work Organisation: Can Europe Realise its Full Potential? Dublin: European Foundation.

Feuer, D., 1989. Quality of work life: a cure for all ills? *Training: The Magazine of Human Resources Development*, 26: 65-66.

Ford, R. (1973). "Job Enrichment Lessons for At and t", *Harvard Business Review,* Vol. Jan- Feb., 15-20

Ganguli, O. N. and Joseph, J.S. (1976). *Quality of working life: work prospects and aspiration of young workers in Air India,* Central Labour Institute: Bombay.

Gani, A. (1993). Quality of work life in a state setting: findings of an empirical study, *The Indian Journal of Labour Economics,* 36 (4), 817-823.

Ghosh and Subratesh (1992). Quality of Work Life in Two Indian Organisations, *Decisions,* 19(2), 89-102.

Ghosh , S. and Karla, S.K. (1982). Perceptual Differences in Quality of Work Life Factors, *Indian Journal of Training and Development, 12* (374), 10-12

Gilgeous, V., (1998), "Manufacturing managers: their quality of working life", *Integrated Manufacturing System,* Vol. 9, No. 3, pp.173-181.

Glasier, E (1976). State of the Art, Questions about Quality of Work Life, Personnel.

Government of India (2004), "Report of the Committee on Revitalisation of Sugar Industry", (Tuteja Committee), Ministry of Food, Consumer Affairs and Public Distribution, Department of Food and Public Distribution, New Delhi.

Groeschl. S. (2003). Cultural Implication for the Appraisal Process, Cross Cultural Management, *An International Journal,* 10(1), 67-79.

Guest R.H. (1979), 'Quality of Work Life-learning from Terry-town', *Harward Business Review,* July-August, 28-39.

Gupta P. and Khandelwal, P. (1988). Quality of Work life in Relation to Role Efficiency, *Psychological Studies,* 33 (1), 34-38, p.73.

Gupta, T.K. (1993). Quality of Work Life, *The Indian Journal of Labour Economics,* Vol. 4, 770-77.

Hackman, J.R. and Lawler, E.E. (1971), Employee Reactions to Job Characteristics, *Journal of Applied Psychology,* 53(3), 259-86.

Hackman, J.R. and G.R. Oldham *et. al.,* (1975), A New Strategy for Job Enrichment, *California Management Review.*

Hackman, J.R. and G.R. Oldham, (1980). *Work Redesign*. Reading, M.A: Addison-Wesley.

Haque, A.B.M.Z. (1992). Quality of Working Life and Job Satisfaction of Industrial workers in relation to size of organisation, Bangladesh. *Journal of Psychological Studies,* 2 (1), 43-55.

Heizel, M.F., Geodale, J.G. Joyner, R.C and Burke, R.J. (1973). 'Development of a Quality of Working Life Questionnaire: Item Discrimination Study', Department of Labour, Ottawa, Canada.

Herrick, N and Maccoby, M. (1972). Humanising Work: A priority Goal of the 1970's', Paper presented at the International Conference on the Quality of Working Life, Adren House, Harrison, New York.

Hofstede, G. (1990). Managerial Culture and work-related values in India. *Organisation Studies,* 11(1), 103-106.

Hossain, J. A. (1997). Quality of working life of Industrial worker in Bangladesh: A case study in Greeter Kush.

Hossain Md. Mosharraf and Islam Md. Tariqual (1999). Quality of Working Life and Job Satisfaction of Conventional Hospital Nurses in Bangladesh, *Indian Journal of Industrial Relations,* 34 (3).

Huang, T.C., Lawler, J., and Lei, C.Y. (2007). The effects of quality of work life on commitment and turnover intention. *Social Behaviour and Personality*, *35*, 735-750.

Igbaria, M., and Greenhaus, J.H. (1992). Determinants of MIS employees' turnover intentions: A structural equation model. *Communications of the ACM, 35* (2), 34-51.

International Labour Organisation (1982). Condition of Work: A cumulative Digest, ILO, Geneva.

International Labour Office (1984) "Introduction to Social Security", Geneva, p. 3.

Jenkins, D.(1981). QWL: Current Trends and Directions. A series of occasional papers No. 3. Ontario: Quality of Working Life Centre.

Joanne Profetto-McGrath *et. al.*, 2003 "A study of Critical thinking and research utilisation among nurses", *Western Journal of Nursing Research,* Sage Publications, 25: 322.

Jonston, R. (1975). Pay and job satisfaction: A study of sum research finding. *International Labour Review, 111* (5), 441-49.

Johnsrud, L. 2002. Measuring the quality of faculty and administrative work life: implications for college and university campuses, *Research in Higher Education,* 43(2), 379 – 95.

Joseph, J.S. (1978). Quality of Working Life (QWL) and job attitudes of Indian Craftmen, *Bombay Psychologists,* 11 (1), 28-34.

Kalbers, L.P., and Cenker, W.J. (2007). Organisational commitment and auditors in public accounting, *Managerial Auditing Journal, 22*, 34-36.

Kalra, S. and Ghosh, S. (1984). Quality of Work Life; A study of associated factors. *The Indian Journal of Social Work,* 45-54.

Kanagalakshmi, L. and Devei, N. B. (2003), "A Study on Perception of Quality of Work Life among Textile Manufacturing Workers in Tirunelveli".

Khalique, A. and Rehman, M.A. (1987). Perceived importance of job facets and overall job satisfaction of industrial workers, *Human Relation,* 40 (7), 401-416.

Lau, T., Y.H., Wong, K.F., Chan, and M., Law, (2001). Information Technology and the work environment – Does it Change the Way People Interact at Work, *Human Systems Management, 20* (3), 267-280.

Lawler, E.E.III., (1982). Strategies for improving the quality of work life. *Am. Psychologist,* 37: 486- 493.

Livneh, A. (1978). Life-cycle approach to the Quality of work experience. *Dissertation Abstracts International,* 39, 2578-A.

Loscocco, K.A. and Roschelle, A.R. (1991). Influences on the quality of work and non-work life: two decades in review, *Journal of Vocational Behaviour,* 39 (2), 182.

Macy, B.A. and Mervis, P.H. (1976) 'A Methodology for Assessment of Equality of Working Life and Organisational effectiveness in Behavioural Economic Terms' *Administrative Science Quarterly,* 21, 215-226.

Majumdar, N. (1978). Industrial pollution in proceedings of the national seminar on Quality of working life, Organised jointly by Central Labour Institute Bombay and National Labour Institute: New Delhi.

Mathur, R.N. (1989). QWL of women construction workers, pp. 22-24.

May, B.E., Lau, RSM., and Johnson, S.K. (1999). A longitudinal study of quality of work life and business performance. *South Dakota Business Review, 58,* 3-7.

Mehta, P. (1987). Administrative- Organisation Structure, Perceived Quality of Work Life and Development Related Bureaucratic Behaviour, New Delhi: Participation and Development Center Mimeographed.

Mehta, P. (1976) 'From Economism to Democratic Commitment, The Role of Working Participation', *Vikalpa,* 1 (4), 39-46.

Mirvilis and Mehta, P. (1977). The role of workers participation' *Vikapla* 1976, 1 (4), 39-46 and Employee motivation and work satisfaction in Public Enterprises, *Vikapla* 2(3), 236.

Mirvis, P.H. and Lawler, E.E. (1984) Accounting for the Quality of Work Life. *Journal of Occupational Behaviour.* 5, 197-212.

Murthy S.R.S. (2010). National Bank for Agriculture and Rural Development Department of Economic Analysis and Research, Mumbai 3.

Nadler, D.A. and Lawler E.E. (1983). 'Quality of Work Life, Perspective and Direction', *Organisational Dynamics,* Winter, *11 (3),.* 20-30.

National Federation of Co-operative Sugar Factories Ltd., New Delhi, *Co-operative Sugar,* 40 (10) June 2009.

National Seminar on Improving the Quality of Work Life (1982) Proceeding and recommendation. New Delhi: Participation and Development Centre, *Mimeographed.*

National Symposium on Quality of Working Life (1983). Summary of deliberation and recommendation. July 25-26, Hyderabad. *Mimeographed.*

Opperman, C.S. (2002). Tropical Business Issues. Partner Price Water House Coopers.

Pandey, A.P. (2007) 'Indian sugar industry: A strong industrial base for rural India' Banaras Hindu University MPRA Paper No. 6065.

Parthasarthy, J. (1988). "Resources and Quality of life: A case study of the Irulas of Nilgiris." *The Eastern Anthropologist*, 41 July-Sept 3: 240-249.

Paul, W.L. *et. al.* (1969), "Job Enrichment Pays Off", *Harvard Business Review*, Vol. March- April, 1-15.

Rahman, A. (1984). QWL as perceived by industrial shift worker' thesis, Osmania University: Hyderabad.

Rainaye R. (2005). Quality of Work Life in Banks: A micro-level Comparative Analysis, *The Indian Journal of Commerce*, 58 (4), 113-121.

Rao, M.G. (1993). Quality of working life and Quality circle, *Human Behaviour at Work*, (1) 43-54.

Rao, M.G. (1993), Quality of Working Life and Quality Circles, Vol. 1. *Human Behaviour at Work*, 43-54.

Razali, M.Z. (2004). Perception of professional engineers towards quality of work life and organisational commitment, a case study. *International Journal of Business,* 6, 323-334.

Richard Walton, E. (1977). Criteria for Quality of Working Life, in Davis L., *et.al.* The Free Press London, 91-112.

Rhoades, L and Eisenberger, R. (2002). Perceived Organisational Support: A Review of the Literature, *Journal of Applied Psychology*, 87 (4), 698-714.

Rice, A.K. (1953). Productivity and social organisation in an Indian weaving shed. *Human Relation,* 6, 297-329.

________. (1958). Productivity and social organisation: The Ahemdabad Experiment. London and Tavistock.

Robert F. Craver, AT & T, (1983). QWL Experiment- A Practical case study, *Management Review,* Summer, 91-112.

Robert, H. Guest. (1979). Quality of Work Life - Learning from Tarrytown, *Harvard Business Review,* 28-39.

Rosow, J.M. (1977) 'Quality of Working Life and Productivity', The double pay off, A paper presented at Conference held at America Institute Inc., Chicago.

Runcie, J.F. (1980). Dynamic Systems and the Quality of Work Life, *Personnel,* 57(6), 13–24.

Ryan, G.M. (1995). Theoretical Basis for the QWL Concept. University of Siena: Quality, (Esprit Project 8162) Working Paper.www.yahu.com.

Saklani, D.R. (2004). Quality of work life in the Indian context: An empirical investigation. *Decision* 31.

Sandrick K (2003). Putting the emphasis on employees as an award winning employer, Baptist health care has distant memories of the work force shortage, *Trustee*, 6-10.

Sanyal, A. and Singh, B.R. (1982). Improving the quality of work-life, *Lok Udyog,* 27-35.

Sanyal, N., Bhagria, R.P. and Ray, S.C. (2008), "Indian Sugar Industry", *Yojna,* 52(4), 13-17.

Sashkin, M and Lengermann, J.J. (1984). 'Quality of Work Life Conditions/Feelings (ed.) Pfeiffer, J.M and Goldstein, L.D. (1984), Annual Developing Human Resources, 13th Annual, University Associates Inc., California,131-144.

Sayeed, O.B. and Sinha, P. (1981). QWL in relation to Job Satisfaction and performance in two organisations, *Managerial Psychology*, 2(1), 15-30.

Sekaran, Uma (1985). The Perceived Quality of Working Life in Banks in Major Cities in India,*Prajan,* 14 (3), 273-284.

Sengupta and Sidique (2001). The effect of Quality of work life on Group Cohesiveness: An Empirical Analysis, *Labour and Development,* 7(2), 126-36.

Shamir, B. and I. Salomon, 1985. Work-at-home and the quality of working life. *Acad. Manag*., 10: 455-64.

Sharma, Ajay and Ghosh, Siladitya (1993), Quality of Work Life and Productivity, *The Indian Journal of Labour Economics,* Vol. 36 (4), 785-88.

Sinha, Prakash (1982). Quality of working life and quality of life, *Indian Journal of Industrial Relation, 17* (3), 373-94.

Singhal, Sushila. (1983). Quality of Work Life: A re-examination of assumption, Hyderabad, *National Symposium on Quality of Working Life,* 25-26.

Singhal, Sushila (1983), Quality of Work Life: A re-examination of Assumptions, Hyderabad: National Symposium on Quality of Working Life, *Mimeographed*, 25-26.

Singh, A. (1992). Collective Bargaining in Sugar Industry in UP Unpublished Thesis, Banaras Hindu University, UP, India.

Singh, J.P. (1982). Improving Quality of working life in the Indian context, *Productivity,* 22 (4), 13-20.

Singh, J.P. (1983). QWL experiments in India-trails and Triumphs, A*bhigyan*, Vol. Autumn, 23-37.

Singh, SP (2006a), "Technical and Scale Efficiencies in the Indian Sugar Mills: An Inter-state Comparison", *The Asian Economic Review,* Vol. 48 (1), pp. 87-100.

Sinha, J.B.P., (1977). 'Quality of Working Life in the Indian setting' *Journal of Social and Economic Studies,* 2, 235-247.

Sinha, Prakash (1982). Quality of Working Life and Quality of Life, *Indian Journal of Industrial Relation, 17(3),* 373-394.

Sinha, Prakash and Sayeed, Omer Bin (1980). Measuring Quality of Work Life: Development of an Inventory, *Indian Journal of Social Work, 41(3),* 221-26.

Sirgy, M.J., Efraty, D., Siegel, P. and Lee, D. (2001). A new measure of quality of work life based on need satisfaction and spillover theories. *Social Indicators Research*, 55, 241-302.

Sirota, D. (1973). Production and services personnel and job Enrichment, *Work Study,* 22(1) January, 9-15.

Sprin, P. (1975). 'Some comment on the Quality of Working Life', *Journal of Occupational Psychology, 48*, 179-184.

Srivastava, A.K. (2007). Perceived Work Environment and Employees' Health, *Psychological Studies,* 52, (4), 345-347.

Straw, R.J. and C.C. Heckscher, (1984). QWL: New working relationships in the communication industry. *Labour Studies J.* (9), 261-274.

Taylor, J. C. (1973). 'Concept and Problems in Studies of the Quality of Working Life': Graduate School of Management, UCLA.

Thorsrud, E. (1976). 'Democracy at the Work and Prospective on the QWL in Scandinavia', Research Studies, No. 8, IIILS, Geneva.

Triandis H.C. (1982). Review of culture's consequences. *Human Organization*, 41, 86-90.

Turner, A. N. and P.L. Lawrence (1965). Industrial jobs and the Worker, Boston, Harvard Graduate School Business Administration.

Tandon, Rajesh and Dhawan, K. Sunil (1987), Variations in Job Satisfaction with age Among Blast White Collor Indian Workers, *Indian Journal of Industrial Relations*, 16(4), 615-622.

UNESCO 38. "Indicators of Environmental Quality and Quality of Life" Reports and Papers in the Social Sciences.

Varadaraj S. and Sellappan R. (2008). Quality of Work Life of Employees in Engineering Industry, *The Management Accountant,* 711-717.

Verwayen, H. (1978). 'The Specification and Measurement of the Quality of Life in OECD Countries, The Quality of Life-comparative Studies (Ed.) Szalai, A and Andrews, F.F. Sage Publication, California, 235-24.

Wadud, N. (1996). Job stress and QWL among working women, *Bangladesh Psychological Studies,* 6, 31-37.

Walton, R. (1973). Quality of Work life Indicators -- Prospects and Problems - A Portugal Measuring the Quality of working life, 57-70, Ottawa.

Walton, R.E. (1973). 'Quality of Working Life: What Is It?' *Sloan Management Review, 15(1):* 11-21.

Walton, R.E. (1975). Criteria for Quality of Working Life. In L.E. Davis, A.B. Cherns and Associates (Eds.) The Quality of Working. New York: The Free Press, Life, 1: 91-104.

Willmott, H. (1993). "Strength is Ignorance, Slavery is Freedom: Managing Culture in Modern Organisations', *Journal of Management Studies, 30 (4)*, 515-52.

Winter, R.,T. Taylor and J. Sarros, (2000). Trouble at mill: quality of academic work life issues within a comprehensive Australian university. *Studies in Higher Education*, 25: 279-294.

Worrall, L. and Cooper, C.L. (2006). The Quality of Working Life: Managers' Health and Well-being. Executive Report, Chartered Management Institute.

Wright, T.A. and Bonett, D.G. (2007). Job Satisfaction and Psychological Well-being as Non-additive Predictors of Workplace Turnover, *Journal of Management, 33*(2), 141-160.

Wright, T.A. and Cropanzano, R. (2004), The Role of Psychological Well-being in Job Performance: A Fresh Look at an Age-old Quest, *Organisational Dynamics*, 33(4), 338-351.

Wyatt, T.A. and Wah, C.Y. (2001). Perceptions of QWL: A Study of Singaporean Employees Development, *Research and Practice in Human Resource Management,* 9(2), 59-76.

Yusuf, Anwar (1996), Evaluating the Quality of Working Life, Management and Labour Studies, 21(1), 8-15.

WEBSITES:

http://www.seattlepi.com
http://www.sitescraper.co.uk/include/m.js/html).
http://www.indiansugar.com
www.careratings.com
www.upfed.org
www.upcane.org
www.indiasugaronline.com
www.usda.gov
www.sugarnet.com
www.wsro.org.

Index

R

S